Representing Violence against Women

EUROPA PERIODICA

Edited by
Patrizia Delpiano, Fabio Forner, Giovanni Lamartino,
Viola Corrado, Sabine Schwarze

VOL. 5

Sara Delmedico

Representing Violence against Women

A Case Study from Early Twentieth-Century Italy

PETER LANG
Berlin - Lausanne - Bruxelles - Chennai - New York - Oxford

Bibliographic Information published by the Deutsche Nationalbibliothek
The Deutsche Nationalbibliothek lists this publication in the Deutsche Nationalbibliografie; detailed bibliographic data is available online at http://dnb.d-nb.de.

Library of Congress Cataloging-in-Publication Data
A CIP catalog record for this book has been applied for at the Library of Congress.

Cover image © Sara Delmedico

Funded by the Irish Research Council and Gerda Henkel Foundation

ISSN 2749-215X
ISBN 978-3-631-90629-3_HC 290629_HC (Print)
ISBN 978-3-631-90630-9 (E-PDF)
ISBN 978-3-631-90631-6 (E-PUB)
DOI 10.3726/b21063

Published by Peter Lang GmbH, Berlin (Germany)

info@peterlang.com

This publication has been peer reviewed.

www.peterlang.com

Contents

List of images

Acknowledgement

I would like to express my deepest gratitude to the Irish Research Council and to the Gerda Henkel Foundation for generously supporting my research for this study and for enabling me to write it.

My thanks also go to the School of Languages, Cultures and Linguistics at University College Dublin for creating the supportive environment in which I had been able to work during the first stages of this research.

I am also extremely grateful to the anonymous reviewers who gave me significant suggestions to improve this book.

Sincere thanks also go to Katherine Powlesland for sharing her expertise and providing me with helpful comments, and to Giovanni Iamartino for helping me throughout the publication process.

I would also like to thank the staff of Biblioteca Braidense, Biblioteca Sormani, Biblioteca della Fondazione Anna Kuliscioff, Biblioteca del Circolo Filologico Milanese, Biblioteca Nazionale in Rome, Biblioteca di storia moderna e contemporanea in Rome, Cambridge University Library, Biblioteca APICE and Milan State Archive for their help and support.

My warmest thanks go to my family and friends for their unwavering love and support.

Note to the reader

Primary sources have been transcribed, adopting conservative criteria and following the original as closely as possible (e.g. 'a dirittura' instead of 'addirittura'). Any apparent incongruities in spelling and morphology that have been preserved are part of the original text. The original spelling of titles in the body of the text and the bibliography has been preserved as far as possible.

Some changes have been made, however, for ease of reading. They are as follows:

- some abbreviations have been expanded;
- accents follow modern usage;
- some minor changes have been introduced in terms of punctuation;
- uppercase is left as in the original text.

Translations are the author's own, unless otherwise indicated.

Translations of texts included both in the body and in the appendix of the book have been made adopting conservative criteria.

Quotations in American English have been left as such.

Introduction

'Siamo nel secolo della emancipazione della donna' [we are in the century of female emancipation].[1] With this comment, Alberto Olivo explained to the court why he could not force his wife, Ernesta Beccaro, to obey him and added that *they saw what had happened in the end*.[2] Taking as its subject the representation in the Italian printed press of the case of the murder of Ernesta Beccaro by Alberto Olivo in 1903, and by examining the works of scientists and jurists across centuries, this book seeks to explore how the society of early-twentieth-century Italy envisioned the relationship between men and women and how reputation, honour and their understanding intertwined to mould the values by which people lived. Specifically, it investigates how scientific and juridic literature, together with newspapers, magazines and journals, had an oblique power to manipulate and reinforce stereotypes and prejudices – thereby distorting perceptions and rendering acceptable inequalities, discrimination and violence – at a time in which new ideas and new sciences, and new approaches, challenged certainties and redefined the sense of self.

Historically, women have been treated and represented differently from men. Leveraging a centuries-old construction of female inferiority, societal behaviours towards women continued to rely on a *habitus*, 'internalized

1 *Il Secolo*, 3–4 June 1904, p. 2.

2 Legal documents and the press referred to Beccaro by using randomly Ernesta or Ernestina. See, for example, Milan State Archive, Assise, 1904–1906, 1904, Sentenze, 2134.

and converted into a disposition that generates meaningful practices and meaning-giving perceptions', in Pierre Bourdieu's terms.[3] This habitus, for Bourdieu both 'a structuring structure' and 'a structured structure', is 'an infinite capacity for generating products – thoughts, perceptions, expressions and actions – whose limits are set by the historically and socially situated conditions of its production'.[4] In this lies the masculine order he so clearly exposed: a habitus that perpetuates hierarchies of the dominant and the dominated by investing the order of 'the objectivity of a common sense' and of neutrality.[5] It also continually perpetrates a symbolic violence that manifests itself in the bulk of societal norms shared by the dominant and by the dominated, who 'apprehend all reality, and in particular the power relations in which they are held, through schemes of thought that are the product of embodiment of those power relations and which are expressed in the founding oppositions of the symbolic order'.[6]

However, this order, together with its norms, could not be regarded as natural. Instead, it entailed a detailed social and cultural construction of identities in opposition – the masculine and the feminine – each with specifically prescribed features that validate themselves, and each with a range of potential sub-identities. In his *The Image of Man: The Creation of Modern Masculinity*, historian George Mosse defined masculinity as 'the way men assert what they believe to be their manhood', its ideal being 'invoked on all sides as a symbol of personal and national regeneration, but also as

3 Pierre Bourdieu, *Distinction: A Social Critique of the Judgment of Taste* (Cambridge: Harvard University Press, [1979] 1984), p. 170. On the notion of *habitus*, see also in this text pp. 168–74 and Pierre Bourdieu, *The Logic of Practice* (Stanford: Stanford University Press, 1990), pp. 52–65.

4 Bourdieu, *The Logic of Practice*, p. 55.

5 Pierre Bourdieu, *Masculine Domination* (Bloomington: Stanford University Press, [1998] 2002), pp. 33–4. This concept has also been highlighted in relation to history by John Tosh, a historian who posited that the crucial feature of masculinity is 'its relative invisibility. Men were the norm against which women and children should be measured' [John Tosh, 'What Should Historians Do with Masculinity? Reflections on Nineteenth Century Britain', *History Workshop Journal*, 38 (1994), 179–202 (p. 180)]. A similar concept has recently been emphasised by sociologist Cirus Rinaldi, who observes that masculine invisibility reveals its hegemony because it is implicit, general, abstract and universalising [Cirus Rinaldi, *Maschilità, devianze, crimine* (Milan: Meltemi, 2018), p. 14].

6 Bourdieu, *Masculine Domination*, pp. 33–34.

basic to the self-definition of modern society'.[7] Linking this image to the symbolic also meant envisioning attitudinal patterns that would frame this symbol within the boundaries of normativity, thus designating acceptable and unacceptable behaviour. This process of standardisation and of 'stereotyping meant that men and women were homogenized, considered not as individuals but as types'.[8]

But this process is not immutable and eternal. Historian Angus McLaren, for example, in *The Trials of Masculinity: Policing Sexual Boundaries, 1870–1930*, contended that 'new boundaries of normal male and female behavior were freshly established' by experts in the late nineteenth century, not creating but selecting and exploiting 'the stereotype of a virile, heterosexual, and aggressive masculinity' and declaring 'preeminent one particular model of masculinity from an existing range of male gender roles'.[9] The notion of 'one preeminent model' implies that, within this model of masculinity, there are other less eminent sub-models, suggesting hierarchies and hegemonies not only in relation to femininity but also to other masculinities.[10] Such a categorisation of identities at the time was tightly connected to the codification of sexual behaviour, which created and enforced further strata of power, transcending the individual and existing 'in a certain concerted distribution of bodies, surfaces, lights, gazes; in an arrangement whose internal mechanisms produce the relation in which individuals are caught up'; and thereby devising a society in tension between 'discipline and punishment'.[11]

---

7 George Mosse, *The Image of Man. The Creation of Modern Masculinity* (Oxford: Oxford University Press, 1996), p. 3. On masculinity, see also David Gilmore, *Manhood in the Making: Cultural Concepts of Masculinity* (New Haven: Yale University Press, 1990).

8 Ibid., p. 6.

9 Angus McLaren, *The Trials of Masculinity: Policing Sexual Boundaries, 1870–1930* (Chicago: University of Chicago Press, 1997), p. 2.

10 Michael S. Kimmel, *The Gendered Society* (Oxford: Oxford University Press, 2011), p. 7. See, also Michael S. Kimmel, 'Invisible Masculinity', *Society*, 30 (1993), 28–35 (p. 30). Sociologist Raewyn W. Connell coined the term 'hegemonic masculinity' to designate masculinity that prevails over others. On this, see Raewyn W. Connell, *Masculinities* (Cambridge: Polity Press, 1995), especially, pp. 76–81. See also, Raewyn W. Connell, *Gender and Power. Society, the Person, and Sexual Politics* (Cambridge: Polity Press, [1987] 2002).

11 Michel Foucault, *Discipline and Punish: The Birth of the Prison* (New York: Pantheon, 1977), p. 202.

Construction of identities

Today, it is widely accepted that women and men are the product of their societies. They reproduce and reinforce their own societal values, ambitions and expectations, which standardise themselves by means of a hegemonic 'heterosexual matrix',[12] and in the realm of what social critic Michael Warner called 'heteronormativity'.[13] Resistance to male dominion – which was previously assumed to be the 'natural' order – is a long-term phenomenon, but it is precisely when women attempted to reconceive of their role in the private sphere and crossed boundaries in the public sphere that it gained momentum. Especially from the nineteenth century, women's substantial and increasing participation in the modern labour market led to a reconfiguration of the image of women, both in physical and non-physical terms,[14] and, together with the many gendered challenges of that era – arguably most notably, the women's rights movement – threatened 'that gender division so crucial to the construction of modern masculinity'.[15] This gendered divide, reliant for its status quo on inequality and discrimination, was formed of tangible and intangible elements, establishing different standards for the sexes and shaping the identities of women and men alike.

Identity was a central concept and was tightly linked to a notion of honour, itself a concept that was fluid and gendered and whose definition was constantly revised. Anthropologist Julian Pitt-Rivers has described honour as the estimation of worth by individuals and in the eyes of the society to which they belonged,[16] a nuanced definition to which Susan E. Cross and

---

12 See Judith Butler, *Gender Trouble. Feminism and the Subversion of Identity* (London: Routledge, 1990), particularly, pp. 45–48.

13 Michael Warner, 'Introduction: Fear of a Queer Planet', in *Fear of a Queer Planet. Queer Politics and Social Theory*, ed. By Michael Werner (Minneapolis: University of Minnesota Press, 1993), pp. vii–xxxiii.

14 Sandro Bellassai, *L'invenzione della virilità. Politica e immaginario maschile nell'Italia contemporanea* (Rome: Carocci, 2011), pp. 84–5; Alessandra Pescarolo, *Il lavoro delle donne nell'Italia contemporanea* (Rome: Viella, 2019), pp. 163–76.

15 Mosse, *The Image of Man*, pp. 78. On the perception of the 'new women', see also, Bellassai, *L'invenzione della virilità*, p. 44. On the construction of genders, see Simonetta Stella Piccone and Chiara Saraceno, eds, *Genere. La costruzione del femminile e del maschile* (Bologna: Il Mulino, 1996).

16 Julian Pitt-Rivers, 'Honour and Social Status', in *Honour and Shame: The Values of Mediterranean Society*, edited by J. Peristiany (London: Weidenfeld and Nicholson, 1965), pp. 19–77 (p. 21).

Ayşe K. Üskül added conceits of respectability and morality.[17] The concept of honour remained closely allied with ownership:[18] anthropologist Salvatore D'Onofrio defined as honourable those individuals who were able to defend and grow the integrity of their own goods, with the latter understood as an extension of their corporal dimension.[19] And it was precisely upon the body – a problematic site embedded with symbolic values – that honour inscribed its sprawling meanings: as Antonino Buttitta expressed it, for women, honour is understood as purity and sexual fidelity; for men, it is constituted by the purity and sexual fidelity of their women.[20]

Predictably, this understanding has its reverberations throughout time (and also affects the present) and yielded an unbalanced world that found its equilibrium in the reproduction of inequality and discrimination, in the deployment of male dominance, and in praise for power dynamics in every aspect of life, and additionally, through violence. As sociologist Elisa Giomi has observed, under such conditions, it is an individual's gender that 'regola il rapporto con la violenza' [rules the relation with violence].[21]

This might suggest that gender can also rule the perception of violence.

---

17 Susan E. Cross and Ayşe K. Üskül, 'The Pursuit of Honor: Novel Contexts, Varied Approaches, and New Developments', in *Handbook of Advances in Culture & Psychology*, ed. by Michele J. Gelfand, Chi-Yue Chiu and Ying-Yi Hong (Oxford: Oxford University Press, 2022), pp. 189–243.

18 Maurice Daumas, *Adulteri e cornuti. Storia della sessualità maschile tra Medioevo e modernità* (Bari: Dedalo, 2008), p. 31.

19 Salvatore D'Onofrio, 'Onore e disonore in Sicilia', in *La antropologia como pasión y como práctica: ensayos in honorem Julian Pitt-Rivers*, ed. by Honorio M. Velasco, Dominique Fournier, Luiz Díaz Viana (Madrid: CSIC, 2004), pp. 201–28 (p. 204).

20 Antonino Buttitta, *Semiotica e antropologia* (Palermo: Sellerio, 1979), p. 135. Honour, women's honour, in particular, has often been linked to nation and its honour. On this, see Alberto Mario Banti, *La nazione del Risorgimento. Parentela, santità e onore alle origini dell'Italia unita* (Turin: Einaudi, 2000); Alberto Mario Banti, 'Discorso nazional-patriottico e ruoli di genere (Europa, secoli XVIII-XIX)', in *Innesti. Donne e genere nella storia sociale*, ed. by Giulia Calvi (Rome: Viella, 2004), pp. 121–46; Alberto Mario Banti, 'Nations, Sexuality, and Violence in Nineteenth-Century National Narratives', in *European Modernity and the Passionate South. Gender and Nation in Spain and Italy in the Long Nineteenth Century*, ed. by Xavier Andreu-Miralles and Mónica Bolufer-Peruga (Leiden: Brill, 2022), pp. 73–91.

21 Elisa Giomi, 'Introduzione', in *Relazioni brutali. Genere e violenza nella cultura mediale*, ed. by Elisa Giomi and Sveva Magaraggia (Bologna: Il Mulino, 2017), pp. 14–15.

This is particularly the case in relation to matrimony, in which, according to historian Marco Cavina, violence was 'un elemento fisiologico e accettato' [a physiological and accepted element].[22] Violence was personally and socially accepted and acceptable and, within marriage, was 'emblematico delle relazioni asimmetriche tra uomini e donne e inscritto nella loro esperienza quotidiana' [emblematic of the asymmetrical relationships between men and women and inscribed in their daily experience].[23] Further, it had long been enshrined in Italy's legal framework and was located within blurred boundaries of tolerability, so long as it did not extend into what was deemed to be abuse. Violence was often adjudged a necessary corrective for behaviour perceived to be unacceptable and a legitimate means to ensure individual compliance with societal norms and expectations.[24]

In this scenario, the production and reproduction of gender relations was consistent with what jurist Lama Abu-Odeh has called a 'complex triangular interaction', in which social violence came into contact with the state's attempt to regulate such violence and with 'the response by contemporary men and women to the balance between these two types of violence'.[25] The boundaries of such a triangulation defined the extent to which behaviour that was non-compliant with social norms and values could devalue the worth of an individual and the degree of violence that society saw as tolerable and acceptable. For example, in the case of adultery, the murder of one's wife was given what historian Christel Radica has termed a 'cornice di legittimità' [frame of legitimacy], since adulterous women, in the eyes of many, were deserving of murder at the hands of their husbands.[26]

---

22 Marco Cavina, *Nozze di sangue: storia della violenza coniugale* (Rome-Bari: Laterza, 2011), p. XII. See, also, Cesarina Casanova, *Per forza o per amore: storia della violenza familiare nell'età moderna* (Rome: Salerno, 2016).

23 Simona Feci and Laura Schettini, 'Storia e uso pubblico della violenza contro le donne', in *La violenza contro le donne nella storia: contesti, linguaggi, politiche del diritto (secoli XV-XXI)*, ed. by Simona Feci and Laura Schettini (Rome: Viella, 2017), pp. 7–39 (p. 17).

24 On this see also Guglielmo Gulotta, *Famiglia e violenza: aspetti psicosociali* (Milan: Giuffrè, 1984), p. 46, who raises the question of 'violenza strumentale' [instrumental violence].

25 Lama Abu-Odeh, 'Comparatively Speaking: The "Honor" of the "East" and the "Passion" of the "West"', *Utah Law Review* (1997), 287–307 (p. 287).

26 Christel Radica, 'Onore, follia e amore: storie di assassini e Firenze (1866–1914)', *Genesis*, XVIII, 2 (2019), *Maschilità e violenza di genere*, 63–82 (pp. 81–82).

In recent decades, several scholars contributed to investigate the history of discrimination, with many studies engaging with notions of violence, including several major and groundbreaking works that address questions of violence from several diverse viewpoints. The edited volume *Crime and Culture: An Historical Perspective* by René Lévy and Amy Gilman Srebnick, for example, analyses historical discourses of crime in Europe and the United States from the sixteenth to the late twentieth century from an international and interdisciplinary perspective; whilst it does not set out specifically to explore violence against women, the phenomenon is nonetheless investigated meticulously.[27] *Victims, Crime and Society*, edited by Pamela Davies, Peter Francis, and Chris Greer, focuses on victims of crime from a sociological perspective and considers the construction of victim identity across categories of social class, race, age, and gender;[28] and Jane Kilby and Larry J. Ray's edited volume, *Violence and Society: Toward a New Sociology*, which aims 'to better understand the world we live in', features interdisciplinary analyses additionally incorporating questions of honour, identity, and domestic and gender-based violence.[29]

Analysis of crime in history is also investigated in *Men and Violence: Gender, Honor, and Rituals in Modern Europe and America*, edited by Pieter Spierenburg, which examines masculinity and violence between the seventeenth and the twentieth centuries.[30] Julius R. Ruff's monograph, *Violence in Early Modern Europe*, considers the role of the modern state at the time of its formation, the ways in which it sought to control violence, and the effect of violence upon women.[31] The modern state and criminality are also the topic of two other notably thought-provoking edited volumes: *Problems of Crime and Violence in Europe 1750–2000: Essays in Criminal Justice*, edited by Shani D'Cruze, Efi Avdela, and Judith Rowbotham, and *Shame, Blame, and Culpability: Crime*

27 René Lévy and Amy Gilman Srebnick, eds, *Crime and Culture: An Historical Perspective* (Farnham: Ashgate, 2005).

28 Pamela Davies, Peter Francis and Chris Greer, eds, *Victims, Crime and Society* (London: Sage, 2007).

29 Jane Kilby and Larry J. Ray, eds, *Violence and Society: Toward a New Sociology* (Malden: Wiley-Blackwell, The Sociological Review, 2014).

30 Pieter Spierenburg, ed., *Men and Violence: Gender, Honor, and Rituals in Modern Europe and America* (Columbia: Ohio State University Press, 1998).

31 Julius R. Ruff, *Violence in Early Modern Europe* (Cambridge: Cambridge University Press, 2001).

and Violence in the Modern State, edited by Marianna Muravyeva, David Nash, and Judith Rowbotham.[32]

Several works relating to Italy in particular also deal specifically with the topic of violence against women. These include two issues of the journal *Genesis*, edited, respectively, by Maria Clara Donato and Lucia Ferrante and by Domenico Rizzo and Laura Schettini; edited volume by Simona Feci and Laura Schettini entitled *La violenza contro le donne nella storia. Contesti, linguaggi, politiche del diritto (secoli XV–XXI)*; the afore-mentioned *Nozze di sangue. Storia della violenza coniugale*, by Marco Cavina, and Cesarina Casanova's *Per forza o per amore. Storia della violenza familiare nell'età moderna* – both of which latter provide robust studies of conjugal and familial violence throughout history, based on extensive archival research.[33] In addition, Emilia Musumeci's work, *Emozioni, crimine, giustizia: un'indagine storico-giuridica tra Otto e Novecento*, gives a precise analysis of the development of the legal debate on emotion and violence in the decades between the late nineteenth and early twentieth centuries in Italy.[34] Elsewhere, the sociological aspect of the phenomenon has been explored as in the two monographs by Cristina Oddone and by Carlotta Vagnoli, respectively.[35]

---

32 Shani D'Cruze, Efi Avdela and Judith Rowbotham, eds, *Problems of Crime and Violence in Europe 1750–2000: Essays in Criminal Justice* (Lewiston: Mellen, 2010) and Marianna Muravyeva, David Nash and Judith Rowbotham, eds, *Shame, Blame, and Culpability: Crime and Violence in the Modern State* (Abingdon: Routledge, 2013).

33 Maria Clara Donato and Lucia Ferrante, eds, *Violenza. Genesis*, IX/2 (2010); Marco Cavina *Nozze di sangue: storia della violenza coniugale* (Rome-Bari: Laterza, 2011); Cesarina Casanova, *Per forza o per amore: storia della violenza familiare nell'età moderna* (Rome: Salerno, 2016); Feci and Schettini, eds, *La violenza contro le donne nella storia: contesti, linguaggi, politiche del diritto (secoli XV–XXI)*; Domenico Rizzo and Laura Schettini, eds, *Maschilità e violenza di genere, Genesis*, XVIII/2 (2019). See also Guido Panico, 'La violenza giustificata. Il racconto dell'uccisione di una femme fatale: un case study', in *Il genere nella ricerca storica*, ed. by Saveria Chemotti and Maria Cristina La Rocca, 2 vols (Padua: Il Poligrafo, 2015), II, pp. 889–900; Laura Schettini, 'La violenza maschile contro le donne', *Storia delle donne nell'Italia contemporanea*, ed. by Silvia Salvatici (Rome: Carocci, 2022), pp. 135–61.

34 Emilia Musumeci, *Emozioni, crimine, giustizia: un'indagine storico-giuridica tra Otto e Novecento* (Milan: FrancoAngeli, 2015).

35 See Cristina Oddone, *Uomini normali: Maschilità e violenza nell'intimità* (Turin: Rosenberg & Sellier, 2020); Carlotta Vagnoli, *Maledetta sfortuna: vedere, riconoscere e rifiutare la violenza di genere* (Milan: Fabbri, 2021). See also the thought-provoking

Constructing the 'true victims' and the 'true culprits'

Central to this current study is the case of an act of violence perpetrated against a woman: a murder that happened in Italy at the beginning of the twentieth century,[36] and shows how the categories of 'victims' and 'culprits' were constructed and structured. The time period is particularly important for a number of reasons. Since the late eighteenth century, major disruptive

---

scholarly works by Sonja Plesset, *Sheltering Women: Negotiating Gender and Violence in Northern Italy* (Stanford: Stanford University Press, 2006); Chiara Gius and Pina Lalli, '"I loved her so much, but I killed her". Romantic love as a representational frame for intimate partner femicide in three Italian newspapers', *ESSACHESS. Journal for Communication Studies*, 7, 2/14 (2014), 53–75; Daniela Bandelli, *Femicide, Gender and Violence: Discourses and Counterdiscourses in Italy* (Cham: Palgrave, 2017); and Giovanna Parmigiani, *Feminism, Violence, and Representation in Modern Italy: "We are Witnesses, not Victims"* (Bloomington: Indiana University Press, 2019). On a European and global perspective, alongside the groundbreaking works by Jill Radford and Diana E.H. Russell, eds, *Femicide. The Politics of Woman Killing* (New York: Twayne, 1992) and Diana E.H. Russell and Roberta Harmes, eds, *Femicide in Global Perspective* (New York: Teacher's College Press, 2001), highly significant are also the edited volume by Shalva Weil, Consuelo Corradi and Marceline Naudi, eds, *Femicide across Europe: Theory, Research and Prevention* (Bristol: Bristol University Press, 2018). See also, Laura J. Shepherd, ed., *Handbook on Gender and Violence* (Cheltenham: Edward Elgar, 2019); Consuelo Corradi and Heidi Stöckl, 'Intimate Partner Homicide in 10 European Countries: Statistical Data and Policy Developments in Cross-national Perspective', *European Journal of Criminology*, 11/5 (2014), 601–18; Myrna Dawson and Michelle Carrigan, 'Identifying Femicide Locally and Globally: Understanding the Utility and Accessibility of Sex/Gender Related Motives and Indicators', *Current Sociology* (2020), 1–23; Nicoletta Mandolini, Caroline Williamson Sinalo, eds, *Representing Gender-Based Violence: Global Perspectives* (Cham: Palgrave, 2023).

36 I elect not to use the terms 'femicide' or 'feminicide' in this study, but instead the terms 'murder', 'uxoricide' or 'homicide', specifically to reflect the terminology used at the time. This notwithstanding, in my opinion, the case is undoubtedly a feminicide, and indeed was perceived as such by the people of time.

On the terms femicide and feminicide, see, Marcela Lagarde, '*Identidades de género y derechos humanos. La construcción de las humanas*', VII curso de verano, *Educación, democracia y nueva ciudadanía*, Universidad Autónoma de Aguascalientes, 1997, Cátedra UNESCO de Derechos Humanos de la UNAM, online resource <http://www.derechoshumanos.unlp.edu.ar/assets/files/documentos/identidad-de-genero-y-derechos-humanos-la-construccion-de-las-humanas.pdf> [accessed on 30 April 2024]; Diana E.H. Russell, 'Femicide: Politicizing the Killing of Females', in *Strengthening Understanding of Femicide: Using Research to Galvanize Action and Accountability*, Report of the Conference held in Washington on 14–16 April 2008, pp. 26–31 (p. 27).

change had been affecting society. New ideas – social, scientific, legal – had begun to influence the way individuals perceived themselves within the family unit, within society, and within their quotidian worlds.[37] In particular, women's voices were becoming louder, demanding greater inclusion and participation, and women were questioning inequality and discrimination, hithertofore conceived as the natural, normative order, and challenging male-female hierarchies.

It is within this context that the construction of the victim and the culprit could be precisely delineated by standardising categories of 'good' and 'bad'. On the one side were those who abided by the shared values of society, conformed to societal expectations, and occupied – and aspired to continue to occupy – the place assigned them by the natural order of things. On the other side were the disruptors of society: those unable, or unwilling, to comply with prescribed roles and hierarchies. A 'good' woman, then, was submissive, embodying the eternal feminine; obedient, pious, honourable, keenly aware of her role in society and of her own finiteness; a 'good' man was dominant, virile, strong, and able to offer guidance to a woman. The 'bad', by contrast, were violators of boundaries, the disobedient who did not understand limits, and the dominated who, themselves, wanted to dominate.

Within the populations of the time period of this study, and beyond, the internalisation of these categorisations led to a precise locating of victim and culprit in the common understanding. As a result, those not abiding by the behaviours expected of 'the goods' risked being perceived

---

[37] On this point, see, for example, Marzio Barbagli, ed., *Famiglia e mutamento sociale* (Bologna: Il Mulino, 1977); Marzio Barbagli, *Sotto lo stesso tetto. Mutamenti della famiglia in Italia dal XV al XX secolo* (Bologna: Il Mulino, 1984); Luciano Guerci, *La discussione sulla donna nell'Italia del Settecento: aspetti e problemi* (Turin: Tirrenia Stampatori, 1987); Luciano Guerci, *La sposa obbediente: donna e matrimonio nella discussione dell'Italia del Settecento* (Turin: Tirrenia Stampatori, 1988); Piero Melograni and Lucetta Scaraffia, eds, *La famiglia italiana dall'Ottocento a oggi* (Rome and Bari: Laterza, 1988); Daniela Calanca, *Storia della famiglia italiana: ruoli e passioni nel XX secolo* (Pesaro: Metauro, 2005), in particular, pp. 1–63; Angela Carbone, ed., *Scritti in onore di Giovanna Da Molin. Popolazione, famiglia e società in età moderna* (Bari: Cacucci, 2017); Sara Delmedico, "I Forgive my Sons for any Disgust They Might Have Caused Me'. Alvise I Mocenigo and the Decline of Paternal Authority in Nineteenth-Century Venice', *Journal of Family History*, 44/4 (2019), 347–65; Alessandra Samoggia and Francesco Scalone, eds, *La famiglia tra mutamenti demografici e sociali* (Udine: Forum, 2019).

as accomplices to the violence they might suffer, effectively experiencing a transfer from the position of victim to that of culprit. This is the rationale behind the notion of 'the power to correct and discipline' included in the Italian penal code, which permitted a certain degree of violence, and led the Supreme Court to state that 'la circostanza del flagrante adulterio è a reputarsi una scusante nel senso di legge, che non immuta il carattere del reato d'omicidio' [the circumstance of flagrant adultery is to be considered an excuse in the sense of the law, which does not change the character of the crime of murder].[38] The term 'scusante' precisely conveys the understanding of such a murder and also illuminates the words of Scipio Sighele in relation to a particular case of murder: 'è difficile dire quali siano le vere vittime, quali i veri colpevoli' [it is difficult to distinguish the true victims from the truly culpable].[39] So, the principle was unquestionable: people had to conform to social norms and expectations if they did not wish to lose their societal worth.

This present work intends to contribute to the historiography of discrimination by showing how beliefs, prejudices, and stereotypes were triggered, reinforced, reproduced, and conveyed by treatises and by the printed press in ways that reinvigorated hierarchies and maintained inequalities. If, in the words of Mark Seymour, 'it is unlikely that we will ever truly reconstitute, on a broad scale, the emotional experience of the past', it is nonetheless possible that exploring changes 'in emotional language, expression, "style", and norms' could be fruitful.[40] In particular, it is productive to understand how the use and manipulation of words, which 'are not ephemeral in affecting

38 Supreme Court of Rome, 20 February 1893, *Il Foro Italiano*, 18/2 (1893), 185–90 (p. 190).

39 Augusto Guido Bianchi, Guglielmo Ferrero and Scipio Sighele, eds, *Il mondo criminale italiano*, 2 vols (Milan, Omodei Zorini, 1893), I, p. 45.

40 Mark Seymour, *Emotional Arenas: Life, Love, and Death in 1870s Italy* (Oxford: Oxford University Press, 2020), p. 9. On emotions, see also, Barbara Rosenwein, 'Problems and Methods in the History of Emotions', *Passions in Context*, 1/1 (2010), 1–32; Benno Gammerl, 'Emotional Styles – Concepts and Challenges', *Rethinking History*, 16/2 (2012), 161–75; Mark Seymour, 'Emotional Arenas: From Provincial Circus to National Courtroom in Late Nineteenth-Century Italy', *Rethinking History*, 16/2 (2012), 177–97; Caroline Braunmühl, 'Theorizing Emotions with Judith Butler: Within and beyond the Courtroom', *Rethinking History*, 16/2 (2012), 221–40; Laurajane Smith, Margaret Wetherell and Gary Campbell, eds, *Emotion, Affective Practices, and the Past in the Present* (Oxon and New York: Routledge, 2018), pp. 1–22.

encounters',[41] contribute to the construction of mentalities and values. This is particularly true in relation to the general subject of this study and particularly the individual case study explored. In this case, at the close of the trial, the murder victim – a woman – underwent a process of depersonalisation: no longer conceived of as a person and a victim, she was instead read through a voyeuristic lens, one that focused attention on her reported behaviour and non-adherence to social conventions, rather than on the violence she had suffered. As a consequence, her murder was received as something tolerable, acceptable, and, to a certain degree, predictable and merited.

In this work, the analysis of the representation and perception of mentalities as produced and reproduced by the printed press proves key to understanding a society and its values. In late-nineteenth- and early-twentieth-century Italy, newspapers started to be major information sources for the lower and middle classes.[42] Increasing literacy rate together with a lowering of newspapers' price contributed to this tendency. Moreover, new visual layouts and more streamlined texts' styles improved their usability and attractiveness.[43] This is why the role of newspapers and the printed press is so significant.

In recent years, a number of studies have analysed varying media, with their logic and practices, positing the power of the news and other media to influence and mould beliefs, values and, more broadly, mentalities.[44]

---

41 Margaret Wetherell, Laurajane Smith and Gary Campbell, 'Introduction: Affective Heritage Practices', in *Emotion, Affective Practices, and the Past in the Present*, pp. 1–22 (p. 14). See also, Ute Frevert, 'Defining Emotions: Concepts and Debates over Three Centuries', *Emotional Lexicons. Continuity and Change in the Vocabulary of Feeling 1700–2000*, ed. by Ute Frevert, Christian Bailey, Pascal Eitler, Benno Gammerl, Bettina Hitzer, Margrit Pernau, Monique Scheer, Anne Schmidt, and Nina Verheyen (Oxford: Oxford University Press, 2014), pp. 1–31.

42 Valerio Castronovo, *Stampa e opinione pubblica nell'Italia liberale*, in *Storia della stampa italiana*, ed. by Valerio Castronovo and Nicola Tranfaglia, 5 vols (Rome-Bari, Laterza, 1979), III, *La stampa italiana nell'età liberale*, pp. 1–54 (p. 43).

43 Ibid., pp. 128–54.

44 Andreas Hepp, 'Mediatization and the 'Molding Force' of the Media', *Communications: The European Journal of Communication Research*, 37/1 (2012), 1–28; David L. Altheide, 'Media Logic, Social Control, and Fear', *Communication Theory*, 23/3 (2013), 223–38; Kent Asp, 'News Media Logic in a New Institutional Perspective', *Journalism Studies*, 15/3 (2014), 256–70; Aspa Baroutsis, 'Understanding Media Mentalities and Logics: Institutional and Journalistic Practices, and the Reporting of Teachers' Work', *Discourse: Studies in the Cultural Politics of Education*, 40:4 (2019), 545–59.

As highlighted by sociologists David L. Altheide and Robert P. Snow, the media respond to a logic that determines the organisation, style, focus on characteristics, and grammar of information delivered in order to present, transmit, and 'promote a particular kind of presentation and understanding'.[45] Indeed, by considering 'the media as a dominant and powerful cultural text that creates the realities it describes', scholars Martin Mills and Amanda Keddie have suggested that the media 'are highly problematic in their polarising discourses that distort, conflate and re-signify assumptions'.[46] This, together with the ways news is sensationalised, plays a significant role in the reception and understanding of reported events, thereby contributing to what criminologist David Garland has called the construction of 'collective representations rather than accurate information',[47] that is, the dissemination of stories, not facts, and stories that are deeply influenced by authorial point of view and values.

Recently, some scholarly works have specifically addressed the issue of crime and its representation in the press in Italy. In relation to the late nineteenth century, Thomas Simpson's *Murder and Media in the New Rome: The Fadda Affair*, and Mark Seymour's *Emotional Arenas: Life, Love, and Death in 1870s Italy*, along with Stefano Serafini's article, 'Immagini e criminalità nell'Italia di fine secolo tra stampa, letteratura e scienza', are of great relevance

---

45 David L. Altheide and Robert P. Snow, *Media Logic* (Beverly Hills: SAGE, 1979), p. 197.

46 Martin Mills and Amanda Keddie, 'Cultural Reductionism and the Media: Polarising Discourses around Schools, Violence and Masculinity in an Age of Terror', *Oxford Review of Education*, 36/4 (2010), 427–44 (p. 429).

47 David Garland, *The Culture of Control: Crime and Social Order in Contemporary Society* (Chicago: University of Chicago Press, 2001), p. 158. See also, Richard Mc Mahon, ed., *Crime, Law and Popular Culture (1500–1900)* (Portland: Willan Publishing, 2009). On sensationalisation, see Henrik Örnebring and Anna Maria Jönsson, 'Tabloid Journalism and the Public Sphere: A Historical Perspective on Tabloid Journalism', *Journalism Studies*, 5/3 (2004), 283–95. On the representation of crime in the media, see also: Robert Reiner, 'Media Made Criminality: The Representation of Crime in the Mass Media', in *The Oxford Handbook of Criminology*, ed. by Rod Morgan, Mike Maguire, and Robert Reiner (Oxford: Oxford University Press, 2007), pp. 376–416; and Nikitha Suresh and Lucy Sara George, 'Trial by Media: An Overview', *International Journal of Law Management and Humanities*, 4/2 (2021), 267–72. On the symbolic meaning of transgressive stories in the media, see Cristine Penedo, 'O Crime nos Media. Impacto e valor simbólico das historias transgressivas', *Media & Jornalismo*, 3 (2003), 89–102.

to the current work.[48] With regard to violence against women and its representation in the press, some works have recently been published, but these deal only with the present era: for example, Cristina Gamberi's article 'Retoriche della violenza. Il femminicidio raccontato dai media italiani', Elisa Giomi and Sveva Magaraggia's edited volume, *Relazioni brutali. Genere e violenza nella cultura mediale*; Marina Bettaglio, Nicoletta Mandolini, and Silvia M. Ross's edited volume, *Rappresentare la violenza di genere: sguardi femministi tra critica, attivismo e scrittura*; and Nicoletta Mandolini's monograph, *Representations of Lethal Gender-based Violence in Italy between Journalism and Literature*.[49]

In relation to the time period covered by the present study – an important period for understanding how new ideas brought in by Positivism dialogue with the past and with our present – Dominique Kalifa has produced some significant works on the context in France.[50] These investigate how crimes were described in the press with a focus on the late nineteenth century, although Kalifa's topic is not specifically gendered violence. Further, a work by Kalifa with Philippe Artières, *Vidal le tueur de femmes. Une biographie sociale* examines the case of a murderer who killed many young women at the first turn of the twentieth century.[51] This thought-provoking book examines the

---

48 Thomas Simpson, *Murder and Media in the New Rome: The Fadda Affair* (New York: Palgrave Macmillan, 2010); Mark Seymour, *Emotional Arenas: Life, Love, and Death in 1870s Italy* (Oxford: Oxford University Press, 2020); Stefano Serafini, 'Immagini e criminalità nell'Italia di fine secolo tra stampa, letteratura e scienza', *The Italianist*, 42/1 (2022), 1–23. See, also, Stefano Serafini, *Gothic Italy. Crime, Science, and Literature after Unification, 1861–1914* (Toronto: University of Toronto Press, 2024).

49 Cristina Gamberi, 'Retoriche della violenza. Il femminicidio raccontato dai media italiani', in *La violenza contro le donne nella storia*, ed. by Simona Feci and Laura Schettini (Rome: Viella, 2017), pp. 261–78; Giomi and Magaraggia, eds, *Relazioni brutali. Genere e violenza nella cultura mediale*; Marina Bettaglio, Nicoletta Mandolini and Silvia M. Ross, eds, *Rappresentare la violenza di genere: sguardi femministi tra critica, attivismo e scrittura* (Milan: Mimesis, 2018); Nicoletta Mandolini, *Representations of Lethal Gender-based Violence in Italy between Journalism and Literature* (London: Routledge, 2021). See also the special issues edited by Gregoria Manzin and Barbara Pezzotti, 'Women and Violence in Italian Literature', *Spunti e Ricerche*, 33 (2018), 1–168; and Giorgia Alù and Sarah Patricia Hill, 'Mini special Issue: Violence Against Women in Italian Literature', *Italian Studies*, 76/3 (2021), 302–06.

50 Dominique Kalifa, *L'Encre et le sang. Récits de crimes et société à la Belle Époque* (Paris: Fayard, 1995); Dominique Kalifa, *Crime et culture au XIXe siècle* (Paris: Perrin, 2005).

51 Dominique Kalifa and Philippe Artières, *Vidal le tueur de femmes. Une biographie sociale* (Paris: Perrin, 2001).

construction of a male criminal but within this does not specifically explore societal stereotyping and prejudices about gender and behaviour. Eliza Earle Ferguson's book, *Gender and Justice: Violence, Intimacy, and Community in Fin-de-Siècle Paris*, analyses crimes of passion in late nineteenth-century Paris (1871–1900).[52] It foregrounds women but takes as its evidence base judicial proceedings and does not analyse how these crimes were reported in the press. Sharon P. Johnson's article 'Cultural Blindness and Ambiguity: Reading (for) and Writing about Rape' is about crimes against women in late nineteenth-century France. It highlights the ways in which rape was reported in the printed press, exposing the cultural blindness and ambiguities embedded in nineteenth-century society.[53] An interesting article summarising how violence has been tackled in literature and in the press in France and Spain was published in 2011 by historian Jordi Luengo López and considers the early decades of the twentieth century.[54]

However, an extended examination of the topic is merited. With my article, '"He Saw what He Wanted to See": Reputation, Jealousy and the Law. The Uxoricide of Giselda Zanolo', published in 2021, I made a first attempt to address the representation of violence against women in the context of the early-twentieth-century Italian press.[55] The article explores a case of violence against a woman in the 1920s, but the context of Fascism and its rhetoric of masculinity informed every aspect of life at the time, distorting a wider understanding of the picture. The status of women in the 1920s was also different from the preceding period, since marital authorisation had been removed from the juridical framework in 1919, an act that could be considered a first important step in the path towards equality for women in Italy.

---

52 Eliza Earle Ferguson, *Gender and Justice: Violence, Intimacy, and Community in Fin-de-Siècle Paris* (Baltimora: John Hopkins University Press, 2010).

53 Sharon P. Johnson, 'Cultural Blindness and Ambiguity: Reading (for) and Writing about Rape', *French Cultural Studies*, 27/2 (2016), 113–34.

54 Jordi Luengo López, 'El siniestro gusto literario del Neronismo. Un estudio comparativo en la producción franco-española sobre la violencia contra las mujeres', *AnMal Electrónica*, 31 (2011), <https://dialnet.unirioja.es/servlet/articulo?codigo=4043411> [electronic resource, accessed on 28 October 2024].

55 Sara Delmedico, '"He Saw what He Wanted to See": Reputation, Jealousy and the Law. The Uxoricide of Giselda Zanolo', *Papers of the British School at Rome* (2021), 319–33.

Sources, structure and methodology

The core of this work, as mentioned earlier, is a single case study. It concerns a uxoricide committed in 1903 and serves to show how a stereotyped vision of women and expectations of women's behaviour were reinforced in the printed press and how a peculiar rhetorical manipulation concluded with the release of a man who had admitted his guilt. Initially acquitted on a judicial technicality, a second trial against the murderer descended into a spectacle, and his second acquittal was welcomed with frenetic applause in a packed courtroom.

Among the many cases appeared in the printed press and examined for preliminary investigations for this book, the specific case study has been chosen for two key reasons. The first relates to the time period. Throughout the nineteenth century, Italian society, like Europe as a whole, had faced new changes and challenges that were reflected in many aspects of life. New possibilities and expectations were making individuals reconsider their ambitions and their places in society; new movements – in the arts, science, politics, the law… – were inviting fresh thinking about people's roles within their own worlds. The call for the emancipation of women was growing, increasingly part of the very fabric of Italian society. The path towards equality would still be long and continuing, but change was coming and perceived as possible.[56] This period was also particularly important for the rise and decline of new 'sciences', such as the studies propounded by Cesare Lombroso,[57] which also had a strong role in the judicial process.

The second reason for choosing this particular case is the wave of sentiment it triggered amongst the general public and the role of jurists and scientists of the time. Alongside the journalists who reported on the trials, which quickly became a spectacle, the views and opinions of jurists and scientists were also sought and published in interviews, conveying, implicitly and

---

[56] See, for example, the bills for women's suffrage presented to the Italian Parliament from the late nineteenth century onwards. For the history of women's vote in Italy, see Anna Rossi-Doria, *Diventare cittadine. Il voto alle donne in Italia* (Florence: Giunti, 1996); Giulia Galeotti, *Storia del voto alle donne in Italia* (Rome: Biblink, 2006); Marisa Ferrari Occhionero, ed., *Dal diritto di voto alla cittadinanza piena* (Rome: Casa editrice Università La Sapienza, 2008).

[57] On the rise and decline of "new sciences", see Silvano Montaldo, *Donne delinquenti. Il genere e la nascita della criminologia* (Rome: Carocci, 2019), pp. 151–83.

explicitly, the societal and moral values espoused by such professionals and experts. Throughout the two trials that made up the case, the circumstances of the crime, its victim and the accused were all examined from manifold perspectives, rendering the courtroom an arena in which, as was also noticed by the press, renowned scientists of the time intervened – with the Positivist School representing the new and the Classic School, the old, brought into confrontation – and a locus for the exhibition of skill and expertise. The eventual liberation of Alberto Olivo, the defendant who had admitted all along to murdering his wife from his very first interrogation by the Milanese police, serves as a representative case and a powerful reminder of how, outside the sphere of the law itself, society was able to ambiguously and equivocally interpret and assess those who did not abide by its rules: that is, in its evaluation of the victim in this case, who conversely herself would be adjudged a culprit in relation to her own murder.

This study relies on firsthand investigation of primary printed sources and is composed of this introduction, three parts each divided into three chapters, and a conclusion. The first part consists of three chapters entitled, respectively, *Women in the Theories of Scientists*, *Women and the Law* (*Women and Civil Law*, *Women and Crimes*), and *Scientists Entering Tribunals. Explaining Violence against Women*. The analysis begins by taking into account the works of scientists across the centuries to locate more precisely the roots of the discriminatory notions of women that characterise the treatment of this particular case. From antiquity onwards, there is evidence of prejudice and stereotyping and projection in the construction of the other. Scientific study of the human body and mind was frequently used to justify particular perceptions, inequalities, and discriminatory behaviours and to standardise normative notions of expected human behaviour. Almost entirely neglecting cultural and social factors, the scientists behind such studies insisted on linking bodily characteristics to states of mind and behaviours. Consequent discrimination against women (characterised as weak, irrational, and untrustworthy, for example) resulted in their unequal status in society, and their debarment from equal rights and access to and management of even their own wealth. In the nineteenth century, many works by jurists leaned heavily on such purportedly scientific studies to provide a strong theoretical basis for the different legal status of women, particularly in regard to their ability to undertake obligations. Works by such scientists and jurists are typically in the form either of treatises (for example, the manifold books published by Cesare Lombroso and his colleagues, or by Giovanni Carmignani, Bernardino Alimena, or Giuseppe Orano); commentaries (such as Giulio Crivellari's work on the 1889 Italian criminal code); or articles in the legal and scientific journals of the time (Cesare Pagani's observations, for example).

Since the law and society are in mutual and continuous dialogue, unwritten norms, attitudes, behaviours, and values can be seen to exist and influence changes in the law and society. Consequently, this book also considers the examination of certain legal norms, given that the study of the letter of the law at any given moment may be pivotal in casting light on the unwritten habits and values that caused those specific norms to be enacted.

The second and third parts of the book engage with the case study itself. The sources for this analysis are various newspapers, magazines and journals. The newspapers – specifically, the *Corriere della Sera*, *La Stampa*, *Il Secolo*, *Avanti!*, *La Tribuna*, *Il Giornale d'Italia* and *Il Messaggero* – were published daily and also often included articles by eminent experts.[58] Weekly and monthly magazines considered are *Il Buon Cuore, La Civiltà Cattolica, Il Caffaro, Pasquino, Il Secolo XX* and *L'Illustrazione Italiana*, although these only gave brief accounts at the end of both trials.[59] Key legal journals are also taken into account, namely *I Tribunali. Giornale di cronaca e critica giudiziaria*, *Il Filangieri. Rivista giuridica,*

---

[58] For a study of the press in late-nineteenth and early-twentieth-century Italy, see Castronovo, *Stampa e opinione pubblica*, pp. 128–47. See also Paolo Murialdi, *Storia del giornalismo italiano. Dalle gazzette a Internet* (Bologna: Il Mulino, 2006); Franco Della Peruta, *Il giornalismo italiano del Risorgimento* (Milan: FrancoAngeli, 2011); Mauro Forno, *Informazione e potere: storia del giornalismo italiano* (Rome: Laterza, 2012); Ann Caesar, Gabriella Romani, and Jennifer Burns, eds, *The Printed Media in Fin-de-Siècle Italy: Publishers, Writers, and Readers* (Abingdon: Routledge, 2017); Morena Corradi and Silvia Valisa eds, *La carta veloce. Figure, temi e politiche del giornalismo italiano dell'Ottocento* (Milan: Franco Angeli, 2021).

[59] *Il Buon Cuore* (1901–1917) was the official publication of the Society of Friends of Good, a Milanese association dedicated to protecting abandoned children. *La Civiltà Cattolica*, founded by the Society of Jesus in 1850, is still in publication today. *Il Caffaro* (1875–1943), established in Genoa, adopted positions aligned with Fascism and ceased publication with the fall of the regime. *Pasquino* (1856–1930) was a satirical magazine founded in Turin and suppressed by Fascist government in 1930. *Il Secolo XX (1902–1933)* was a monthly magazine published in Milan, primarily focused on news and literature. *L'Illustrazione Italiana* (1874–) was a weekly magazine published in Milan. It continues to be published with no set frequency.

dottrinale e pratica, *La Giustizia penale: rivista mensile di dottrina, giurisprudenza* and *Monitore dei tribunali*: with the exception of *I Tribunali*, the accounts in these journals are also brief.[60] Certain magazines from the mid-nineteenth century took as their subject court cases: such titles included *I processi celebri* (published in 1867), *Rivista dei dibattimenti celebri* (1872), *La corte d'assise. Rivista popolare giudiziaria* (1879), and *I grandi processi illustrati* (1896).[61] Each of these magazines had a short life and, in 1904, as far as I can ascertain, only *I grandi processi illustrati* was published, with the legal journal *I Tribunali* observing that *I grandi processi illustrati* had closed many years previously, but had been temporarily reopened specifically to report on the trial of Alberto Olivo.[62] After publishing 13 issues on Olivo's first trial, its publication stopped again.

Notwithstanding efforts to be as exhaustive as possible in consultation of relevant material, not every source has been used in every part of the book. Indeed, I principally deploy those sources that overtly demonstrate how stereotypes and prejudices were constructed and reinforced through the use of a peculiar lexicon and style and by highlighting or adjusting details and circumstances in grey areas. Court records have been examined but are not included in this book.[63]

---

60 The journal *I Tribunali* was edited by Enrico Valdata and had a narrative style addressing both the specialist and the popular public. See, Marco Unia, 'I periodici giuridici milanesi dal 1848 al 1946', in *Avvocati a Milano: sei secoli di storia*, ed. by Ada Gigli Marchetti, Alceo Riosa and Francesca Tacchi (Milan: Skira, 2004), pp. 191–97 (p. 194). See, also, Claudia Storti and Cristina Danusso, eds, *Figure del Foro lombardo tra XVI e XIX secolo* (Milan: Giuffrè, 2006).

61 Patrizia Caccia, '"Giustizia sia fatta: e giustizia sia". Giustizia e avvocati nella letteratura popolare milanese', in *Avvocati a Milano*, pp. 179–89. On the use of images in the media, see Roberto De Romanis and Rosamaria Loretelli, eds, *Il delitto narrato al popolo. Immagini di giustizia e stereotipi di criminalità in età moderna* (Palermo: Sellerio, 1999); Paola Pallottino, *Storia dell'illustrazione italiana: cinque secoli di immagini riprodotte* (Florence: Usher Arte, 2011); Alberto Mario Banti, 'Media e immagini nel mondo contemporaneo (XIX-XXI sec.)', *Società e storia* (2016), 529–32; Serafini, 'Immagini e criminalità nell'Italia di fine secolo tra Stampa, letteratura e scienza'.

62 *I tribunali*, 5 June 1904, p. 5.

63 Court records relating to the case are held at the Milan State Archive (only the sentence, see Milan State Archive, Assise, 1904–1906, 1904, in which there are also documents from the Supreme Court). According to Bergamo State Archive, court records from the second trial held in Bergamo do not exist: documents are only preserved from 1911 onwards.

The second part of the book is divided into three chapters: *The Case and the Press*, *The Trial and the Account of the Murder* and *The Defence and the Verdict*. The third part is also composed of three chapters: *After the First Trial's Verdict*, *The Second Trial* and *"Science"*. As already observed, there were two trials against Alberto Olivo, the first at the Court of Assize of Milan. Following Olivo's acquittal on a technicality (a purported misinterpretation of the counts by the jurors against which Olivo was to be judged), a second trial took place before the Court of Assize of Bergamo a few months later. The structure of parts two and three follows the various steps of the two trials. These parts examine how newspapers, magazines and journals constructed the images of the victim, Ernesta Beccaro, and the culprit, Alberto Olivo, and shifted the responsibility of the murder from Olivo to Beccaro, thus creating an equivocal misrepresentation of the reality.

PART 1

CHAPTER 1

Women in the theories of scientists

Notions that the body affects the mind have led to women being discriminated against since the earliest times. Historically, physicians, philosophers, and scholars in a range of academic fields stressed that the normatively less physically powerful build of a woman corresponded to a weaker mental capacity to develop and elaborate ideas, and such a theory was used to justify the different roles and positions held by women and men in society. The inferior status of women was enshrined in many aspects of life, affecting the way women were judged and expected to behave. In addition to being taken as a basis to describe women's alleged *infirmitas*, *imbecillitas*, and *levitas*,[1] however, the study of the body and physical appearance has also been used more broadly to explain personality in both men and women. This has been so since antiquity, including in treatises such as the pseudo-Aristotelian *Physiognomonics* that sought, through the observation of physical traits, to explain inclinations, behaviours, and models of personality.

---

1 On notions of *infirmitas*, *imbecillitas*, and *levitas*, see Ian Maclean, *The Renaissance Notion of Woman: A Study in the Fortunes of Scholasticism and Medical Science in European Intellectual Life* (Cambridge: Cambridge University Press, 1980), p. 8. See also Gail Kern Paster, 'Unbearable Coldness of Female Being: Women's Imperfection and the Humoral Economy', *English Literary Renaissance*, 28 (1998), 416–40. On medicine in the Renaissance, see, also, Nancy G. Siraisi, *Medicine and the Italian Universities: 1250–1600* (Leiden: Brill, 2001); Nancy G. Siraisi, *History, Medicine, and the Traditions of Renaissance Learning* (University of Michigan Press, 2007); William Eamon, 'The Scientific Renaissance', in *A Companion to the Worlds of the Renaissance*, ed. by Guido Ruggiero (Oxford: Blackwell, 2002), pp. 403–24.

These types of studies flourished with variable success for centuries.[2] The sixteenth-century Neapolitan scholar Giambattista Della Porta argued, for example, in his *De humana physiognomonia* (1586),[3] that, since *physin* means 'nature' and *gnome*, 'rule', then 'da tal forma di corpo, si conosce tal passion dell'animo' [from the shape of the body, it is also possible to know the passion of the soul].[4] In this context, the face, in particular, was considered the undisputed mirror of the inner self: the most noble part of the body, receiver of the body's 'sangue, e spiriti' [blood and spirits].[5] This made Della Porta claim that 'le passioni di tutto il corpo, e dell'animo si conoscono nella faccia' [the passions of the whole body, and soul are evident in the face].[6] Analysis of facial traits further permitted him to understand types of animals with which a person might be identified. This led him to warn, for example, that despite the softness and tenderness of a woman's body, she was in reality 'ladra e piena d'inganni' [a thief and full of deceptions],[7] since women were to men as leopards were to lions: the man, like a lion, 'magnanimo, generoso, disioso di vincere, mansueto, giusto' [magnanimous, generous, eager to win, meek, just]; the leopard, 'delicato, effeminato, iracondo, insidioso, fraudolente, audace e timido insiememente' [delicate, effeminate, irascible, insidious, fraudulent, bold and shy all at once] – just

---

2 On this, see Lucia Rodler, *Il corpo specchio dell'anima: teoria e storia della fisiognomica* (Milan: Mondadori, 2000). See, also, Paolo Savoia, *Early Modern Surgery: Faces, Men, and Pain* (London: Routledge, 2020).

3 Giambattista Della Porta, *De humana physiognomonia libri sex*, ed. by Alfonso Paolella (Naples: Edizioni scientifiche italiane, 2013), p. 88. Della Porta (1535–1615) was a philosopher from Naples, most known for *De humana physiognomonia* (1586) and *Coelesti Physiognomonia* (1603). On Della Porta, see, also, Katherine MacDonald, 'Humanistic Self-Representation in Giovan Battista Della Porta's "Della Fisonomia Dell'Uomo": Antecedents and Innovation', *The Sixteenth Century Journal*, 36/2 (2005), 397–414; Eugenio Refini, 'Bodily Passions: Physiognomy and Drama in Giovan Battista Della Porta', *Renaissance and Reformation*, 40, 1 (2017), 121–39.

4 Della Porta, *De humana physiognomonia libri sex*, p. 96. On the link between physiognomy and grace, see Martino Monti Rossi, 'Fisiognomica e grazia: da Bernardo di Chiaravalle a Giovan Battista Della Porta', *Bruniana & Campanelliana* 21, 2 (2015), 330–45.

5 Della Porta, *De humana physiognomonia libri sex*, p. 97.

6 Ibid.

7 Ibid., p. 88.

like a woman.[8] Moreover, leopards were treacherous, like women, a characteristic easily remarkable in a leopard, maintained Della Porta, because of its habit of secretly following other animals.[9] For Della Porta, the correct way to understand the true personality of a person was to compare them with such animals and to deduce if feminine or masculine traits predominated. A man who tried to conceal his evil and wicked mind, for example, would nonetheless manifest characteristics of the leopard and, consequently, characteristics similar to those of women.[10]

The study of physical traits was also key for the British philosopher Thomas Browne (1605–1682).[11] In his *Christian Morals*, written around 1675 and published posthumously, Browne argued that, '[s]ince the Brow speaks often true, since Eyes and Noses have Tongues, and the countenance proclaims the Heart and inclinations; let observation so far instruct thee in physiognomical lines'.[12] In a fundamentally misogynistic approach, Browne stressed that, '[s]ince Men and Women have their proper Virtues and Vices, and even Twins of different sexes have not only distinct coverings in the Womb, but differing qualities and Virtuous Habits after; transplace not their Properties and confound not their Distinctions[;] Let Masculine and feminine accomplishments shine in their proper Orbs, and adorn their Respective subjects'.[13] Insisting that he did not speak 'in prejudice, nor [...] averse from that sweet sex, but naturally amorous of all that is beautiful',[14] Browne emphasised that women's accomplishments were less important than those of men, given that '[t]he whole world was made for man, but the twelfth part of man for woman: man is the whole world, and the breath of God; woman the rib, and crooked piece of man'.[15] A significant aspect of Browne's theories was the idea of the existence of a 'national face'; indeed, he argued that '[t]here are

8 Ibid., pp. 87 and 89.
9 Ibid., p. 89.
10 Ibid., p. 90
11 Thomas Browne, *Religio Medici: Or, the Christian Religion, as Professed by a Physician; Freed from Priest-Craft and the Jargon of Schools*, 2 vols (London: Curll, 1736), II, p. 92. Browne was a British philosopher; his *Religio Medici* was published in 1643, followed by *Pseudodoxia Epidemica* in 1646, and *Hydriotaphia* in 1658.
12 Thomas Browne, *Christian Morals* (Cambridge: Cambridge University Press, 1716), p. 47.
13 Ibid., p. 29.
14 Thomas Browne, *Religio Medici* (Boston: Roberts Brothers, 1878 [1643]), p. 137.
15 Ibid., p. 137.

therefore Provincial Faces, National Lips and Noses, which testify not only the Natures of those Countries, but of those which have them elsewhere'.[16]

Particularly from the end of the eighteenth century, assumptions like these were further theorised and developed. The works of Swiss physiognomist Johann Kaspar Lavater (1741–1801), including *Physiognomische Fragmente zur Beförderung der Menschenkenntnis und Menschenliebe* (1775–1778), became extremely popular and were translated into English and French and reprinted many times. Alongside his endorsement of Browne's ideas on nationality as a biological characteristic,[17] Lavater was complicit with the misogynistic vision of the time, claiming that female temperament was highly mutable and that women were 'easy to conduct and to tempt; so ready of submission to the enterprise and power of the man', as well as lacking the profundity of thought that Lavater considered a man's prerogative.[18]

The body, and particularly the female body, continued to be the locus for discussion used to justify prejudices and inequality. In parallel with these new disciplines, 'traditional' physicians also continued to study the influence of the body on the mind. In a major study, *Système physique et moral de la femme* – a work widely known at the end of the eighteenth century that was translated into Italian – French physician Pierre Roussel set out theories suggesting that women were less likely than men to be able to engage in higher mental concepts.[19] The 'weakness' that characterised a

---

16 Browne, *Christian Morals*, pp. 47–8.

17 Lavater's ideas on the national character were manipulated to endorse Eurocentrism. Upholding the primacy of one nationality over another served to support the aim of justifying colonialism and suprematism. During Fascism, for example, the idea of race as an immanent characteristic was highlighted to the extent that 'Italian origins made a person *Italian* even if these origins were unknown to that person' [Sara Delmedico and Manuela Di Franco, 'Fascism and "Italians Abroad": National Identity and the Building of the Fascist State', *Chronica Mundi*, 14 (2019–2020), 81–119 (p. 99)].

18 Johann Kaspar Lavater, *Physiognomy, Or, the Corresponding Analogy between the Conformation of the Features and the Ruling Passions of the Mind* (London: Tegg, 1866), pp. 181–2. A Swiss physiognomist and philosopher, Lavater is best known for his *Physiognomische Fragmente zur Beförderung der Menschenkenntnis und Menschenliebe*, published between 1774 and 1778.

19 Pierre Roussel, *Sistema fisico e morale della donna*, 2 vols (Naples: Manzi, 1829 [1775]), II, p. 65. Pierre Roussel (1742–1802), a French physician, studied women from a physical and moral stance. His best-known work, *Système physique et moral de la femme* (1775), went through several editions until 1845.

woman's physical body was also reflected in her mental capacities, impeding her from undertaking the necessary effort and developing the restraint of spirit necessary for the study of the abstract sciences. Whilst men were readily able to hold the broader views required for debate in politics and for an appreciation of fundamental moral principles, women were not. Roussel theorised that, because of their fickle imagination, women were unable to hold a firm mental position, rendering them unequal to the study of those arts that required such discipline. By contrast, their essential nature was to be found in the sweet and fond feelings that could arise from their very weakness: a weakness that made them feel powerless and, by consequence, enabled them to empathise with the unfortunate people of the world. This natural piety was the basis for their social virtues. Therefore, argued Roussel, whilst women's qualities may not be as dazzling as those of men, they are more beneficial to society.[20]

Similar theories were expressed by French physiologist Pierre Jean George Cabanis (1757–1808).[21] He believed that the women's physical make-up deeply affected their psychological capacities and tendencies, explaining, in particular, that women's:

> pulpe cérébrale participe de la mollesse des autres parties [...]. Tous les mouvements s'y font d'une manière plus facile, et par conséquent plus prompte [...]. Or, la promptitude et la vivacité d'action dans le système nerveux sont la mesure de la sensibilité générale du sujet
>
> [cerebral pulp is similar to the softness of their other parts [...]. All movements are made in an easier manner, and consequently more promptly [...]. Now, the promptness and vivacity of action in the nervous system are the measure of the general sensibility of the subject].[22]

He went further, arguing that women's 'weakheadedness' was made yet worse by their tendency to feel insecure. As a result, they were in constant pursuit of attention so as to fortify their own existence through the attention of those

---

[20] Roussel, *Sistema fisico e morale della donna*, pp. 66–7.

[21] Pierre Jean George Cabanis (1757–1808) was a French physiologist. In his *Rapports du physique et du moral de l'homme* (1802), he studied men and women from several points of view, highlighting the intellectual predominance of men.

[22] Pierre Jean George Cabanis, *Rapports du physique et du moral de l'homme* (Paris: Fortin, Masson, 1843 [1802]), p. 201.

they considered more able to protect them.[23] Their essential nature, already weak, was further eroded by such repeated behaviour. Even in childhood, where the nature of male and female character appeared more similar, they were not equal, and an attentive eye was already able to discern certain differences:

> les garçons ont quelque chose de plus emporté dans leurs mouvements; ils donnent moins d'attention aux petites choses [...]; leurs attitudes ne sont pas seulement plus libres et plus prononcées, mais qu'elles diffèrent aussi par la disposition habituelle à tel mouvement plutôt qu'à tel autre
>
> [boys have something more fiery in their movements; they pay less attention to small things [...]; their behaviours are not only freer and more emphatic, but also differ in their habitual disposition to one movement rather than another].[24]

Little girls, on the contrary, were already entirely caught up in the impression they wanted to make on those around them, preferring to play games more aligned with the role for which nature had destined them. In particular, 'l'art de la conversation par lequel elles doivent un jour assurer leur empire commence à leur devenir familier; elles s'y exercent incessamment' [the art of conversation, by which they must one day ensure their empire, begins to become familiar to them; they practise it incessantly].[25] Furthermore, he claimed, women would reject any effort of mind because they understood that those things that necessitated deep cogitation were not designed for them. And since women were unable to bear fatigue, confront challenges, or tolerate the tumultuous clash of great assemblies of men, they left such hard work and its associated perils to men. Women turned away from discussions of public affairs, for which great rationality, character, and energy were prerequisites. Cabanis further argued that women left not only political or civilian jobs to men but also all tasks exterior to the home environment, keeping for themselves the labour of the care of the family and home, that 'sweet domestic domain' that made them both respectable and gave them worth.[26] Women were strongly dependent on men; their happiness was always

---

23 Ibid., p. 197.
24 Ibid., p. 195.
25 Ibid.
26 Ibid.

tightly linked to the impression they made on men.[27] In everyday life, a man would comport himself according to the ascendancy of his intelligence; a woman would seek always to influence a man through the seductiveness of her manner and by constant alertness to anything that might flatter his heart and captivate his imagination.[28] Cabanis endorsed the idea that women who abandoned the role assigned them by nature to pursue ephemeral triumphs by studying the sciences would gain not knowledge, but merely the pedantry of these studies. He also directed his critiques towards those philosophers who thought that the cause of women's subjugation was insufficient education. He claimed that erudite women merely pretended to know things, but in reality knew nothing: they confused and confounded all objects and ideas, were unable to fix their attention sufficiently long on one thing, were unable to experience the lively and profound pleasures of deep thought, and were incapable of deep meditation. What was more, the fate of those few women who could achieve genuine success would be even worse, since they would fail to find a place for themselves in society. Too intelligent to be real women, but physically still female, the most successful in fact belonged to neither sex.[29]

Throughout the nineteenth century, this physiognomical discourse pervaded and gave ground to collateral kinds of analysis such as phrenology.[30] Influenced by physiognomy,[31] phrenology explored cerebral localisation. By analysing the skull, German physicians Franz Joseph Gall (1758–1828) and Johann Caspar Spurzheim (1776–1832), 'inventors' of this new discipline, identified particular sites in the brain reportedly responsible for specific psychic functions.[32]

27 Ibid., p. 215.

28 Ibid., pp. 209–10.

29 Ibid., pp. 214–15.

30 For an overview, see, also, in the first instance: Richard Twine, 'Physiognomy, Phrenology and the Temporality of the Body', *Body & Society*, 8/1 (2002), 67–88 (p. 74); and Jan Verplaetse, *Localising the Moral Sense: Neuroscience and the Search for the Cerebral Seat of Morality, 1800–1930* (Dordrecht: Springer, 2009), pp. 33–35.

31 Twine, 'Physiognomy, Phrenology and the Temporality of the Body', p. 74.

32 The major work of Franz Joseph Gall and Johann Gaspar Spurzheim is *Anatomie et physiologie du système nerveux en général, et du cerveau en particulier*, 4 vols (Paris: Schoell, 1810–1819). The term 'phrenology' was used by Spurzheim from the early decades of the nineteenth century. For an overview of Gall and Spurzheim's thinking and biography see, in the first instance: Georges Lantéri-Laura, *Histoire de la phrénologie* (Paris:

This new discipline's reach also extended to the United States of America. Establishments for the pursuit of phrenology were created in New York and Philadelphia by brothers Lorenzo Niles Fowler and Orson Squire Fowler, their members studying the subject and disseminating its theories. Together with another proponent, Samuel Wells, the brothers founded a printing house and published their own studies on the topic, alongside Spurzheim's and George Combe's works.[33] Lorenzo Fowler's *Marriage, its History and Ceremonies, with a Phrenological and Physiological Exposition of the Functions and Qualifications for Happy Marriages* is one such output. In this book, he gave advice on marriage by considering physical suitability. For example, if a man had 'a predominance of the reflective intellect, with uncommon perseverance and concentration of mind', he should avoid marrying a woman with too much abstractedness, because, otherwise, he would not hear the call to dinner, and she would forget preparing it.[34]

PUF, 1970); Giovanni Pietro Lombardo, Marco Duichin, and François Azouvi, eds, *Frenologia, fisiognomica e psicologia delle differenze individuali in Franz Joseph Gall: antecedenti storici e sviluppi disciplinari* (Turin: Bollati Boringhieri, 1997); Marc Renneville, *Le langage des crânes: histoire de la phrénologie* (Paris: Institut d'edition Sanofi-Synthelabo, 2000); John Van Whye, 'The Authority of Human Nature: The "Schädellehre" of Franz Joseph Gall', *The British Journal for the History of Science*, 35/1 (2002), 17–42; and James Poskett, *Materials of the Mind: Phrenology, Race, and the Global History of Science, 1815–1920* (Chicago: University of Chicago Press, 2019). On the influence of Gall's theories in Italy, see the letter of Giuseppe Maria De Rolandis ('Lettre de M. le docteur De Rolandis, de Turin, a M. le docteur Fossati, sur un criminel convaincu de plusieurs viols, suivis de meurtre', *Journal de la Société Phrénologique de Paris*, 3 (1835), 244–8); a work also known to the jurist and sociologist Enrico Ferri (1856–1929), who particularly acknowledged De Rolandis' studies in 'Necroscopia di un delinquente', *Repertorio medico-chirurgico del Piemonte* (1835) (see Enrico Ferri, *Sociologia criminale*, 3rd ed. (Turin: Bocca, 1892), p. 51). On analysis of corpses, see, also, Silvano Montaldo, 'The Medicalisation of the Corpse in Liberal Italy. National Legislation and the Case of Turin', in *Public Uses of Human Remains and Relics in History*, ed. by Silvia Cavicchioli and Luigi Provero (New York-Abingdon: Routledge, 2019), pp. 230–45.

33 Among the works of the Scottish phrenologist George Combe (1788–1858), his *Notes on the United States of North America during a Phrenological Visit in 1838–39–40* (1841) recounts his travels across and lectures in America, and his analysis of American society.

34 Lorenzo Fowler, *Marriage, its History and Ceremonies, with a Phrenological and Physiological Exposition of the Functions and Qualifications for Happy Marriages* (New York: Fowlers and Wells, 1848), p. 203.

The climate of the time supported the flourishing of several other pseudo-sciences, including Francis Galton's eugenics.[35] Such theories were used as conceptual building blocks by which it was possible to construct ideas of superiority and inferiority across individuals: through theories of eugenics, one individual could infer grounds for a sense of superiority over another in justification of racism; men could locate a basis for arguing for inherent superiority over women, justifying sexual discrimination on a putative basis of science and rationality.

Differences between men and women were also the object of several scholarly investigations in other geographical areas and in other disciplines, including the work of British anthropologist James McGrigor Allan (1827–1916). Seeking to explain the 'mental and moral as well as material, arising from a difference in material structure, in texture and temperament as well as organic, which no similarity of education can ever remove, no identity of circumstances can ever serve to annihilate',[36] McGrigor Allan argued that '[i]n reflective power, woman is utterly unable to compete with man; but she possesses a compensating gift in her marvellous faculty of intuition'.[37] The inherent prejudice of this so-called 'gift' had been clearly explained by Pierre Bourdieu as 'a particular form of the special lucidity of the dominated [...] needed to anticipate desires or avoid unpleasantness'.[38] Therefore, this 'faculty', far from being 'marvellous', was nothing more than the correct and praised virtue a good woman – obedient and submissive – had to have to please the man.

Charles Darwin also advanced certain views now likely to be considered misogynist. Whilst his studies and observations led him to claim that man

---

[35] Francis Galton (1822–1911) believed that certain human traits were hereditary and could be improved by selective breeding. He used the term "eugenic" to describe his theories (Francis Galton, *Inquiries into Human Faculty and its Development* (London: Macmillan, 1883), p. 24).

[36] James McGrigor Allan, 'On the Real Differences in the Minds of Men and Women', *Journal of the Anthropological Society of London*, 7 (1869), cxcv–ccxix (p. cxcv). On McGrigor Allan's ideas on women see, also, his *Woman Suffrage, Wrong in Principle, and Practice: An Essay* (London: Remington & Company, 1890). For an analysis of his work, see Cynthia Eagle Russett, *Sexual Science: The Victorian Construction of Womanhood* (Cambridge, MA: Harvard UP, 1989), pp. 30–1, p. 55, and pp. 75–6.

[37] McGrigor Allan, 'On the Real Differences in the Minds of Men and Women', cxcvii.

[38] Bourdieu, *Masculine Domination*, p. 31.

had a more inventive genius, whereas 'woman seem[ed] to differ from man in mental disposition, chiefly in her greater tenderness and less [sic] selfishness',[39] he further observed that:

> the chief distinction in the intellectual power of the two sexes is shewn by man attaining to a higher eminence, in whatever he takes up, than woman can attain – whether requiring deep thought, reason, or imagination [...]; [and] some of the pure mental faculties have been modified or strengthened through sexual selection [...]. [T]thus man has ultimately become superior to women.[40]

In late nineteenth-century Italy, the works of scientists such as Cabanis and Darwin were beginning to be known and widely examined. Women were still the object of sustained attention; the findings of such observation continued to serve the goal of justifying their subordination and promoting a hierarchical order within families and society.

Paolo Mantegazza, holder of the first university Chair of anthropology in Italy, took women as his subject from the earliest days of his career. In his dissertation, *Fisiologia del piacere*, he claimed that a woman 'è troppo distratta, e per la sua organizzazione intellettuale troppo avversa all'analisi delle sensazioni' [is too distracted, and, due to her mental structure, too averse to the analysis of sensations].[41] He thought women were, and always would be, less intelligent than men, since the general characteristics of female thought were childlike.[42]

---

39 Charles Darwin, *The Descent of Man, and Selection in Relation to Sex* (London: Murray, 1871), p. 326.

40 Ibid., p. 327.

41 Paolo Mantegazza, *Fisiologia del piacere* (Milan: Bernardoni, 1874 [1854]), p. 117.

42 Paolo Mantegazza, *Fisiologia della donna*, 2 vols (Milan: Bietti, 1945 [1893]), II, p. 207. A Lombardian physiologist, anthropologist, and member of the Italian Parliament from 1865 to 1876, Mantegazza (1831–1910) supported Darwin's theories of evolution. His major works are: *La fisiologia del piacere* (1854), *La fisiologia dell'amore* (1873), and *Fisiologia della donna* (1893). On Mantegazza's early studies, see: Maria Gloria Roselli, 'Paolo Mantegazza: la prima cattedra di Antropologia in Italia e la fondazione del Museo', in *L'Istituto di Studi Superiori e la cultura umanistica a Firenze*, 2 vols, ed. by Adele Dei (Ospedaletto-Pisa: Pacini, 2016), II, pp. 601–55; Nicoletta Pireddu, 'Paolo Mantegazza: ritratto dell'antropologo come esteta', in *Paolo Mantegazza: medico, antropologo, viaggiatore: selezione di contributi dai Convegni di Monza, Firenze, Lerici*, ed. by Cosimo Chiarelli and Walter Pasini (Florence: Florence University Press, 2002), pp. 1–11; and Paul M. Taylor and Cesare Marino, 'Paolo Mantegazza's Vision: The Science of Man

Such visions were key in the work of other scientists, including Italian anthropologist Giuseppe Sergi, who endorsed ideas on women's inferiority, offering evidence from his own studies. In a letter to the Italian criminologist Cesare Lombroso published in *Archivio di psichiatria, scienze penali ed antropologia criminale* (1892), Sergi wrote that the cerebral capacity of women was smaller than that of men and that women had fewer red blood cells than men.[43] Sergi contended that the general nature of the woman was somewhere between that of an adult and a young boy, 'non come essere inferiore, patisce cioè anche in questo un arresto di sviluppo rispetto all'uomo' [not as an inferior being, but also in this she suffers an arrest in development compared to man].[44] By a lag inherent in their nature – 'in uno stadio che per l'uomo è imperfezione, per lei è la condizione naturale' [in a stage which for man is an imperfection, for her is the natural condition],[45] Sergi's 'normative woman' was one who

> ama di esser corteggiata e amata dall'uomo, ma cede come una vittima alle di lui voglie sessuali [...]. Si sa che bisogna far molte carezze e molto solletico per indurre

---

behind the World's First Museum of Anthropology (Florence, Italy, 1869)', *Museum Anthropology*, 42 (2019), 109–24. See, also, Giovanni Landucci, *Darwinismo a Firenze. Tra scienze e ideologia (1860–1900)* (Florence: Olschki, 1977), and Giovanni Landucci, *L'occhio e la mente. Scienza e filosofia nell'Italia dell'Ottocento* (Florence: Olschki, 1987).

43 Giuseppe Sergi, 'Sensibilità femminile. Lettera all'illustre Prof. C. Lombroso', *Archivio di psichiatria, scienze penali ed antropologia criminale per servire allo studio dell'uomo alienato e delinquente*, 13/1 (1892), 1–8 (p. 2). Ezechia Marco Lombroso (1835–1909), known as Cesare, was an Italian criminologist and physician. He was best known for his theories on correspondences between physiognomic characteristics and likelihood to commit crime. Among the many works on Lombroso, see, for example: Mary Gibson, *Born to Crime: Cesare Lombroso and the Origins of Biological Criminology* (Westport, CT; London: Praeger, 2002); Nicole Hahn Rafter, *The Criminal Brain: Understanding Biological Theories of Crime* (New York: New York University Press, 2008); Silvano Montaldo, ed., *Cesare Lombroso. Gli scienziati e la nuova Italia* (Bologna: il Mulino, 2010); Peter Becker and Richard F. Wetzell, eds, *Criminals and Their Scientists: The History of Criminology in International Perspective* (Cambridge: Cambridge University Press, 2013); *The Cesare Lombroso Handbook*, ed. by Paul Knepper and Per Jørgen Ystehede (London: Routledge, 2013); Silvano Montaldo, 'Lombroso: The Myth, The History', *Crime, Histoire & Sociétés / Crime, History & Societies*, 22/2 (2018), 31–61; and Liliosa Azara and Luca Tedesco, eds, *Donna delinquente e la prostituta: l'eredità di Lombroso nella cultura e nella società italiane* (Rome: Viella, 2019); Montaldo, *Donne delinquenti*, pp. 109–254.

44 Sergi, 'Sensibilità femminile', p. 4.

45 Ibid., p. 8.

> la donna a cedere con piacere ed a farle sentire il piacere sessuale; senza questi mezzi rimane fredda, né dà, né ha soddisfazione
>
> [loves to be courted and loved by a man, but cedes like a victim to his sexual desires [...]. It is known that a woman needs many caresses and much tickling to induce her to give in with pleasure and make her feel sexual pleasure; without these means she remains cold, she neither gives nor has satisfaction].[46]

Sensitivity was a pivotal element around which investigations of some scholars revolved and that served to support ideas on the inferiority of women. According to historian Mary Gibson, these scholars believed that 'external, biological traits and internal, psychological states were directly related, experimenters equated sensitivity of touch, emotion, and morality'.[47] Lombroso, for example, endorsed this vision through his support of the work of Salvatore Ottolenghi (1861–1934), who maintained that 'non pensa chi non sente' [those who do not feel cannot think],[48] contending that women had minimal sensitivity.[49] Women were described as appearing of equal or superior strength and stature to men before puberty and often also in intelligence too, but then it could be observed that they began to fall behind, and this momentary preponderance was evidence of a precociousness normally associated with the inferior races.[50] In his *The Criminal Woman, the Prostitute, and the Normal Woman*, written with Guglielmo Ferrero in 1893, Lombroso expanded his ideas on sensitivity by postulating an 'ottusità dolorifica' [dullness to pain]:[51] this was the reason why women so readily fell pregnant, despite the

---

46 Ibid., p. 5.

47 Mary Gibson, 'On the Insensitivity of Women: Science and the Woman Question in Liberal Italy, 1890–1910', *Journal of Women's History*, 2/2 (1990), 11–41 (p. 15).

48 Salvatore Ottolenghi, *La sensibilità della donna* (Turin: Bocca, 1896), p. 3. Lombroso mentioned Ottolenghi's work in an article published in 1891 (see footnote below), some years before this publication.

49 Cesare Lombroso, *Tatto sensibilità generale e dolorifica, e tipo degenerativo in donne normali, criminali e alienate: seduta del 2 gennaio 1891* ([n. p..]: [n. pub.], 1891), pp. 81–2.

50 This point had already been expressed by other scientists, including James McGrigor Allan. See: McGrigor Allan, 'On the Real Differences in the Minds of Men and Women', p. cxcvii. Lombroso and Ferrero, *La donna delinquente, la prostituta e la donna normale*, p. VI. Guglielmo Ferrero (1871–1942) was an Italian historian and sociologist. Professionally, he collaborated with Lombroso, and he also married Lombroso's daughter, Gina.

51 Lombroso and Ferrero, *La donna delinquente, la prostituta e la donna normale*, p. 66. Lombroso and Ferrero noted that 'anche nel sangue pare chiara l'inferiorità' [even in

well-known pain of giving birth and the little pleasure they took from love. Lombroso and Ferrero were convinced that 'l'uomo non farebbe altrettanto' [a man would not do the same].[52]

Driven by an anxiety to explain and justify theories of the inferiority of women, such remarks suggested that women had a degree of control over whether or not they fell pregnant and that it was only their dullness that made them insist on becoming pregnant and, consequently, experiencing pain. Alongside liberating the man from any active role in making a woman pregnant, similar to Sergi's ideas, Lombroso and Ferrero were convinced that women enjoyed sexual pleasure only with a man for whom they felt love: this was deemed evidence that women's love was a condescension composed of those instincts of devotion that existed in a relationship between superior and inferior.[53]

The historian Matteo Loconsole has observed that, for scientists such as Lombroso and Sergi, men's sexuality was rendered complete through sexual intercourse, whilst the sexuality of women revolved around motherhood, which was their natural occupation.[54] Such ideas on women's sexual pleasure meant that those who were not compliant with the role assigned them by nature were seen as deviant. This deviant sexuality was to be controlled and limited to avoid harm and disruption to society.[55]

Sergi, however, in fact considered women's lower acuity of sexual desire a natural and useful brake for the greater masculine desire,[56] arguably a barrier

---

the blood the inferiority seems clear], pointing out that women had fewer red blood cells. Specifically, they argued that, on average, men had five million red blood cells per cubic millimetre of blood compared to four million for women. Cesare Lombroso and Guglielmo Ferrero, *La donna delinquente, la prostituta e la donna normale* (Turin: Bocca, 1903 [1893]), pp. 21–22.

52 Ibid., p. 66.

53 Ibid., pp. 127 and 130.

54 Matteo Loconsole, 'Laws and sexual prejudices in the Italian positivist culture: murderous mothers and the education to infanticide', *Studi sulla Formazione*, 22/2 (2019) 355–74 (p. 360).

55 On this point, see Annamaria Tagliavini, 'Il fondo oscuro dell'anima femminile', in *La donna nelle scienze dell'uomo: immagini del femminile nella cultura scientifica italiana di fine secolo*, ed. by Valeria P. Babini, Fernanda Minuz, and Annamaria Tagliavini (Milan: Franco Angeli, 1986), pp. 78–113 (p. 102). See, also, Loconsole, 'Laws and sexual prejudices', p. 357.

56 Sergi, 'Sensibilità femminile', p. 6.

to the male tendency to destruction assumed by Lombroso and Ferrero.[57] Moreover, women were focused on pursuing the goal nature had assigned them: that is, marriage. This could be inferred by the fact that, according to Sergi, in Europe young women were happier if they were able to find young husband but nonetheless they would rarely hesitate to marry an old man. Sometimes they would even abandon a younger man for an older one if the latter were wealthier.[58] Their weakheadedness was also demonstrated by their keenness to marry even a man they despised if he were to insist and if the possibility of marriage were real.[59] Female inferiority was also manifest in the words of Galton, as reported by Sergi, as evidence of the different ways in which women and men loved: 'il desiderio dell'uomo è per la donna, ma il desiderio della donna è per il desiderio del desiderio dell'uomo' [the man's desire is for the woman, but the woman's desire is for the desire of the man's desire].[60]

Drawing on contemporaneous notions of femininity, Sergi highlighted those characteristics considered 'female': a tendency 'al capriccio, alla vanità e all'infantilità, in forme più o meno chiare' [to caprice, vanity and childishness, in more or less clear forms].[61] Vanity was also considered a key characteristic by Lombroso and Ferrero, who argued that civilisation caused men's vanity to decrease but made the vanity of women increase.[62]

Situating his thinking in common ideas of his time, Sergi explained his view of female emancipation. Referring to the habitual dichotomy of roles, he argued that any person who sought to dislocate women from their practical social life would make 'di questo sesso, così ben delineato e definito dalla natura, una forma sessuale mista, la donna-maschio, che come è facile a comprendere, sarebbe una mostruosa anomalia' [of this sex, so well delineated and defined by nature, a mixed sexual form, the man-woman, which, as can easily be understood, would be a monstrous anomaly]:[63] a distortion of

---

57 Lombroso and Ferrero, *La donna delinquente, la prostituta e la donna normale*, p. 98.

58 Sergi, 'Sensibilità femminile', p. 5.

59 Ibid., p. 5.

60 Giuseppe Sergi, *Per l'educazione del carattere*, 2nd ed. (Milan: Dumolard, 1893 [1884]), p. 234.

61 Sergi, *Per l'educazione del carattere*, p. 238.

62 Lombroso and Ferrero, *La donna delinquente, la prostituta e la donna normale*, p. 140. Lombroso and Ferrero also considered vanity as something to be used to punish women's crimes. See footnote 49, p. 69.

63 Sergi, *Per l'educazione del carattere*, p. 226.

the human ideal, and would cause female influence in the general sphere of humanity to decrease rather than increase.[64] Sergi praised what he considered 'true' female emancipation: namely, a liberation 'dalle influenze superstiziose di ogni genere, le quali rendono schiavo l'animo gentile e flessibile, e danno adito a penetrare nel seno della famiglia, a chi ne abusa e tenta di avviluppare con una rete strettissima la società intera' [from superstitious influences of all kinds that enslave the gentle and pliable soul, and allow to penetrate in the heart of the family those who abuse them and try to envelop in them the whole of society in a very tight net].[65] Once again, Sergi's words focused on what was key to the society of the time: a patriarchal family, led by a man, in which the woman's role revolved around domesticity and motherhood. The family was to be protected from the malign behaviours and actions of which women could be capable. Identified as the weak element, women had to be be guided and, if necessary, corrected, as we shall see, also by using violence.[66]

These theories served to justify the inferior status of women in everyday life and across all contexts. Men and women were to comply with specific roles; non-compliance meant a loss of value in the eyes of society. However, whilst noncompliance for men might in some cases have been excusable, for women, the approach was not so kind. Indeed, given that women were

---

64 Ibid., p. 227.

65 Ibid., p. 246.

66 The power to correct was grounded in the idea of discrimination and inequality. Considering a person inferior to another also implied that the latter was allowed to correct and discipline the former. Some degree of violence was accounted as a means of correction and discipline and was fully tolerated, but, as contended by the historian Christel Radica, from the nineteenth century, female voices increasingly denounced domestic violence, and, on a legislative level, the Zanardelli code introduced the crime of spousal abuse (see, Radica, 'Onore, follia e amore', p. 81). Indeed, Articles 390 and 391 of the 1889 Penal Code ruled about abuse of means of correction or discipline and family mistreatment, thus, on the one hand, clearly affirming that a person had the power to use violence over others if aimed at correct or discipline them; on the other hand, envisioning a blurred idea of abuse of this power and the boundaries within which violence could be exercised (only to correct or discipline). As the historian Laura Schettini explained, the ratio of these two articles relied on the idea that, for what concerned abuse of the means of correction and discipline, the perpetrator, moved by feelings of benevolence, aimed to improve the victim, but used means that exceeded the measure. In cases of mistreatment, instead, the perpetrator was moved by resentment and adversity (Schettini, 'La violenza maschile contro le donne', p. 139).

allegedly 'made for men', their happiness was deemed to revolve around men and the impression they made on men. This meant that it was implicit that women not abiding by these ideas of functionality were considered 'abnormal'.

Many men and women of the time, living in a context in which these ideas were accepted and endorsed, conformed to this vision. For example, Paola and Gina Lombroso, the daughters of Cesare, even contributed to their father's studies. In Paola's work, despite her positing in her *Caratteri della femminilità* that women had 'una superiorità organica' [an organic superiority],[67] we nonetheless find the usual topoi of female sentimentality and garrulousness. For Paola, women were unable to write drama because they needed instead a genre that 'permetta di estendersi piuttosto che di concentrarsi, di analizzare piuttosto che di sintetizzare' [allows them to elaborate rather than to concentrate, to analyse rather than synthesise].[68] Moreover, she wrote, women composed bad poetry because they were too poetic and too emotional, when poetry required inspiration, a poetic temperament, laborious cultivation, an education in aesthetics, and rigorous discipline – elements of which women were not possessed.[69] Furthermore, 'il desiderio di piacere, che si proietta nella civetteria, per la donna è ormai diventato un istinto perché è la condizione per esser ricercata dall'uomo, condizione essenziale al suo destino fisiologico e sociale' [the desire to please, which is projected into coquetry, has now become instinctual for women, because it is the condition for being pursued by a man, an essential condition for her physiological and social destiny].[70] Paola's sister Gina also wrote on women and the female character, focusing in particular on 'alterocentrism', which she

---

67 See Guglielmo Gambarotta, *Inchiesta sulla donna* (Turin: Bocca, 1899), pp. 133–40. See, also, Paola Lombroso, 'Superiorità organica della donna', *L'Italia femminile: corriere delle donne italiane: mode, letteratura, arte, varietà*, I/1, 15 January 1899.

68 Paola Lombroso, *Caratteri della femminilità* (Turin: Bocca, 1909), p. 32. On the life and works of Paola Lombroso (1871–1954) and Gina Lombroso (1872–1944), see Delfina Dolza, *Essere figlie di Lombroso. Due donne intellettuali tra '800 e '900* (Milan: Franco Angeli, 1990); Michela De Giorgio, 'Madri del "secol novo". Sfide, lotte, scelte', in Maria Teresa Mori, Alessandra Pescarolo, Anna Scattigno, Simonetta Soldani, eds, *Di Generazione in Generazione: Le Italiane Dall'Unità a Oggi* (Rome: Viella, 2014), pp. 139–66 (p. 143); Montaldo, *Donne delinquenti*, pp. 185–97.

69 Lombroso, *Caratteri della femminilità*, p. 33.

70 Ibid., p. 91.

deemed 'la chiave di volta dell'animo femminile' [the keystone of the female soul].[71] Alterocentrism, or the instinct for altruism, was considered pivotal for humanity, because 'la creazione e l'allevamento dei figli presuppongono un genitore determinato a sacrificare tutta o parte della sua esistenza ai nuovi esseri, e questo genitore non può essere che il genitore che crea: la femmina' [the creation and rearing of children presupposes one parent compelled to sacrifice all or part of their existence to these new beings, and this parent can only be the parent who creates: the female].[72] This altruism was meant to respond to specific needs such as, again, the desire to please men.

71 Gina Lombroso, *L'anima della donna*, 3 vols (Bologna Zanichelli, 1917–1926), I, *Gli enigmi più oscuri*, p. 215.

72 Ibid. p. 12. In Cesare Lombroso's work, *La donna delinquente, la prostituta e la donna normale*, written with Gina's husband Guglielmo Ferrero, Cesare Lombroso also reported Gina's observations; for example, that 'le ragazze fin da bambine hanno meno bontà per le compagne che non i maschi. Esse sono pietose, ma per le persone di un'altra casta, di un altro sesso, un'altra età. Per es., esse non aiutano una compagna anche quando questo non recherebbe loro danno' [from childhood, girls are less kind to their female peers than to male peers. They are sympathetic, but towards those of another caste, another sex, another age group. For example, they do not help a female peer even when this would not cause themselves harm] (Lombroso and Ferrero, *La donna delinquente, la prostituta e la donna normale*, p. 152).

CHAPTER 2

Women and the law

Notwithstanding a minority of voices that were beginning to highlight the misogyny of a vision that considered women inferior to men, the great majority of late nineteenth-century society continued to endorse ideas that foregrounded female domesticity and inherent feebleness.

In complex rhetoric that also encompassed honour and reputation, women were considered, on the one hand, unable to understand the value of goods and to correctly manage their patrimony; but, on the other, in the eyes of criminal law, they were to be punished in an identical way to men.[1] A number of theories were advanced in support of this, reinforcing a variable inability of women to comprehend the law depending on circumstance.

Women and civil law

Since antiquity, law has not been kind to women. The male-dominated society was driven by the goal of accumulating or at least preserving wealth for those who were going to take forward the family name. For this reason, the different legal status of men and women responded to specific economic needs. Inequality was thus enshrined in civil law and was evidenced in institutions such as marital authorisation and the dowry.[2]

1 Sara Delmedico, *Opposing Patriarchy: Women and the Law in Action in Pre-Unification Italy (1815–1865)* (London: Institute of Modern Languages Research, 2021), pp. 77–8.

2 For a general overview on the legal status of women, see the studies by Paolo Ungari, *Il diritto di famiglia in Italia dalle costituzioni giacobine al Codice civile del* 1942 (Bologna: Il Mulino, 1970) and *Storia del diritto di famiglia in Italia (1796–1942)* (Bologna: Il Mulino,

For centuries, women had needed the permission of either a man in their family and/or a judge to dispose of their own goods. With the enactment of the Napoleonic Code and its extension to the Italian peninsula, this authorisation was restricted just to married women, thereby freeing single women and widows from the requirement. When Napoleon was defeated, the French code was repealed, and the Italian rulers, returning to their thrones, reinstated the previous legal system. With the exception of the Kingdom of Lombardy-Venetia, this meant, once again, that contracts made by women were valid only with the approval of a male relative or a judge.[3]

1974). See, also, Manlio Bellomo, *La condizione giuridica della donna in Italia. Vicende antiche e moderne* (Rome: Il Cigno, 1996 [1970]); and Delmedico, *Opposing Patriarchy*.

3 Marital authorisation was included in Article 1124 of the *Codice Civile di Napoleone il Grande pel Regno d'Italia*, the translated version of the 1804 *Code Civil des Français*. See 'Codice Civile del Regno d'Italia', in *Collezione Completa dei Moderni Codici Civili* (Turin: Minerva Subalpina, 1845), p. 65. In the Kingdom of the Two Sicilies, the Duchy of Parma, Piacenza and Guastalla, as well as in the Kingdom of Sardinia, married women needed their husbands' authorisation to make contracts (Art. 1078, Sezione II, 'Codice pel Regno delle Due Sicilie', in *Collezione Completa*, p. 298; Art. 1073, Capo Primo, 'Codice civile per gli Stati di Parma, Piacenza e Guastalla', in *Collezione Completa*, p. 435; Art. 1211, Sezione II, 'Codice civile per gli Stati del Re di Sardegna', in *Collezione Completa*, p. 668). In the Duchy of Modena, judges provided authority to married women, and single or widowed women, only after first granting it to their husband or closest male relative, respectively (Art. IX, Titolo IV, 'Codice di leggi e costituzioni pel Ducato di Modena', in *Collezione Completa*, p. 794). In the Papal States, the judge's authorisation was necessary for all women, regardless of status (Art. 52, 'Regolamento Legislativo e Giudiziario per gli affari civili', in *Collezione Completa*, p. 878). In the Grand Duchy of Tuscany, women had to ask for the authorisation of both their father and the judge; married women also had to ask for their husbands' authorisation (Art. 1–3, 'Delle obbligazioni delle donne, Leggi sopra la patria potestà, la tutela, l'interdizione, le obbligazioni delle donne, i testamenti i codicilli e la porzione legittima, 15 novembre 1814', in *Collezione Completa*, p. 906). On marital authorisation, see: Monica Fioravanzo, 'Sull'autorizzazione maritale. Ricerche attorno alla condizione giuridica della donna nell'Italia unita', *Clio*, 30 (1994), 641–725; Victor Crescenzi, 'L'autorizzazione maritale e il problema storico della capacità della donna coniugata di disporre dei propri beni', in *Mujeres y derecho. Una perspectiva histórico-jurídica. Encuentro de historiadores del derecho. Actas*, ed. by Francisco L. Pacheco Caballero (Barcelona: Associació Catalana d'Història del Dret, 2015), pp. 127–85; Giulia Galeotti, 'L'autorizzazione maritale nel primo codice civile unitario: un istituto "estraneo" alla tradizione italiana?', *Dimensioni e problemi della ricerca storica*, 2 (2005), 155–82; Delmedico, *Opposing Patriarchy*, pp. 114–16; and *Cittadinanze incompiute: la parabola dell'autorizzazione maritale*, ed. by Stefania Bartoloni (Rome:

Alongside being enshrined in law, discrimination against women was the subject of several legal treatises that commented on existing laws and, aware of new demands for justice, sought to avoid the granting of further rights.

In the Enlightenment, in particular, as new ideas began to pave the way for a new understanding of the place of the individual in society, jurists used centuries-old prejudices about the minds of women to support their arguments.

The jurist and philosopher Gaetano Filangieri (1752–1788) dedicated a chapter of his major work, *La scienza della legislazione*, to women's education. He contended that women shaped their children's future, conditioning 'la gioia o la tristezza delle domestiche mura' [the joy or the sadness in the four walls of the home].[4] Filangieri entrusted women with a key role, but it still laid with men, as the undisputed head of the family, to direct them. Society was built from families, whose direction required vigilance and the care of only one of its members, namely the man.[5] In Filangieri's view, as for almost all nineteenth-century theorists, women's social function was fulfilled within the household, and, consequently, a woman's education needed to be neither public nor extensive. In his *La scienza della legislazione*, Filangieri particularly highlighted the need, in law, for public education, but an education in which women would not be asked to participate. Their education was to be mediated and indirect, because:

> formando gli uomini, la legge verrebbe a formare indirettamente anche le donne. È un errore il credere che l'uomo si modifichi sulla donna. Questa sarebbe una contraddizione a quella legge eterna e costante della natura, che ha stabilito, che il più forte sia sempre il primo a dar la legge al più debole
>
> [in shaping men, the law would also indirectly shape women. It is a mistake to believe that a man modifies himself because of a woman. This would be a contradiction to that eternal and constant law of nature, which has established that the strongest always leads in imposing laws on the weakest].[6]

Viella, 2021), and particularly, in this volume, Maria Rosa Di Simone, 'Le italiane tra Code Napoléon e Allgemeines Bürgerliches Gesetzbuch', pp. 35–53, and Monica Fioravanzo, 'L'autorizzazione maritale e la sua abrogazione nel quadro europeo tra guerre e rivoluzioni (1919–1945)', pp. 223–42.

4 Gaetano Filangieri, *La scienza della legislazione*, 8 vols (Milan: Borroni and Scotti, 1856 [1780–1791]), II, p. 360.

5 Ibid., p. 217.

6 Ibid., p. 361.

Consequently, the dichotomy strong–weak was used to justify varying gender roles and marginalisation within different spaces. At the same time, the emphasis on strength implicitly contributed to a construction of violence as a tolerable, perhaps even indispensable, element of daily life, to be deployed when correction and direction were necessary. References to eternal laws and natural constraints also helped convey a perception that such ideas were elaborated not only by human individuals and society as a whole but further were also given by a superior entity – divine law – and, for this reason, were indisputably right and apt.

The Roman jurist Filippo Maria Renazzi (1745–1808) had similar ideas, believing that it was 'divina lege sancitum foeminas viris subjectas esse debere' [sanctioned by divine law that women were to be subject to men].[7] Another who considered the female mind 'weaker' than the male, he believed men had a particular duty to direct women, and this was why marriage had to have a hierarchical structure.[8]

Pisan criminalist Giovanni Carmignani (1768–1847) argued, in his *Juris criminalis elementa* and *Teoria delle leggi della sicurezza sociale*, that women lacked the physical means to develop strong concepts. However, notwithstanding their softer and weaker 'cerebralis medulla' [spinal brain], which implied a more feeble capacity in women to develop ideas,[9] Carmignani maintained that women were not entirely inferior to men, but instead merely

7 Filippo Maria Renazzi, *Elementa juris criminalis*, 4 vols (Bologna: Francisci Cardinali and Caroli Frulli, 1826 [1773–1775]), I, *Liber primus. De delictis generatim*, pp. 198–99.

8 Ibid., pp. 198–99. On Filippo Maria Renazzi, see: Margherita Scoliere, 'Il giureconsulto Filippo Maria Renazzi: presentazione di un inedito', *Studi Romani*, 46/3 (1998), 375–98; Beatrice Maschietto, 'Il problema penale nella dottrina italiana del secondo Settecento: Filippo Maria Renazzi', in *Criminalità e giustizia in Germania e in Italia. Pratiche giudiziarie e linguaggi giuridici tra tardo medioevo ed età moderna*, ed. by Marco Bellabarba, Gerd Schwerhoff, and Andrea Zorzi (Bologna: Il Mulino, 2001), pp. 235–52; Maria Rosa Di Simone, 'L'influenza di Beccaria nello Stato pontificio: il trattato di Filippo Maria Renazzi', *Rivista di storia del diritto italiano*, 87 (2014), 365–98; and Marco Cavina, 'Il dolo latente nell'animo. Filippo Maria Renazzi nel dibattito giuridico intorno alla graduazione del dolo fra XVIII e XIX secolo', in *Filippo Maria Renazzi: università e cultura a Roma tra Settecento e Ottocento*, ed. by Paolo Alvazzi Del Frate, Maria Rosa Di Simone, and Carla Frova (Bologna: Il mulino, 2019), pp. 227–39.

9 Giovanni Carmignani, *Juris criminalis elementa*, 5th ed. (Pisa: Nistri, 1833 [1808]), p. 44. On Carmignani, see Paolo Comanducci, 'La scuola criminalistica pisana tra Sette e Ottocento', in *Illuminismo e dottrine penali*, ed. by Luigi Berlinguer and Floriana Colao

several steps behind in achievement of full human maturity.[10] This argument was a standard approach that envisioned women not as full adults but rather as minors to be protected and guided throughout their lives. Despite allowing that 'la supposta imbecillità d'intelletto nelle femmine debba essere valutata, qualora sussista, come mancanza di senno squisito [the supposed imbecility of intellect in females must be evaluated, if it does exist, as a lack of exquisite sense],[11] Carmignani claimed that women lacked the firmity of mind necessary for an understanding of civil law and to enable the undertaking of an obligation.[12] For this reason, he contended that the perpetual protection to which women had been subject in the past may have been a public guarantee against offences caused by corrupt men taking advantage of women's tendency to wickedness.[13] In this context, a key role was played by the family, 'ordigno di pubblico ordine, e di pubblica prosperità ma di costruzione e di maneggio difficile per la legge' [instrument of public order and public prosperity, but difficult to construct and handle in law],[14] as well as a moral body, with its hierarchical structure consecrated and preserved through centuries and via which its members had a clear and defined role.

The Venetian jurist Francesco Foramiti was also occupied by relations between family members. For him, it was not necessary that in a society of two – a marriage being such – the deliberative voice of one or the other should prevail; but, since he considered men more capable than women of governing certain affairs, he thought it prudent to establish a general rule that the husband's voice should prevail when the two did not reach agreement.[15] Moreover, men, 'avendo maggior forza di mente e di corpo, contribuisc[ono] assai più al bene comune; di maniera che la moglie deve essere necessariamente

(Milan: Giuffrè, 1990), pp. 241–304; and Marco P. Geri, *Il magistero di un criminalista di foro. Giovanni Carmignani "avvocato professore di Leggi"* (Pisa: ETS, 2015).

10 Giovanni Carmignani, *Teoria delle leggi della sicurezza sociale*, 3 vols (Pisa: Nistri, 1831–1832), II, p. 172.

11 Carmignani, *Teoria delle leggi della sicurezza sociale*, III, pp. 311–12.

12 Carmignani, *Juris criminalis elementa*, p. 44.

13 Carmignani, *Teoria delle leggi della sicurezza sociale*, III, pp. 311–12.

14 Ibid., pp. 323–4.

15 Francesco Foramiti, *Enciclopedia legale ovvero lessico ragionato di gius naturale, civile, canonico*, 4 vols (Venice: Co' Tipi del Gondoliere, 1842), II, p. 928. On Francesco Foramiti, see Laura Casella, 'Foramiti, Francesco', in *Dizionario biografico dei giuristi italiani (XII-XX secolo)*, 2 vols (Bologna: Il Mulino, 2013), I, pp. 886–87.

subordinata al marito od obbedire ai di lui ordini in tutti gli affari domestici' [having greater strength of mind and body, contribute much more to the common good, such that the wife must necessarily be subordinate to her husband or obey his orders in all domestic affairs].[16] Foramiti also identified the precise duties that a wife must fulfil:

> 1. l'astinenza dal cercare di dominare sul marito e di togliergli la sua legittima autorità; 2. Una sollecita amministrazione delle cose domestiche; 3. la deferenza ai consigli ed obbedienza agli ordini del marito. Laonde quando nasca un dispiacere tra i due coniugi sulla scelta di una cosa da farsi o da ommettersi, o da farsi in un determinato modo piuttostoché in un altro, dovrà la moglie seguire l'opinione del marito come suo superiore e capo della società coniugale
>
> [1. Abstinence from any attempt to dominate her husband and take away from him his legitimate authority; 2. Prompt administration of domestic affairs; 3. Deference to the advice of her husband and obedience of his orders. Therefore, when a disagreement arises between the two spouses regarding choosing to do or avoid doing a certain thing, or to do it in one way rather than another, the wife must follow the position of her husband as her superior and as head of the marital institution].[17]

The Lombardian jurist Carlo Francesco Gabba expressed similar views in his work *Della condizione giuridica delle donne nelle legislazioni francese, austriaca e sarda. Studio di legislazione comparata*. Considering ideas on emancipation, he argued that this would impose on women an artificial life of passions and cares that were not theirs to bear, damaging and destroying their spirit, and making women imperfect imitators of men.[18] Indeed, Gabba contended that women's 'sentimenti, i pensieri, la coscienza infine di sé medesima non si trovano nel loro stato normale e in un perfetto equilibrio, se non quando essa può dedicarsi tutta all'adempimento de' suoi doveri verso il marito ed i figli' [feelings, thoughts, and, ultimately self-awareness, do not find themselves in their normal state and in perfect equilibrium, unless [a woman] can dedicate herself entirely to fulfilling her duties towards her husband and children].[19] Interestingly, Gabba considered the family as a society of equals in which women, because of their specific role and own sense of weakness,

---

16 Foramiti, *Enciclopedia legale*, p. 928.

17 Ibid., p. 582.

18 Carlo Francesco Gabba, *Della condizione giuridica delle donne nelle legislazioni francese, austriaca e sarda. Studio di legislazione comparata* (Milan: Redaelli, 1861), p. 12.

19 Ibid., p. 12.

saw in men both their representative and guardian, to whose authority they could eagerly submit.[20] Further, Gabba described a model woman who 'non si isola quindi da lui in nessun rapporto, né dentro né fuori della famiglia' [thus does not isolate herself from him in any relationship, neither inside nor outside the family].[21]

By insisting on a model in which women and men were equal yet, at the same time, describing a context distant from any ideas of equality, theorists and jurists of the time continued to reproduce the historical dichotomy that juxtaposed obedience and submission as values to be pursued under all circumstances: a powerful reminder of the unequal status of women within marriage, as in every sphere of life, and of the inherent hierarchy within the institution of marriage.

As mentioned earlier, women in the Kingdom of Lombardy-Venetia were permitted to manage their own goods without needing the permission of a man. However, despite this legal provision, jurists in the region still attempted to challenge these norms, perceiving them to threaten not only the family order but, more widely, the order of society as a whole.

Those who supported restriction of the agency of women typically highlighted not only a woman's need for guidance but also argued that her reputation could be at stake. Francesco Forti, a jurist from Tuscany, stressed the importance of the 'Quintus Mucius presumption',[22] arguing that because of:

---

20 Ibid., p. 13.

21 Ibid., p. 179.

22 Named after the Roman jurist Quintus Mucius Scaevola, this "presumption" implied that the assets belonging to a woman were presumed to have been purchased with her husband's money. See, in *Digest* 24.1.51, *Pomponius 5 ad Quintus Mucius*: 'Quintus mucius ait, cum in controversiam venit, unde ad mulierem quid pervenerit, et verius et honestius est quod non demonstratur unde habeat existimari a viro aut qui in potestate eius esset ad eam pervenisse. evitandi autem turpis quaestus gratia circa uxorem hoc videtur quintus mucius probasse' [Quintus Mucius says that when a controversy arises as to whether anything has come into the hands of a wife, it is better and more honourable to hold that the property came into her hands through her husband, or through someone under his control, where it is not proven from what source she acquired it. Quintus Mucius appears to have adopted this opinion, for the purpose of avoiding any disgraceful inquiry with reference to a wife]. (Translation sourced from <https://droitromain.univ-grenoble-alpes.fr/Anglica/D24_Scott.htm?>). See, further: Francesco Forti, *Trattati inediti di giurisprudenza* (Florence: Viessieux, 1854), pp. 456–57; See, also, Delmedico, *Opposing Patriarchy*, p. 76. On Francesco Forti, see Leopoldo

> [la] poca abitudine delle donne ad acquistare per lecita industria, e la loro mancanza di capitali [...] non par possibile che il sistema della comunione venga adottato da alcun savio legislatore in Italia. Ma a questa generale riforma pare che si opponga la frivolezza ed il puttanesimo del sesso. Si dirà forse, che i vizj ed i difetti delle donne sono conseguenza dei vizj e de' difetti degli uomini; e gli uni e gli altri, conseguenza delle sociali instituzioni: ma codesta risposta non basterebbe a sciogliere le obiezioni. Perocché le leggi posson precedere alquanto la riforma dei costumi, darvi un impulso, e tracciarne la via; ma perché non gli posson mutare di sana pianta, se troppo oltre si avanzano, rischiano di produrre un male maggiore.
>
> [[the] paucity of practice among women of acquisition through lawful work and their lack of capital [...], it does not seem possible that the system of common property [of goods] would be adopted by any wise legislator in Italy. But in opposition to this general reform appears to be the frivolity and whoredom of the [female] sex. Perhaps it will be said that the vices and defects of women are the consequence of the vices and defects of men; and both, a consequence of social institutions: but this answer would not suffice to resolve the objections. However, laws can actively precede the reform of habits, give them an impulse, and set out a path; but, because they cannot change habits at base, if they proceed too far, they risk producing greater evil].[23]

Together with the centuries-old characterisation of women as being possessed of *infirmitas*, *imbecillitas*, and *levitas*, the 'angel–devil' dichotomy was a constant element in narratives about women. As established earlier, female sexuality was to be confined within the boundaries of their claimed natural role of motherhood. In their weakheadedness, Forti also identified female inferiority in a lower capacity to take charge of their own bodies. This led to them being considered potentially uninhibited and prone to indulgence in luxury, bringing a risk not only to personal and familial reputation but also to familial order, affecting the very structure of society. Correspondingly, this brought reminders of blurred boundaries between the private and the public sphere and of the intrusiveness of societal control and judgement, and particularly over women.

Further criticism of the *Codice civile universale austriaco pel Regno Lombardo-Veneto* came from Giovanni Carcano, a Milanese jurist, in an entangled discourse linking honour, wealth, weakheadedness, and perceived capacity to

---

Galeotti, *Discorso intorno agli scritti editi e inediti di Francesco Forti*, in Forti, *Trattati inediti di giurisprudenza*, pp. IX–XXVI.

[23] Forti, *Trattati inediti di giurisprudenza*, pp. 456–57.

understand the law. Carcano focused on an idea that granting married women the ability to manage their goods would jeopardise their reputation and their role within the family. Interestingly, this point implicitly admitted that power dynamics were guided not by mental capacity or firmness but instead by the control an individual had over wealth, thus highlighting the hidden goal of preserving wealth in the male hands, not because of women's incapability but for matters of lineage and societal stability. For Carcano, the man should be the woman's 'guardia e tutela' [guard and protection],[24] watching over her behaviour in case her honour was at risk, given that, in being free, she 'dona agli amanti, riceve il prezzo dell'adulterio' [gives to lovers, receives the price of adultery], and 'fomenta gli scialaqui e le insubordinazioni dei figli, disperde il proprio patrimonio, e ciò tutto senza che sappia, senza che abbia diritto di divieto il marito' [encourages the profligacy and insubordination of her children, disperses her own patrimony, and all this unwittingly, with her husband having no right to prohibit it].[25] Moreover, the man was bound to grant the woman his guardianship since it was such freedom that would render all equal, and this equality would move everyone into a lower position.[26] Essentially, Carcano was arguing that a woman's dignity was recognised partly through a clearly outlined role as wife and mother, but, above all, by her location in a subaltern position and under the rule of the man. As a consequence, he wrote, for granting the possibility of managing her goods, the woman found herself in a position of substantial economic equality, thus losing her guide and becoming 'destituita in questo Codice d'ogni dignità, come moglie e come madre, destituita pure di ogni dignità nella sua selvaggia libertà, come donna' [deprived of all dignity in this Code, as a wife and mother, and deprived too of all dignity in her savage freedom as a woman].[27] Carcano's paternalistic and misogynistic views were again upheld through his insistence on the domestic role of the woman. He contended that:

> grandi parole furono fatte per emancipare la donna: facciamo di meglio: eleviamola, coordinandola. Ora come la natura diede alla donna vivacità di immaginazione e lo squisito sentire, e pose invece specialmente nell'uomo vigore di ragione; e come tutte queste facoltà sianno pari tra loro, poiché tutte elemento del completo nostro

[24] Giovanni Carcano, *Il codice civile austriaco ed i suoi caratteri* (Milan: Manini, 1860), p. 29.
[25] Ibid., p. 28.
[26] Ibid., p. 29.
[27] Ibid., p. 28.

> essere umano, ma la ragione governa; così la donna, eguale all'uomo, partecipi alla sua dignità, ma insieme onori il consiglio virile che la natura le pone compagno ai suoi fianchi; lo onori con fiducia ed affetto, poiché è sua guardia e tutela. E la donna lochiamola altamente nella famiglia sui figli, poiché, sebbene debole, non vi ha più vigile sguardo che quello di una madre
>
> [great words have been said to emancipate women: let's do better: let us elevate her, coordinating her. Given that nature gave women a liveliness of imagination and exquisite feeling, and specifically imbued man with the vigour of reason. And as all these faculties are equal to each other, since they are all elements of the full nature of the human condition, but it is reason that rules; thus, let the woman, equal to the man, participate in her dignity with him, but at the same time honour the masculine advice that nature places as a companion at her side. May she honour him with faith and affection, since he is her guard and protection. And let us locate women highly in the family, above children, because, although she is weak, there is no more vigilant gaze than that of a mother].[28]

Marital authorisation was one of the two methods enshrined in the law by which women were marginalised and distanced from access to wealth and agency; the other being the dowry. For centuries, the dowry was considered the only right to which women were entitled as far as their fathers' patrimony was concerned, indicating a precise boundary of discrimination between the sexes and perpetuating the patriarchal order. Over time, the institution of the dowry underwent few changes and contributed to the shaping of an economic, social, and legal imbalance between men and women, providing women with more limited access to wealth than men.

For this reason, the Napoleonic Code, which stated that sons and daughters might receive the same inheritance, was strongly opposed. By introducing the possibility that men and women might share access to equal wealth, Article 745 disrupted the order of society of the Italian peninsula of the time, an order that rested on inequality and discrimination. Among the various criticisms of the Napoleonic Code was jurist Giovanni Maria Negri's argument that 'le primitive leggi di natura costituiscono uguali li figli maschj alle figlie femmine: ma già si sa in quanti casi le leggi naturali abbiano ricevuta una utile modificazione dal diritto civile, e dai sistemi sociali' [primitive laws of nature make sons equal to daughters: but it is already known that in many cases the natural laws have been subject to a useful modification by civil

---

[28] Ibid., p. 29.

law and by the social systems].[29] Praising municipal statutes that ruled that a daughter should be excluded from an inheritance in favour of a son, Negri argued that it is 'universalmente radicato nell'animo dei padri di famiglia, che le loro facoltà passino possibilmente nei loro maschj' [universally rooted in the mind of the family fathers that their wealth should pass to their male children].[30] However, if a father died intestate, Article 745 of the Napoleonic Code would exercise 'una violenza alla volontà e all'affetto di un proprietario' [an act of violence against the will and affection of a proprietor], since it ruled that daughters and sons would each be entitled to the same share.[31] In a society that still revolved around the name and prestige of the *casato*, that is, the Italian extended familial house, the passing on of goods was a central concern to such an extent it was deemed a concern shared by every father. The Restoration and enactment of the ABGB, or Allgemeines bürgerliches Gesetzbuch,[32] in the Kingdom of Lombardy-Venetia confirmed equal inheritance rights to sons and daughters, while in the great majority of the states of the Italian peninsula there was a return to the dowry system.

With the Unification of Italy, the Civil Code of the Kingdom of Sardinia (1837) was extended to the whole country, thereby imposing once again a model of unequal distribution among children also in areas such as Lombardy-Venetia. Shortly afterwards, though, in 1865, the new *Codice civile del Regno d'Italia* was promulgated. Known as the Pisanelli Code, this new code was based on the structure of the Napoleonic Code and introduced no substantial innovations. However, although it reconfirmed the centuries-old hierarchical order that saw women subjugated to men, sons and daughters were now permitted to receive equal financial inheritances. The new code continued to endorse dowry and marital authorisation – those key instruments of

29 Giovanni Maria Negri, *Dei difetti del Codice Civile Italico, che porta il titolo di Codice Napoleone e dei pregj del Codice Civile Austriaco* (Vicenza: Parise, 1815), pp. 76–77. On Giovanni Maria Negri (1748–1818), see Chiara Valsecchi, *L'avvocatura veneta tra diritto comune e codici: il caso del vicentino Giovanni Maria Negri*, in *Avvocati e avvocatura nell'Italia dell'Ottocento*, ed. by Antonio Padoa Schioppa (Bologna: Il Mulino, 2009), pp. 521–624.

30 Negri, *Dei difetti del Codice Civile Italico*, p. 77.

31 Ibid.

32 On the enactment of this code, see Ettore Dezza, Ettore and Pio Caroni, *L'ABGB e la codificazione asburgica in Italia e in Europa* (Milan: Cedam, 2006); Paolo Grossi, *A History of European Law* (Chichester: Wiley-Blackwell, 2010), pp. 90–93.

the patriarchal order – but the dowry was now considered rather a form of advance on a daughter's inheritance. The rule could still be circumvented through the writing of a will, but equivalent inheritance was nonetheless becoming increasingly accepted. The historian Ida Fazio argued that this phenomenon could be noticed since the mid-nineteenth century, when families started to privilege other forms of transmission of wealth – donations or wills – rather than dowries.[33]

Where marital authorisation was concerned, the new code of a united Italy ruled that married women must ask for their husbands' approval to undertake any legal act.[34] However, whilst the legal status of married women in regions such as the former Kingdom of Lombardy-Venetia grew even weaker, in the rest of the Italian peninsula, single women, both the unmarried and widows, were now permitted to freely manage their own goods and capital, without the requirement to seek any male authorisation.[35] That the new rule affected only married women was again linked to the importance of the family in Italian society, a point that may also be inferred from other sections of the civil code, such as those dealing with 'l'ordine delle famiglie' [family order].[36] The model of the family at that time was still deeply influenced by ideals of the past: a moral body composed of members with a common identity, and in which reputation and honour inscribed their worthiness in society. The preservation of the family and of its name was a major goal, and one to be pursued through sacrifice of personal ambition and expectations. In this context, although the Napoleonic and Pisanelli Codes were starting to attach greater standing to the individual, the moral significance of the family remained strong and deemed worthy of protection, even to the detriment of the individual.

The dowry system was abandoned with the code of 1865,[37] but marital authorisation continued to be deemed an essential institution, as it permitted

33 Ida Fazio, 'Valori economici e valori simbolici. Il declino della dote nell'Italia dell'Ottocento', *Quaderni storici*, 78 (1992), 291–317 (pp. 297–311).

34 Art. 134–7, *Codice civile del Regno d'Italia: corredato della relazione del Ministro Guardasigilli fatta a S. M. in udienza del 25 giugno 1865* (Turin: Botta, 1865), p. 28.

35 Marital authorisation remained in force until 1919, when the law 17 July 1919, n. 1176, removed it from the Italian juridical framework.

36 Delmedico, *Opposing Patriarchy*, pp. 27–31.

37 Although it was still possible to constitute dowries, these were considered as an advance on inheritance. Dowry was formally abandoned with Law 19 May 1975, n. 151, Art. 166.

the family to protect its patrimony from those not bearing its name and from those considered weak and marginal members. Marital authorisation was also crucial since it minimised the possibility of a challenge to authority, the prerogative of men. Following enactment of this new code, several jurists immediately registered their responses in favour of the importance of this institution. One such was Antonio Scotti, a jurist who had published several articles in the journal of jurisprudence, *Archivio giuridico*. He wrote that marital authorisation was not necessary when:

> scompare il pericolo del dualismo perturbatore, quando l'autorizzazione non serve a mantenere l'unità di direzione, per mancanza di antagonista, la donna ricupera la sua piena libertà giuridica; e non ha d'uopo, come pei precedenti codici, dell'autorizzazione del giudice
>
> [the danger of disruptive dualism disappears, when the authorisation does not serve to maintain unity of direction, due to the lack of an antagonist, the woman recovers her full legal freedom; and the authorisation of the judge, as in the previous codes, is not needed].[38]

This disruptive dualism seems to disappear in the event of the husband being either a minor or an interdict, for example. This suggests that, despite explicitly defending centuries-old views, Scotti and other theorists of the time were tacitly convinced that women were as able to manage a family as a man was, but that society's hierarchical structure was to be preserved. This structure was clearly rooted in inequality and discrimination and depended on a duality of obedience versus command as the routine basis for quotidian life.

In the final decades of the nineteenth century, more voices in support of equal rights began to make themselves heard. For example, jurist Domenico Giuriati believed women were equal to men and considered their *deterior* condition unfair.[39] In his *Le leggi dell'amore*, published in 1881, he described

---

[38] Antonio Scotti, 'Dell'autorizzazione maritale e giudiziale secondo il codice civile italiano', *Archivio giuridico*, IV (1869), 387–435 (p. 425).

[39] Domenico Giuriati (1829–1904) was a patriot and jurist from Venice. He was a supporter of divorce and, while a member of Parliament, acted as a speaker for the draft of the *Legge Villa*, a law on divorce presented in 1882–1883 that was subsequently rejected by Parliament. On drafts of divorce, see Mark Seymour, *Debating Divorce in Italy. Marriage and the Making of Modern Italians, 1860–1974* (New York: Palgrave Macmillan, 2006); Angela Carbone, 'Il dibattito sul divorzio nel lungo Ottocento: Stato, Chiesa

the standing of women in the eyes of the law at the end of the nineteenth century as follows:

> [H]avvi eguaglianza di condizione soltanto nelle leggi penali, dove la donna è ammanettata, custodita, processata, e, dato il caso, impiccata senza distinzione dall'uomo quantunque lo superi [...] in moralità [...]. [N]elle relazioni civili e commerciali dove la donna sa reggere la famiglia e custodire i beni quanto lui, egli è il tutore ed essa la pupilla, anzi in certi casi qualche cosa di più del tutore e qualche cosa meno della pupilla [...]; nella ripartizione dei diritti e dei beni sociali alla quale essa, come l'uomo, aspira con bisogni differenti e con attitudini circoscritte, viene trasandata o reietta a dirittura
>
> [There is equality of condition only in penal law, where the woman is handcuffed, guarded, tried, and, as the case may be, hanged without distinction from the man, although she surpasses him [...] in morality [...]. [I]n civil and commercial relations, where the woman knows how to govern the family and guard her property as well as he does, he is the guardian and she is the pupil, or indeed in some cases he is something more than the guardian and she something less than the pupil [...]; in the distribution of social rights and chattels to which she, like the man, aspires with different needs and limited aptitudes, she is neglected or outright rejected].[40]

Giuriati was convinced that, in elevating his spouse, a man increased his own dignity, increased his value, developed a powerful ally, and 'fa sì che il casato, oggidì ancora grettamente personificato in una egoistica e fittizia individualità, irradii virtù collettiva per gli sforzi concordi di una sposa, della madre, delle sorelle, delle figliuole' [makes the family, today still crudely personified in an egotistical and fictitious individuality, radiate collective virtue through the concerted efforts of a wife, mother, sisters, daughters].[41]

He defined those who maintained that women were inferior to men as a 'compact phalanx of latecomers', hiding behind the objection that opening the 'valve' of rights and powers to the benefit of women would distract women from their role in the household.[42] In opposition to marital authorisation, he contended that if married women needed a 'guardian', reason would suggest guardianship should be imposed upon all women and not only those

---

e opinione pubblica nel Mezzogiorno d'Italia', *Chronica Mundi*, 15 (2021), 103–29 (in particular, pp. 117–23).

40 Domenico Giuriati, *Le leggi dell'amore* (Turin: Roux and Favale, 1881), p. 95.

41 Ibid., p. 97.

42 Ibid.

who were married. Otherwise, it was akin to declaring that the moral and intellectual faculties of women decreased with marriage.[43] Giuriati pointed out that the Italian law system 'schiaccia una persona a benefizio di un'altra, mentre favella di civile filosofia' [crushes one person for the benefit of another, while babbling civil philosophy].[44] It is noteworthy, though, that despite his support of female emancipation, Giuriati still adhered to mainstream ideas of the time that assumed women had roles assigned them by nature.[45]

Women and crimes

For centuries, the study of physical features served to explain behaviours, personality, the ability of an individual to undertake a particular task, and to explain particular concepts or mental firmity. In addition to discriminating between women and men, these studies also served to distinguish between those with and without the propensity to commit crime. From the nineteenth century onwards, many scholars in Europe began to systematically investigate this link, including, in France, widely circulated and examined works by Prosper Despine and Gabriel Tarde; in Britain, James Bruce Thompson, Forbes Benignus Winslow, George Wilson, David Nicholson, and Luke Owen Pike; and, in Germany, Friedrich Christian Benedict Avé-Lallemant.[46]

In Italy, alongside attempts to identify what kind of woman would commit crime and what kind of impulsion could push a woman into crime, scholars discussed whether the crimes of women, given alleged female mental inferiority, should be dealt with differently from the crimes of men. Since criminal

---

43 Ibid., p. 277.

44 Ibid., p. 280.

45 On this point, See, also, Mazzini's 'different functions' (Giuseppe Mazzini, *Dei doveri dell'uomo* (Milan: RCS, 2010 [1860]), p. 81). A brief outline of his writings in this regard can be found in Delmedico, *Opposing Patriarchy*, pp. 81–83.

46 See, Cleobis H. S. Jayewardene, 'The English Precursors of Lombroso', *The British Journal of Criminology*, 4/2 (1963), 164–70; Robert A. Nye, 'Heredity or Milieu: The Foundations of Modern European Criminological Theory', *Isis*, 67/3 (1976), 335–55; Piers Beirne, 'Between Classicism and Positivism: Crime and Penalty in the Writings of Gabriel Tarde', *Criminology*, 25/4 (November 1987), 785–820; and Ruth Triplett, ed., *The Wiley Handbook of the History and Philosophy of Criminology* (Hoboken, NJ: Wiley-Blackwell, 2018), especially, in this volume, Paul Knepper, 'Laughing at Lombroso: Positivism and Criminal Anthropology in Historical Perspective', pp. 49–66.

law permitted no differentiation other than in a few exceptional cases, discussion focused on women's responsibility, imputability, and punishment.

Theories revolved around a stereotypical image of women as vessels of sweetness, love, and domesticity. Giovanni Carmignani, discussed earlier, was convinced, for example, that 'è inopinabile in cor di donna la odiosa forza, che è necessaria al delitto. Sembra perciò aspra troppo la sentenza di chi nella imputazione de' delitti non ammette distinzione di sesso' [the hateful strength that is necessary in the heart of a woman for her to commit a crime is inadmissible. Therefore, the sentence imposed by those who do not admit a distinction by sex in the imputation of crimes seems too harsh].[47] Consequently:

> converrebbe sempre anco nelle materie penali trattar la donna come è trattato il minore per non porle in troppo manifesta contraddizione colle civili; e sebbene la storia denunzi talvolta la femina come capace di crudeltà maggiore del maschio, questi esempj son rari, né mancò chi sulla lor rarità decise dover sempre la forza usare alla bellezza indulgenza
>
> [it would always be appropriate, even in penal matters, to treat women in the way that minors are treated, so as not to place them in too obvious contradiction with civil subjects; and although history sometimes denounces the female as capable of greater cruelty than the male, these cases are rare; nor was there a lack of those who decided that these were so rare that force should also be indulgent to beauty].[48]

The depiction of women criminals was rooted in a stereotypical romanticised image that was complicit with a notion that physical beauty affected the mind. Consequently, an attractive physical form was to be regarded with a degree of respect, or at least leniency, since the union of criminality and beauty was somehow an incongruity, a sort of dissonant union to be excused.[49]

---

47 Carmignani, *Teoria delle leggi della sicurezza sociale*, II, p. 175.

48 Ibid.

49 On this point, also Lombroso and Ferrero gave their perspective. They contended that punishments for female criminals should be different to those for men and argued that:

> nelle donne [...] il carcere e le pene afflittive sono tanto meno necessarie che il loro reato, quasi sempre effetto di suggestione o di passione, le rende meno terribili quando si allontanino dal suggestionatore o dal tormentatore: amante o marito. Vista poi la grande vanità femminile, l'importanza che essa dà al vestito, ai gingilli e ai mobili della sua casa si potrebbe sostituire molte volte nei reati di piccoli furti, di risse, le

The Modenese jurist Bartolomeo Veratti (1809–1889), however, claimed that the reduction of penalties for women would be:

> un incentivo che farebbe aumentare il concorso delle donne in quei gravi delitti, che si commettono appensatamente: perocchè i malvagi farebbero colle donne ciò che fanno coi minori, cui affidano, potendo, la maggior parte nell'esecuzione de' reati
>
> [an incentive that would lead to growth in the involvement of women in those serious crimes committed with premeditation: for the wicked would do with women what they do with minors, to whom they entrust, if they can, the majority of the execution of the crimes].[50]

Discriminated against in many aspects of life, women were not considered even capable of committing a crime on their own initiative. Since their world revolved around men and the impression they wished to make upon men, female criminality could easily be stopped by removing the prime mover of their actions, that is, men.

Giuseppe Orano, a jurist and the author of a study of repeat offending, identified a 'cumulo di motivi' [an accumulation of reasons] that reduced a woman's imputability. Alongside the alleged generic weakness that rendered women inferior to men, women's crimes were supposedly driven by a lower degree of wickedness.[51] Moreover, 'quanto all'aspetto del corpo, la donna ha

---

> pene carcerarie con delle pene afflittive della loro vanità, come il taglio dei capelli, il sequestro degli ornamenti, dei mobili: soprattutto si deve nei ricoveri imporre il lavoro alle oziose collo spauracchio della fame
>
> [For women [...], imprisonment and afflictive sentences are all the less necessary since their crime, which is almost always an effect of suggestion or passion, makes them less terrible when they are distanced from their influencer or tormentor: their lover or husband. Considering then the great female vanity, the importance the woman gives to her dress, her trinkets, to her domestic furnishings, prison sentences for petty theft and brawling could often be replaced with penalties affecting their vanity, such as the cutting of hair, the confiscation of ornamentation and furnishings: above all, in the poor houses, work must be imposed through the bogeyman of hunger upon the idle women].

Cesare Lombroso and Guglielmo Ferrero, *La donna delinquente, la prostituta e la donna normale*, 4th ed., with notes by Gina Lombroso (Turin: Bocca, 1923), p. 450.

50 Bartolomeo Veratti, 'Della mitigazione delle pene per le femmine delinquenti', in *Opuscoli religiosi, letterarj e morali*, serie II, I (Modena: Soliani 1863), pp. 78–103 (p. 101).

51 Giuseppe Orano, *La recidiva nei reati* (Rome: Carlo Voghera, 1883), p. 136.

invero sull'uomo la supremazia della bellezza e della grazia, ma gli è inferiore nello sviluppo della persona; e la stessa venustà la rende più degna di riguardi, di rispetto, e di scusa' [as for the appearance of the body, the woman indeed has the supremacy of beauty and grace over the man, but she is inferior to him in the development of her personage; and this same loveliness renders her more worthy of regard, respect, and excuse].[52] Orano observed that since women lived under the authority of a family – that is, a man's authority – they had barely any opportunity to acquire a clear understanding of their legal duty and the law.[53] Further, for Orano, a woman's uterus played a significant role in relation to her behaviour and character.[54] Her uterus, he claimed, caused her state of natural minority or semi-morbidity; it was an organ that 'ottenebra lo spirito, come una lieve e fuggevole demenza, quando non cagioni speciali manie, la imputabilità della donna non può non essere scemata' [darkens the mind, like a slight and fleeting madness, when it does not cause special manias, the imputability of the woman cannot but be diminished].[55] As the woman's brain, in his view, was located in her uterus ('il cervello nell'utero'), so 'l'isterismo da cui è travagliata eccita in lei periodicamente forti passioni, pravi istinti, e persino tendenze suicide e omicide' [the hysteria by which she is tormented excites in her periodically strong passions, strong instincts, and even suicidal and homicidal tendencies],[56] causing her to be ruled inevitably by passion and feelings – different from men, whose minds are led by analysis and curiosity.[57]

---

52 Ibid., p. 136.

53 Ibid., p. 137.

54 On this point see, also, Petronio Ignazio Zecchini, *Dì geniali della dialettica delle donne ridotta al suo vero principio* (Bologna: S. Tommaso D'Aquino, 1771), in which Zecchini, a physician, maintained that a woman's uterus was perpetually irritated, and that this prevented women from attaining the same robustness as men. In the late nineteenth and early twentieth centuries, this perception was the object of sustained attention. See, for example: Francesco Forlani, *L'isterismo nei suoi rapporti colla follia e colla responsabilità. Memorie medico-legali* (Vienna-Turin-Florence: Loescher, 1869); Luigi Maria Bossi, *A proposito di malattie utero-ovariche e psicopatie: urgenza di riforme nel sistema manicomiale* (Varese: Premiata Tipografia Cooperativa Varesina, 1912); and Muzio Pazzi, *Per la profilassi dell'aborto criminoso e dell'infanticidio* (Bologna: Poligrafico Emiliano, 1913).

55 Orano, *La recidiva nei reati*, p. 138.

56 Ibid., p. 141.

57 Ibid., p. 138.

Another jurist and senator, Pietro Ellero, expressed similar views.[58] He wrote that a woman's entire being was enslaved to her uterus, and that this caused her to be constantly in a state of feverish heat and subject to the onslaught of passions.[59] Therefore, women who committed crimes should be judged in a less harsh way, since they were more sensitive than men, deemed 'perpetui fanciulli' [perpetual children],[60] and minor offences were to be expected from them.[61]

Others, however, contended that women should be judged in the same way as men, proposing a number of reasons. Leveraging the notion that certain crimes were not easily understood by women, jurist Pellegrino Rossi noted that political crimes were more excusable if committed by a woman than a man, since women could not know their importance and immorality; [62] but that since it was not possible to establish a general rule, the law could not differentiate between men and women.[63] Francesco Carrara, another prominent jurist of the time, who contributed to the drafting of the 1889 Italian criminal code, suggested that women criminals should be considered just as responsible for their crimes as men. Since women had a higher sense of morality than men, he suggested, they generally were less inclined to commit crimes; therefore, those women who did commit crimes should be considered even more corrupt and more evil than men who did the same – or at the very least, equally as responsible.[64]

Bernardino Alimena, another reputative jurist of the time, reported official statistics on female criminality between 1885 and 1889, showing

---

58 On Ellero, jurist and senator, see Abele Casetta, ed., *Pietro Ellero un grande pordenonese nella cultura giuridica, sociale e politica dell'Ottocento*, Atti del convegno di Pordenone 26 novembre 2005 (Pordenone: Comune di Pordenone, 2007).

59 Pietro Ellero, *Opuscoli criminali* (Bologna: Fava and Garagnani, 1874), p. 93.

60 Ibid., p. 94.

61 Ibid., p. 96.

62 Pellegrino Rossi, *Trattato di diritto penale*, 2 vols (Milan: Borroni and Scotti, 1832), I, p. 244. Pellegrino Luigi Edoardo Rossi (1787–1848) served as Prime Minister of the Papal States, and was later murdered during the 1848 upheavals.

63 Ibid., p. 244.

64 Francesco Carrara, *Programma del corso di diritto criminale*, 2 vols (Florence: Cammelli, [1857] 1907), I, p. 232. See, also, Ida Ferrero, '"Eva delinquente": la scuola positiva e l'imputabilità al femminile', in *Donne ristrette*, ed. by Giulia Mantovani (Milan: Ledizioni, 2018), pp. 489–501.

that nineteen crimes out of a hundred were committed by women and that criminality was more common in urban than rural areas.[65] A supporter of the idea that a propensity to commit crimes was influenced by social factors,[66] Alimena contended that female criminals were more cruel than their male counterparts for two main reasons. First, in women, sensations and emotions prevailed over reason; second, there was a 'powerful dynamic factor' to be considered.[67] On this latter, Alimena explained that, in all domains in which women find themselves – education, motherhood, religious sentiment, domestic occupations, modesty, their scarce participation in social life, their entire environment, and tradition – there are obstacles to the committing of crimes. Therefore, any woman who does commit a crime is truly exceptional, since she has found a way to overcome all obstacles.[68] Alimena was convinced that the woman was inferior to men – 'tanto per le sue funzioni organiche che per la sua educazione' [both through their organic functioning and their education][69] – but he thought there was no need for particular intelligence to understand the consequences of one's own actions. Thus were women: sufficiently intelligent to understand their own actions and, in committing crimes, not inferior to men, but more cunning, more sophisticated, and more rational.[70] This meant that women could not generally be judged in a more lenient way than men, but that each case must be evaluated on its own merit.[71]

Some jurists were of the view that, given their alleged inferiority and the vital and unstable nature of their feelings, women could scarcely be considered capable of retaining in their memory an understanding of criminal law, to the extent that women were deemed to obey the law without understanding its essence. In an article entitled *Alcune considerazioni sulla minore responsabilità penale della donna*, jurist Luigi Stella emphasised this point to claim that, for this reason, women must be judged differently

---

65 Bernardino Alimena, *I limiti e i modificatori dell'imputabilità*, 4 vols (Turin: Bocca, 1894–1899), II (1896), p. 335.

66 Ibid., p. 338.

67 Ibid., p. 348.

68 Ibid.

69 Ibid., p. 354.

70 Ibid., p. 356.

71 Ibid.

from men as far as criminal law is concerned.[72] In response, in an article published in *La legge*,[73] Cesare Pagani maintained that it could be held that women had a special nature whereby 'l'impulso sensitivo dell'apparecchio generatore della femmina la spinga più dell'uomo alla soddisfazione dei bisogni erotici, e quindi, cagionando una sensibilità animale maggiore, sia una scusa per certi delitti la cui causa riposa nel desiderio di soddisfare questi appetiti' [the sensitive impulse of the female reproductive apparatus pushes woman, moreso than man, to the satisfaction of their erotic needs, and thus, in so causing a greater animal sensitivity, is an excuse for certain crimes whose cause rests in the desire to satisfy these appetites].[74] However, he emphasised that this 'impulse' could darken the mind, agreeing with Stella that menstruation, pregnancy, and puerperium, or early post-natal stage, could disrupt the normal state of life; but this darkening was not 'la conseguenza del sesso, sibbene del dissesto mentale' [the consequence of sex, albeit of mental breakdown].[75]

The analysis of female criminality, then, as in all matters relating to women at the time, was deeply rooted in stereotypes and prejudice, and these varied depending on the context so as to keep centuries-old ideas constant. In the particular case of women's crime, the approach was ambiguous and contradictory. Historian Marina Graziosi has suggested that this was due to what she termed 'symbolic attenuation': women were considered at one and the same time sacred, as bearers of life, and inferior, through weakheadedness and their fundamental but subservient role in the private sphere, in other words, agents whose acts were to be controlled and punished within the family.[76]

The enactment of the 1889 criminal code, known as the Zanardelli code, excluded biological sex as a factor in reducing imputability and punishment but retained the capacity for a different approach for crimes

---

[72] Luigi Stella, 'Alcune considerazioni sulla minore responsabilità penale della donna', *Archivio Giuridico*, 4 (1869), 76–83 (p. 79). See, also, Delmedico, *Opposing Patriarchy*, p. 77.

[73] Cesare Pagani, 'Osservazioni sull'articolo dell'avv. Luigi Stella', *La Legge, monitore giudiziario e amministrativo del Regno d'Italia*, 3/12 (1872), 160–66.

[74] Ibid., p. 163.

[75] Ibid., p. 164.

[76] Marina Graziosi, 'Infirmitas sexus. La donna nell'immaginario penalistico', *Jura gentium*, I/I (2005), electronic resource [accessed 15 October 2024].

affecting familial honour, reputation, or, more broadly, family order ('ordine delle famiglie'). This might be explained by reference to contemporaneous ideas about the female personality and its porosity to the influence of men, suggesting that crimes committed by women also implicated those men who were responsible for educating and controlling them. Moreover, in a society in which the family was a key institution, responsibility and punishment of individuals might also affect the social standing of the family as a whole. The importance attached to social standing, and the blurred boundaries of this notion, might also explain why punishment of some crimes took a different form depending on whether they were committed by a woman or a man.

Adultery was another matter again, and notions of honour, reputation, and possession all had to be taken into account to understand the legal norms.[77] Honour was perceived as part of a system of values that had to be protected to maintain a stable society, complicit with a centuries-old order that rested on inequality. A breach of this system of shared values affected not only the individuals involved but society as a whole. Adultery, which, in the words of Maurice Daumas, was the objective evidence of the

---

77 On the concept of honour, see Julian Pitt-Rivers, 'Honour and Social Status', in *Honour and Shame: The Values of Mediterranean Society*, ed. by John G. Peristiany (London: Weidenfeld & Nicholson, 1965), pp. 19–77. See, also, Michael Herzfeld, *Cultural Intimacy: Social Poetics in the Nation-State* (London: Routledge, 1997). For the understanding of honour as a loss of reputation, see Marianna Muravyeva, '"Verguenza, Vergogne, Schande, Skam and Sram": Litigating for Shame and Dishonour in Early Modern Europe', in *Shame, Blame, and Culpability: Crime and Violence in the Modern State*, ed. by Marianna Muravyeva, David Nash, and Judith Rowbotham (Abingdon: Routledge, 2013), pp. 17–32. On honour in Italy in particular, see: Antonino Buttitta, *Semiotica e antropologia* (Palermo: Sellerio, 1979), p. 135; Peter Burke, *The Historical Anthropology of Early Modern Italy* (Cambridge: Cambridge University Press, 1987); Thomas V. Cohen, 'The Lay Liturgy of Affront in Sixteenth-Century Italy', *Journal of Social History*, 25 (1991), 857–77; D'Onofrio, 'Onore e disonore in Sicilia'; Antonella Bettoni, '"Fama", Shame Punishments and the History of Justice in the Sixteenth and Seventeenth Centuries', in *Shame, Blame, and Culpability*, pp. 32–43; Sara Delmedico, '"Molto meno se la donna non può provare d'essere stata sorpresa". Donne, onore e seduzione nel Regno delle Due Sicilie di metà Ottocento', in *La donna, il matrimonio e la famiglia Aspetti sociali dal XVI al XX secolo*, ed. by Giovanna Da Molin and Angela Carbone (Bari: Cacucci, 2022), pp. 185–97; Schettini, 'La violenza maschile contro le donne', p. 145.

sexual difference that establishes the male order,[78] was a serious issue, to the extent that it was considered a criminal act and was punished as such. Its effects extended upon both the private and public spheres, so rules for its regulation were reported in both the civil and criminal codes. The Italian civil code ruled that separation could be requested by a husband as a result of his wife's adultery; however, a wife was allowed to ask for separation only if her husband 'mantenga la concubina in casa o notoriamente in altro luogo, oppure quando concorrano circostanze tali che il fatto costituisca un'ingiuria grave alla moglie' [keeps the concubine at home or notoriously elsewhere, or when there are circumstances making the act a serious insult to the wife].[79] The criminal code ruled on the punishment of adultery and again made a distinction between men and women. According to Article 353, an adulterous wife could be punished with imprisonment for a period of between three and thirty months.[80] Article 354 stated that a husband would be punished only if he kept a concubine actually within the marital home, or 'notoriously elsewhere', with the same duration of imprisonment of between three and thirty months and the removal of his 'podestà maritale' [marital authority].[81] A wife could not be punished at all if she could prove that, in the five years prior to her own crime, her husband had committed the same crime as provided for in Article 354, or that he had forced, induced, or encouraged her to engage in prostitution.[82] Additionally, punishment would not be meted out to a husband if he could

---

78 See Maurice Daumas, *Adulteri e cornuti. Storia della sessualità maschile tra Medioevo e modernità* (Bari: Dedalo, 2008), p. 70. For an analysis of adultery through time, Sara McDougall, 'The Transformation of Adultery in France at the End of the Middle Ages', *Law and History Review*, 32/3 (2014), 491–524; Sara Beam, 'Gender and the Prosecution of Adultery in Geneva, 1550–1700', in *Women's Criminality in Europe, 1600–1914*, ed. by Manon van der Heijden, Marion Pluskota, Sanne Muurling (Cambridge: Cambridge University Press, 2020), pp. 91–113. On the perception of adultery as a loss of property, see Guido Ruggiero, *The Boundaries of Eros: Sex Crime and Sexuality in Renaissance Venice* (Oxford: Oxford University Press, 1989), pp. 45–46.

79 Art. 150, *Codice civile del Regno d'Italia: corredato della relazione del Ministro Guardasigilli fatta a S. M. in udienza del 25 giugno 1865* (Turin: Botta, 1865), p. 29.

80 Art. 353, *Il codice penale per il Regno d'Italia*, ed. by Giulio Crivellari (Turin: Unione tipografico-editrice, 1889), p. 132.

81 Art. 354, Ibid.

82 Art. 357, Ibid.

prove that, in the five years prior to the crime, his wife had committed the same crime defined in Article 353.[83]

Alongside honour, certain jurists, such as the Piedmontese Pio Viazzi (1868–1914) connected the different legal approaches with the sensitivity and sexual desire of men and women.[84] Viazzi suggested that men and women experience love, and the emotions and behaviours it triggered, in different ways, and that while 'nella donna normale l'amore cresce dal momento in cui si è data, nell'uomo invece diminuisce sensibilmente colla soddisfazione' [in the normative woman, love grows from the moment she gives herself, in the man it decreases significantly with satisfaction].[85] Moreover, men were deemed to be perpetually driven to search for other women, while women would remain faithfully committed to one man since a natural instinct impelled them to find a protector for their future family. Viazzi claimed that these natural instincts explained why fidelity in marriage was artificial for men but natural for women.[86] As a consequence, Viazzi proposed two causes for female adultery:

> 1º le colpe del marito, l'insufficienza, la disonestà, la trascuranza, il malo esempio e simili;
> 2º la anormalità della moglie afflitta da erotismo morboso o da quelle altre forme di deficienza morale che quasi fatalmente conducono al disordine ed alla dissoluzione
>
> [1. The husband's faults, insufficiency, dishonesty, neglect, bad example and similar; 2. An abnormality in the wife, afflicted by morbid eroticism or by such other forms of moral deficiency that lead almost fatally to disorder and licentiousness].[87]

By framing women's adultery only as a consequence of husbands' faults or wives' 'abnormality', Viazzi's misogynistic view implied that adulterous women were only to be pitied or treated as deviant. However, other jurists observed the issue from other perspectives, identifying a 'distance' between wives and husbands. Tommaso Bruno contended, in *La condizione giuridica della donna nella legislazione italiana: studio teorico-pratico*, written to 'giovare

83 Art. 357, Ibid.
84 On the punishment of adultery from the Middle Ages onwards, see Delmedico, *Opposing Patriarchy*, pp. 199–204.
85 Pio Viazzi, *Sui reati sessuali* (Turin: Bocca, 1896), p. 168.
86 Ibid., p. 169.
87 Ibid., p. 171.

alla causa delle donne' [benefit the cause of women],[88] that marriage was not simply a contract between two people, but rather a solemn act of social importance, with personal and patrimonial consequences.[89] Since marriage was a crucial institution, lawmakers were to pay attention to existing imbalances between wife and husband, which, claimed Bruno, were particularly relevant where adultery was concerned, and were required to try to limit the distance between spouses. He pointed out that the different approaches to male and female adultery were due primarily to the possibility of illegitimate births.[90] Were this eventuality excluded, however, there remained 'il danno dello *scandalo* e della *vergogna*, che suole essere maggiore, e non poco, nell'adulterio della moglie' [the damage of scandal and shame, which is usually greater, and not by a little, in the wife's adultery].[91] Bruno ascribed this understanding to false social prejudices.

Among the few voices raised in favour of equality between women and men was that of Guglielmo Gambarotta. As with Domenico Giuriati, discussed earlier, Gambarotta's view was also deeply embedded in stereotypes, despite his laudable efforts to overcome them. In his *L'adulterio e la teorica dei diritti necessari*, he described women as having an atavistic modesty about their nakedness, constructed over centuries by the perception amongst both their husbands and society at large of female bodies as a mechanism of seduction.[92] This ignited a man's jealousy towards his wife and the 'intimi tesori di cui la donna doveva serbare a lui esclusivamente il godimento' [intimate treasures, the enjoyment of which the woman should keep exclusively for him].[93]

Jealousy, therefore, was conceived as a means for avoiding the danger that threatened a husband in the exclusive possession of his wife.[94] Gambarotta interpreted the body as property; adultery, therefore, was theft and violation of

---

88 Tommaso Bruno, *La condizione giuridica della donna nella legislazione italiana: studio teorico-pratico* (Florence: Barbera, 1894), p. v.

89 Ibid., p. 91.

90 Ibid., p. 97.

91 Ibid., p. 98.

92 Guglielmo Gambarotta, *L'adulterio e la teorica dei diritti necessari* (Turin: Bocca, 1898), pp. 12–13. Gambarotta (1877–1961) was a lawyer and member of the Italian parliament. Note also his important work, *Inchiesta sulla donna* (Turin: Bocca, 1899), in which he set out an enquiry on women and their status.

93 Gambarotta, *L'adulterio e la teorica dei diritti necessari*, p. 13.

94 Ibid.

property rights. Acknowledging that 'l'adulterio è sempre una pura e semplice lesione del diritto personale; non mai una lesione alla moralità dei costumi' [adultery is always a pure and simple violation of personal rights; it is never an injury to the morality of customs],[95] Gambarotta analysed differences in the punishment of male and female adultery. Resting on this central idea of adultery as a personal and not public matter, his findings denounced existing inequalities in law and upheld a requirement for reciprocity and equality within marriage that also extended to the punishment of adultery.[96] In fact, the Italian criminal code included adultery under Title VIII: 'Titolo VIII. Dei delitti contro il buon costume e l'ordine delle famiglie' [Title VIII. Crimes against good morals and family order].[97]

Another jurist, Giulio Crivellari, noted, in his commentary on the 1889 criminal code, that the Justice Minister, Giuseppe Zanardelli, permitted the law to crack down on crimes that could cause conspicuous damage to families, but that it should not overrun morality.[98] Treading a fine line between seeking to preserve order within families by preventing and punishing any act against shared values and an anxiety to avoid public scandal and dishonour, adultery was treated as a crime, but the lawsuit itself was to be initiated by the offended party, namely the wife or husband. The issue, therefore, was to be addressed within the private sphere, with the resultant saving of reputation, as far as this was possible.

Notions of honour and reputation were also important in relation to infanticide.[99] Deeming infanticide to be driven by 'un amore imprudent, che

---

95 Ibid., p. 203.

96 Ibid., p. 234.

97 Crivellari, *Il codice penale per il Regno d'Italia*, p. 123.

98 Ibid.

99 Throughout the late nineteenth century, infanticide was studied from a number of perspectives. See, in the first instance: Lino Ferriani, *La infanticida nel codice penale e nella vita sociale: considerazioni* (Milan: Dumolard, 1886); Raffaello Balestrini, *Aborto, infanticidio ed esposizione d'infante: studio giuridico-sociologico* (Turin: Bocca, 1888); and Vincenzo Mellusi, *La madre delinquente: studio di psicologia morbosa* (Rome: Loescher, 1897). For secondary sources on infanticide, see: Adriano Prosperi, *Dare l'anima. Storia di un infanticidio* (Turin: Einaudi, 2005); Loredana Garlati, 'Honour and Guilt. A Comparative Study on Regulations on Infanticide between the Nineteenth and Twentieth Century', in *Family Law and Society in Europe from the Middle Ages to the Contemporary Era*, ed. by Maria Gigliola Di Renzo Villata (Cham, NY: Springer

trascura il rispetto per gli usi sociali' [an imprudent love; one that neglects respect for social mores],[100] Lombroso and Ferrero claimed that such a crime would be committed by a woman assailed by strong emotion; that is, different from the average woman, who was characterised by sexual coldness.[101] In addition to transgressing societal rules and evidencing strong emotion, infanticide was also linked with women's alleged mental weakness, leading them to become victims of unscrupulous seducers.[102] However, punishment for infanticide was relatively modest. Were a baby's name not inscribed in civil status registers and had the baby's life been taken within five days of birth, and for reasons of honour, including that of the family, a wife, a mother, a descendant, an adopted daughter, or a sister, the penalty was imprisonment for three to twelve years,[103] compared with eighteen to twenty-one years for other types of murder.[104] Vito Porto, another jurist of the time, commented that such provision merited praise, as those committing infanticide in pursuit of saving honour could not be considered akin to 'volgari malfattori' [vulgar criminals].[105] Such a pronouncement offers a clear insight into the societal values of the time: honour was an element to be protected at all costs, including even the cost of a life, which, particularly if it came from intercourse outside the sacred boundaries of marriage, could be sacrificed for the higher goal of preserving reputation.

International Publishing, 2016), pp. 257–81; Adriano Prosperi, *Infanticide, Secular Justice, and Religious Debate in Early Modern Europe* (Turnhout: Brepols, 2016); and Delmedico, *Opposing Patriarchy*, pp. 141–46.

100 Lombroso and Ferrero, *La donna delinquente, la prostituta e la donna normale*, p. 495.

101 Ibid.

102 See Ferriani, *La infanticida nel codice penale e nella vita sociale*, p. 73. See, also, Giovanni Cazzetta, *Praesumitur seducta. Onestà e consenso femminile nella cultura giuridica moderna* (Milan: Giuffrè, 1999), pp. 335–36.

103 Art. 369, in Crivellari, *Il codice penale per il Regno d'Italia*, p. 140.

104 Art. 364, Ibid., p. 139.

105 Vito Porto, *Progetto del codice penale presentato dal Ministro Zanardelli alla Camera dei Deputati nella Seduta del 22 novembre 1887* (Rome: Stamperia dell'opinione, 1888), pp. 70–71.

CHAPTER 3

Scientists entering tribunals. Explaining violence against women

Examination of putative connections between the physical and mental features of the sexes was used not only to explain inclination to commit crime and reduced ability to follow moral rules and meet societal expectations but was also used to justify violence against women. As we shall see, a woman's inability to meet societal expectations rendered her valueless. Such a woman was therefore expendable and, even as a victim of violence, to some extent also an accomplice. A man who did not abide by societal rules was inherently some kind of misfortunate: violence in such a man was somehow excusable, thereby facilitating the bestowing of a lenient sentence.

Violence against women was located in a blurred area where overwhelming emotion and honour coexisted. From the nineteenth century, it became the object of a number of investigations by scientists and jurists. Generally defined as crimes of passion, according to Eliza Earle Ferguson, '[s]tereotypically, such crimes were precipitated by abandonment or infidelity, and carried out in a fit of madness or overwhelming emotion'.[1] This overwhelming emotion, or *furor*, had many similarities with the ancient concept of *iustus dolor*, the 'just rage' inflicted upon a husband if a societal value were betrayed by his wife. Use of the word 'just' implied that there were circumstances in which an overwhelming and destructive *dolor* was apt, and its outcomes understandable.[2]

---

1 Eliza Earle Ferguson, 'Judicial Authority and Popular Justice: Crimes of Passion in Fin-de-Siecle Paris', *Journal of Social History*, 40 (2) (2006), 293–315.

2 On *iustus dolor* in ancient times, see: Eva Cantarella, 'Homicides of Honor: The Development of Italian Adultery Law over Two Millennia', in *The Family in Italy: From Antiquity to the Present*, ed. by David I. Kertzer and Richard P. Saller (New Haven/London: Yale University Press, 1991), pp. 229–44; and Giunio Rizzelli, *Lex Julia de*

This *dolor* could be comparable to the 'state of madness' mentioned in the 1810 Napoleonic criminal code and to which, according to Emilia Musumeci, nineteenth-century studies on crimes attempted to give a solid ground.[3]

The idea behind the state of madness meant that individuals could be partially insane, thus implying a temporary alteration of their minds, under which a crime or delict could be committed.[4] In this regard, the key point was to assess if an act was committed intentionally with the will to harm, that is, committed in a state of mind that allowed perpetrators to understand that what they were doing was wrong and had the capacity not to do a peculiar act, thus making them fully responsible for their acts. As a consequence, total insanity was a state beyond any rationality, while a partially insane individual was the one who was deranged by degrees and retained a lower level of understanding than the average individual.

---

adulteriis, Studi sulla disciplina di adulterium, lenocinium, stuprum (Lecce: Edizioni del Grifo, 1997).

3 On this point, see Emilia Musumeci, 'New Natural Born Killers? The Legacy of Lombroso in Neuroscience and Law', in *The Cesare Lombroso Handbook*, ed. by Knepper and Ystehede, pp. 359–73 (p. 359).

4 On insanity, see, Yves Cartuyvels and Aniceto Masferrer, 'The Making of Insane Offenders in the Western Tradition: A Comparative Approach to the Birth and Enforcement of Criminological Positivism (1870–1940)', *GLOSSAE. European Journal of Legal History*, 20 (2023), pp. 1–27; Stefano Vinci, 'Insanity and Criminal Justice in Italy at the End of the 19th Century', *GLOSSAE. European Journal of Legal History*, 20 (2023), 28–44. Article 64 of the Napoleonic Criminal Code (1810) stated that 'Il n'y a ni crime ni délit, lorsque le prévenu était en état de démence au temps de l'action, ou lorsqu'il a été contraint par une force à laquelle il n'a pu résister' [There can be no crime, or delict, where the accused was in a state of madness at the time of the action; or when he has been constrained by a force which he had not the power to resist]. This code was translated and extended to many areas of Italy by a decree of 12 November 1810, and entered into force on the 1st of January 1811. The 1808 *Code d'instruction criminelle* and the 1810 *Code pénal* contained a tripartite classification of offences on the basis of their punishment. Article 1 of the penal code states that offences are 'crime' [crime], 'délit'[delict] and 'contravention' [contravention]. This distinction relies on the punishment of these offences. These are afflictive or infamous penalties for crimes, correctional penalties for delicts, penalties of police from contraventions. Law codes deriving from Napoleonic codes adopted similar classification or bipartite classification. Article 1 of the 1889 Italian penal code distinguished offences into two categories: 'delitti' [delicts] and 'contravvenzioni' [contraventions]. Since anglophone literature usually employs the term "crime", I choose the term crime instead of delicts.

French psychiatrists such as Jean-Étienne Dominique Esquirol (1772–1840), François Achille Cazauvieilh (1788–1857), Etienne-Jean Georget (1795–1828) and Théodule Ribot (1839–1916) significantly contributed to frame the concept of insanity with their studies of mental disorders, emotions, and monomania. Monomania, in particular, was a term used to define the state of partial insanity, a condition that implied the presence of a pathological fixed idea,[5] which deranged a mind that was otherwise rational.[6]

These studies also started to be translated and taken into consideration in the Italian environment.[7] Criminalists began to use these ideas to improve their understanding of criminal minds and the way jurists had to approach cases and circumstances in which criminal acts take place. In the effort to combine the abstraction of a law – and to overcome the impossibility of foreseeing all the possible situations occurring in the reality – with the legal certainty and equal treatment, jurists such as Filippo Maria Renazzi analysed the circumstances in which the state of madness could be used or abused. Provided that '[h]omines sumus, nihil humani a nobis alienum esse putandum' [we are human, and we should think that nothing human is alien to us],[8] Renazzi allowed that penalty should be mitigated for those who committed crimes in an outburst of anger. Instead,

> si quis non incontinenti, sed jam remissa ira venerit ad delinquendum, hic non impetu deliquisse videbitur, sed nequitia se ulciscendi commodum occasionemque expectasse: proinde incassum irae excusatione contendet legitims evadere poenas. *Ira, furor brevis est*

---

5 Fixed-idea (idée fixe) was probably first coined by Gall and Spurzheim. See Gall and Spurzheim, *Anatomie et physiologie*, [1812], II, p. 192. The term was also used by Etienne-Jean Georget, *De la physiologie du système nerveux, et spécialement du cerveau*, 2 vols (Paris: Baillière, 1821) and by Jean-Étienne Dominique Esquirol, *Note sur la monomanie-homicide* (Paris: Baillière, 1827).

6 On French psychiatry and monomania, see Jan E. Goldstein, *Console and Classify: The French Psychiatric Profession in the Nineteenth Century* (Chicago: University of Chicago Press, 1987), pp. 152–96; German E. Berrios, *The History of Mental Symptoms: Descriptive Psychopathology Since the Nineteenth Century* (Cambridge: Cambridge University Press, 1996), pp. 443–50. See also, Trip Finity Taylor, Kortni MacDonald, 'The criminalization of madness', in *The Origins of Criminological Theory*, ed. by Omi Hodwitz (London: Routledge, 2022), pp. 92–110.

7 See for example, *Della alienazione mentale o Della pazzia in genere e in ispecie*, 2 vols (Milan: Rusconi, 1827), a work of Jean-Étienne Dominique Esquirol translated by the Italian physician Luigi Calvetti.

8 Renazzi, *Elementa juris criminalis*, II, *Liber secundus. De poenis generatim*, p. 113.

> [if someone, not in the heat of the moment but after their anger has subsided, proceeds to commit an offence, they will not be seen as having transgressed in a fit of rage, but rather as having eagerly awaited an opportunity for revenge. Consequently, in vain will they seek to escape just punishment by excusing themselves with anger. *Anger is a brief madness*].[9]

By emphasising the idea of anger being something brief and the importance of considering if this anger was just or not, Renazzi concurred to categorise what was acceptable and what was not. Therefore, the rage was just if it was deployed for something that went against the shared social value, that is, for example, adultery.[10]

Scholars like Cesare Lombroso, Guglielmo Ferrero, Scipio Sighele, and others went even further by linking violent emotion not just to adultery, which could be located within the boundaries of honour and possession, but to love, thus elaborating concepts such as 'delitti o pseudo-delitti d'amore' [crime, or pseudo-crime, of love], which clearly asserted that violence could be an intrinsic component of love.[11] In an entangled elaboration of these concepts, the *delitti o pseudo-delitti d'amore* included the notions of crimes of passion and crimes of honour. The latter, the crimes 'of honour', relied on the notion of 'justification' since the act was committed to defend a person's worthiness and reputation in society; the former, the crimes of passion, were instead crimes committed under the heat of passion. According to the historian Anne-Claude Ambroise-Rendu, the perpetrators of these crimes were not perceived as a danger for society, as theirs was a 'crime without criminality', and, once 'the object of their sickness' disappeared, they returned to soundness.[12] This understanding significantly suspended the culpability of the attacker.

According to the *Codice penale per il Regno d'Italia*, the 1889 criminal code of Italy, the murder of the spouse was punishable with a prison sentence from 22 to 24 years, while the murder of any other person was sentenced from 18 to 21 years.[13] However, some mitigations existed: Article 51 stated that

---

9 Ibid., pp. 113–14.

10 Ibid.

11 See Augusto Guido Bianchi, Guglielmo Ferrero and Scipio Sighele, eds, *Il mondo criminale italiano*, 2 vols (Milan: Omodei Zorini, 1893), I.

12 Anne-Claude Ambroise-Rendu, 'Le chroniqueur, la justice et l'opinion publique: les faits divers à la fin du XIXe siècle', *Histoire de la justice*, 1/20 (2010), 69–80 (p. 77).

13 Articles 364–65, *Codice penale per il Regno d'Italia* (Rome: Stamperia Reale, 1889), pp. 127–28.

> Colui che ha commesso il fatto nell'impeto d'ira o d'intenso dolore, determinato da ingiusta provocazione, è punito con la reclusione non inferiore ai venti anni, se la pena stabilita per il reato commesso sia l'ergastolo, e negli altri casi con la pena stabilita per il reato commesso diminuita di un terzo.
>
> Se la provocazione sia grave, all'ergastolo è sostituita la detenzione da dieci a venti anni, e le altre pene sono diminuite dalla metà ai due terzi, sostituita alla reclusione la detenzione e all'interdizione perpetua dai pubblici uffici l'interdizione temporanea.
>
> [Whoever commits the act in the heat of anger or intense suffering, caused by unjust provocation, shall be punished with imprisonment for not less than twenty years if the penalty established for the offence is life imprisonment, and in other cases, with the penalty established for the offence reduced by one-third.
>
> If the provocation is serious, life imprisonment shall be replaced with detention for ten to twenty years, and other penalties shall be reduced by half to two-thirds, with detention replacing imprisonment and temporary disqualification from public office replacing permanent disqualification].[14]

The punishment was reduced if

> il fatto sia commesso dal coniuge, ovvero da un ascendente, o dal fratello o dalla sorella, sopra la persona del conjuge, della discendente, della sorella o del correo o di entrambi, nell'atto in cui li sorprenda in flagrante adulterio o illegittimo concubito,

---

[14] Article 51, *Codice penale per il Regno d'Italia* (1889), p. 291. See also Emilia Musumeci, *Emozioni, crimine, giustizia: un'indagine storico-giuridica tra Otto e Novecento* (Milan: Franco Angeli, 2015), pp. 70–77; Emilia Musumeci, 'L'amore in tribunale: la rilevanza delle emozioni nel diritto penale in Italia tra Otto e Novecento', in *History and Law Encounters. Lezioni per pensare da giurista II*, ed. by Elisabetta Fusar Poli, Aldo Andrea Cassi, Federica Paletti (Turin: Giappichelli, 2022), pp. 167–88. According to the *Codice penale*, imprisonment was the normal punishment for all non-capital crimes. Imprisonment was a temporary prison aimed at the repression together with the education and amendment of the condemned person. Imprisonment provided that the expiation of the sentence took place in a subsequent and progressive form, with the condemned person who, after an initial period of continuous segregation, as a second stage, had to carry out daytime work in common, under the rule of silence and with night segregation. Detention was the punishment for those crimes that did not reveal serious impulses or a perverse nature in their perpetrators. This punishment was similar to imprisonment in terms of duration, but did not provide the progressive and gradual system of expiation, but simple nocturnal segregation and daytime work at the choice of the convicted person. See also art. 11 Titolo II, Delle pene, *Codice penale per il Regno d'Italia* (1889), p. 14. On prisons in post-Unification Italy, see Assunta Borzacchiello, 'La grande riforma. Breve storia dell'irrisolta questione carceraria', *Rassegna penitenziaria e criminologica* (2005), 83–147 (pp. 101–11).

> la pena è ridotta a meno di un sesto, sostituita alla reclusione la detenzione, e all'ergastolo è sostituita la detenzione da uno a cinque anni
>
> [the act is committed by the spouse, or by an ascendant, or by the brother or by the sister, on the person of the spouse, of the descendant, of the sister or of the co-offender or of both, in the act of catching them in flagrant adultery or illegitimate concubinage, the sentence is reduced to less than one sixth, imprisonment is replaced by detention, and life imprisonment is replaced by imprisonment from one to five years].[15]

As can be noticed, when it comes to protecting honour, the law did not explicitly mention the impetus of anger, thus tacitly alluding that in such a situation anger did not need to be shown through external elements.

In the nineteenth century, triggered by European ferments, the Italian legal and scientific environment also started to follow new directions and approaches, which saw their momentum particularly from the second half of the nineteenth century. Scholars like Cesare Lombroso gave rise to a new Italian penal school, the Positivist School, not just a 'simpatica alleanza fra diritto penale e antropologia criminale' [nice alliance between criminal law and criminal anthropology],[16] but, in opposition to the Classic School, proponents of a new approach.[17] Members of the Classic School gathered around the journals *Rivista penale di dottrina, legislazione e giurisprudenza* and *Giurisprudenza italiana*[18] and were renowned jurists of the time, such

---

15 Article 377, *Codice penale per il Regno d'Italia* (1889), p. 133; see also Musumeci, *Emozioni, crimine, giustizia*, pp. 164–72.

16 Enrico Ferri, *La scuola positiva di diritto criminale: prelezione al corso di diritto e procedura penale nella R. Università di Siena pronunciata il 18 novembre 1882* (Siena: Torrini, 1883), p. 15. On the new school, see also Alfredo Frassati, *La Nuova Scuola di Diritto penale in Italia e all'estero* (Turin: Paravia, 1891).

17 On penal schools, see Floriana Colao, 'Le scuole penalistiche', in *Enciclopedia italiana. Il Contributo italiano alla storia del pensiero. Diritto* (Rome: Enciclopedia Italiana Treccani, 2012), pp. 349–56. See also, Renzo Villa, 'Lombroso and his School. From Anthropology to Medicine and Law', *The Cesare Lombroso Handbook*, ed. by Knepper and Ystehede, pp. 8–29.

18 *Rivista penale di dottrina, legislazione e giurisprudenza* was published in the years between 1874 and 1929. *Giurisprudenza Italiana: Raccolta generale, periodica e critica di giurisprudenza, legislazione e dottrina in materia civile, commerciale, penale, amministrativa e di diritto pubblico e rivista di giurisprudenza straniera* was directed by Francesco Carrara, Francesco Gabba, Luigi Maurizi and Emidio Pacifici Mazzoni. A collection of juridical works rather than a journal, it was published from 1874 to 1880.

as Francesco Carrara, who was also entrusted with the elaboration of the new criminal code; Domenico Giuriati; Luigi Maurizi; and Emidio Pacifici Mazzoni, among others. As contended by Musumeci, the Classic School was 'still anchored to a strictly juridical conception of crime, completely disengaged from other disciplines', and looked at the new emerging school and did not avoid making harsh criticisms.[19]

The Positivist School gathered around *Archivio di psichiatria, scienze penali ed antropologia criminale per servire allo studio dell'uomo alienato e delinquente*,[20] and had among its main representatives Cesare Lombroso, Enrico Ferri, Raffaele Garofalo, Enrico Morselli, Salvatore Ottolenghi and Scipio Sighele.[21] Their approach was innovative and interdisciplinary: as highlighted by Enrico Ferri, the Positivist School's aims were the 'studio concreto del reato, non come astrazione giuridica ma come azione umana, come fatto naturale' [concrete study of the crime, not as a legal abstraction but as a human action, as a natural fact].[22] Ferri claimed that this approach had a significant practical and scientific basis because it was the application of the experimental method to the study of crimes and punishments.[23] Therefore, 'mentre porta nel recinto del tecnicismo giuridico astratto l'alito delle nuove osservazioni fatte non solo dall'antropologia criminale, ma dalla statistica, dalla psicologia, dalla sociologia, rappresenta veramente una nuova fase nell'evoluzione della scienza

---

19 Emilia Musumeci, 'New Natural Born Killers? The Legacy of Lombroso in Neuroscience and Law', in *The Cesare Lombroso Handbook*, ed. by Knepper and Ystehede, pp. 359–373 (p. 360).

20 *Archivio di psichiatria, scienze penali ed antropologia criminale per servire allo studio dell'uomo alienato e delinquente* was founded by Lombroso and Raffaele Garofalo in 1880. Raffaele Garofalo (1851–1934) was a jurist and senator. His most renowned work is *Criminologia: studio sul delitto, sulle sue cause e sui mezzi di repressione* (1891).

21 Enrico Morselli (1852–1929) was a psychiatrist and anthropologist. Among his works, there are *Il metodo clinico nella diagnosi generale della pazzia* (1882), *Antropologia generale* (1911), and, co-written with his colleague Giovanni Angelucci, *Parere medico-forense sullo stato mentale di un uxoricida* (1880). See, also, Patrizia Guarnieri, '"La volpe e l'uva": cultura scientifica e filosofia del positivismo italiano', *Physis*, XXV (1983), 301–336; Patrizia Guarnieri, *Individualità difformi. La psichiatria antropologica di Enrico Morselli* (Milan: Franco Angeli, 1986); Bruce DiCristina, 'Criminology and the "Essence" of Crime: The Views of Garofalo, Durkheim, and Bonger', *International Criminal Justice Review*, 26/4 (2016), 297–315.

22 Ferri, *La Scuola positiva di diritto criminale*, p. 28.

23 Ibid., p. 16.

criminale' [while bringing into the realm of abstract legal technicality the breath of new observations made not only by criminal anthropology, but by statistics, psychology, sociology, it truly represents a new phase in the evolution of criminal science].[24] Moreover, according to Ferri, this new school tended to re-establish the balance 'tra l'elemento individuale e il sociale' [between the individual element and the social], opposite to the Classic School, which 'sorgeva in nome dell'individualismo, per rivendicarne i diritti esageratamente soffocati dallo Stato nel Medio Evo' [arose in the name of individualism, to vindicate the rights exaggeratedly suffocated by the State in the Middle Ages].[25]

As we shall see in the next chapters, members of the Positivist School and their disciples also entered the courtroom and, with their theories and studies, proposed new approaches and ways to tackle crimes and individuals who committed crimes. However, discrimination and inequality were persistent elements of their approaches. Women, in particular, were seen through the lens of a centuries-old, stereotyped and prejudicial vision. As in the past, they were asked to comply with the role and behaviour allegedly assigned to them by nature and praised by society. If they did not comply with these expectations, they became expendable, their lives had less value, and their murders were seen as something acceptable.

This understanding was carried forward also by the press, which, with its articles, contributed to perpetuating this vision, manipulating ideas, and reproducing stereotypes, thus forging the notion of the tolerability of a crime.

---

[24] Ibid., p. 15.

[25] Ibid., pp. 28–9.

PART 2

CHAPTER 4

The case and the press

On the night of 16 May 1903, Alberto Olivo killed his wife, Ernestina Beccaro, in Milan. A week later, on 23 May, Olivo arrived in Genoa with a bag containing his wife's remains and disposed of her body during a boat trip. That same day, three young men, fishing in Genoa's port, found the body. The news rapidly circulated. A neighbour of the couple reported Beccaro's disappearance to the police, and, shortly afterwards, Olivo was arrested.

The case instantly triggered a wave of emotion among the general public and the interest of various jurists and scientists. Newspapers of the time wrote widely about the case, creating their own narratives and focusing on the human interest element: each of Olivo's two trials by jury was described in detail,[1] with particular attention devoted to the audience in the public

1 The trials against Olivo were trials by jury. The historian Claudia Passarella pointed out that trials by jury were both criticised – because their judgement might be too irrational and emotional – and defended – because they expressed societal values and voice. See, Claudia Passarella, 'Between Leniency and Severity. Family Life and Criminal Behaviours at the Court of Assize of Venice, 1871–1898', *Crime, Histoire & Sociétés/Crime, History & Societies*, 24/2 (2020), 97–120 (p. 97). On nineteenth-century treatises on juries and jurors, see Carlo Pagani and Filippo De Ferrari, *Il cittadino giurato innanzi alla corte d'assisie (sic!)* (Florence: Stamperia Reale, 1866); Giulio Crivellari, *La giuria in Italia* (Mantua: Segna, 1872); Luigi Casorati, *La nuova legge sul giurì* (Prato: Giacchetti, 1874); Lorenzo Franceschini, *I giurati secondo la nuova legge 8 giugno 1874: osservazioni e commenti* (Rome: Barbera, 1874); Giuseppe Manfredini, *Il giurato italiano dopo il primo gennaio 1875* (Padua: Salmin, 1875); Enrico Ferri, *Cenni critici sulla giuria in Italia* (Venice: Fontana, 1880); Giovanni Battista Impallomeni, *Della giuria* (Palermo: Lo Statuto, 1895); Augusto Setti, *Manuale per il giurato* (Milan: Hoepli, 1903).

gallery, to female participation in all aspects of the trial, and to people's emotions and particular comments. Indeed, as the historian Thomas Simpson argued, 'what was once a formality became instead a debate, a discussion, a drama, and a spectacle',[2] which grew even more sensationalised after criminologist Cesare Lombroso and other scientists began to study the case following Olivo's first acquittal.

After the first verdict, the case was appealed. Olivo was acquitted again and went on to live his life as a free man. As this study will set out, the case was quickly picked up by the general public, jurists, and scientists. Journalists swiftly anticipated the impression the case would have on the general public and on their own readers and dedicated many pages in their publications to the topic every day. Reporting on the investigation and trial was meticulously detailed: context, defendant, victim, and those following the hearings were all minutely described. What emerged as a result was not only the reportage of a trial and its public repercussion but a picture of early-nineteenth-century society, with all its ambition, expectation, prejudice, stereotyping, particular values, cravings, and desires. As historian Anne-Claude Ambroise-Rendu has noted, attendance at a trial was in service of varying goals, according to the individual's position: on the one hand, the defence of order and decency and the revalorisation of the binding nature of oath and marriage; on the other, the triumph of romanticism and the sovereign rights of love, even at the price of violence.[3] People at Olivo's trial had similar goals, and, as a result, the trial became a spectacle, a microcosm of life itself, in which they were able to be part of the performance and to vicariously experience the emotions of the event for themselves.

In this context, the ways in which the protagonists were described were consistent with the model of a standardised, homogenous society:[4] the

---

2 Thomas Simpson, *Murder and Media in the New Rome: The Fadda Affair* (New York: Palgrave Macmillan, 2010), p. 25.

3 Anne-Claude Ambroise-Rendu, *Crimes et délits. Une histoire de la violence de la Belle Époque à nos jours* (Paris: Nouveau Monde Éditions, 2006), p. 41. On the depiction of crimes of passion in the popular press, see: Kalifa, *L'Encre et le sang*; *Imaginaire et sensibilités au XIX siècle: Études pour Alain Corbin*, ed. by Anne-Emmanuelle Demartini and Dominique Kalifa (Paris: Créaphis, 2005). See, also, Giulio Tatasciore, 'Per una storia culturale del crimine. Alcuni recenti studi francesi', *Storica*, 60 (2014), 92–110.

4 Dominique Kalifa, *Les Bas-fonds. Histoire d'un imaginaire* (Paris: Éditions du Seuil, 2013), p. 347. See, also, *Imaginaire et sensibilités au XIX siècle*.

female victim was, as usual, young and beautiful and, in failing to abide by the common behavioural values of her environment, was somehow at least in part an accomplice to, if not the cause itself of, the violence she had suffered; the accused, typically 'heroised' and described as a hard-working individual, loyal, reliable, and the agent of good deeds, was the innocent victim of cruel fate that had brought him into contact with a bad person by whom he had been deceived.

From a few days after the discovery of Ernestina Beccaro's remains and the subsequent arrest of Alberto Olivo, journalists could be found everywhere around Milan making enquiries about the couple's life in a bid to generate as much first-hand news as possible. On 27 May 1903, a number of newspapers published articles with detailed descriptions of the case and those involved in it. In the *Corriere della Sera*, for example, a very long article detailed the lives of Alberto Olivo and Ernestina Beccaro, the events of Beccaro's murder, the nature of Olivo's interrogation, and a raft of further information gathered through questioning the couple's neighbours. Regarding Beccaro, the newspaper had ascertained that she was the daughter of a courageous soldier who had fought in the Crimea; born in Biella on 14 August 1874, the tenth of fourteen children; and that, after the death of her father, she began working as a maidservant. Olivo, they established, was born in Udine, where he was remembered as a cultured and studious young man but of a gloomy and impetuous disposition. Moreover, Olivo 'amoreggiò per quattro o cinque anni, continuando a scrivere alla fidanzata, ora maniaca' [carried on a flirtation for four or five years, continuing to write to his by then maniacal girlfriend].[5] Beccaro settled in Milan in 1895, where she immediately met Olivo, 'che la sposò il 17 gennaio 1896. I due coniugi vissero sempre uniti' [who married her on 17 January 1896. The two spouses always lived together].[6] Analysis of the language used from the very first articles written about the murder clearly indicates the conventional lens of the time through which observation of facts and people was heavily filtered – such as this fact that the two always lived together, for example. Early descriptions of Beccaro and Olivo and their life as a couple suggested an ordinary situation in which two people had met, married, and lived together. However, the disruptive factor

5 *Corriere della Sera*, 27 May 1903, p. 2.
6 Ibid.

that would later emerge would be Beccaro's behaviour: she was sexually ambiguous and an insubordinate wife to her husband.

During the night of 16 May 1903, screams were heard emanating from the apartment in which Olivo and Beccaro lived, followed by a thud. However, it seems that no one paid any particular attention to this, with the matter attributed to a domestic disagreement. The gas that fuelled the light in their apartment continued to burn throughout the night, a detail noted by several of the insomniacs and early risers of the neighbourhood, who recalled wondering why the couple was still awake at that time.[7] Over the following days, certain neighbours noticed Beccaro's absence, wondering where she was. Having questioned Olivo, they recalled being unconvinced by his answers. The following day, on Sunday, one neighbour, by reaching through his window, managed to open one of the shutters of the couple's apartment and saw, to his amazement, that the gas flame was still lit. He then saw the marital bed: 'Questo, mentre era completamente ordinato dalla parte occupata dal marito, presentava uno strano disordine dall'altra, riservata alla moglie, dove il materasso vuoto era sparso superiormente della lana che avrebbe dovuto contenere' [While completely neat and tidy on the side taken up by the husband, there was a strange disorder on the other side, the wife's, where the empty mattress lay thrown on top of the wool it should have contained].[8] He went to the police station, reported everything he had seen, and speculated: 'chissà che il cadavere di Genova, anziché quello di un uomo, sia quello di una donna e che essa possa essere la signora Olivo' [who knows if the body in Genoa might actually be that of a woman, not a man, and if it might even be Mrs Olivo].[9] This instance in the *Corriere della Sera* is one of the very few times when Beccaro is referred to by the title 'signora', Mrs; as we shall see, jurists, scientists, witnesses, and journalists more typically referred to her by her first name alone or by descriptors such as 'the butchered body' 'the female deceased'; her surname was used only infrequently. The neighbour's

---

7 Ibid.

8 Ibid.

9 *Corriere della Sera*, 27 May 1903, p. 2. At first, it was thought that the recovered body of Beccaro was that of a man. *La Stampa* reported that the slim and not obviously female shape of the body led the police to believe that it was that of an eighteen-year-old youth (*La Stampa*, 27 May 1903, p. 2).

speculation encouraged the Police Commissioner to investigate Olivo, and shortly afterwards, Olivo was arrested. The *Corriere della Sera* reported that:

> la sera del 16 corrente disse di essere venuto ad una delle solite questioni con la moglie, con la quale viveva da sette anni in continua discordia.
> – Mia moglie – egli disse – mi tormentava continuamente, ed ogni cosa, dato il suo carattere bisbetico, le serviva di pretesto. Sabato, 16 maggio, essa, mentre si stava pranzando, rinnovò una delle sue solite scene, alla quale non era estranea una gelosia, fondata sovratutto nel fatto che io ero costretto a rimanere poco in casa
>
> [on the evening of the 16th of this month he said one of the usual rows had started with his wife, with whom he had lived in constant discord for seven years.
> 'My wife', he said, 'tormented me constantly, and everything, in light of her ill-tempered character, was a pretext for her. On Saturday 16 May, while we were having lunch, she launched into one of her usual scenes, which was not unrelated to jealousy, based chiefly on the fact that I was forced not to stay long at home'].[10]

The newspaper went on to describe how Olivo said that he had felt unwell in the night and had asked his wife to make him a lemonade. He reportedly said, 'Ricordo solo che essa mi rispose male, chiamandomi vigliacco e meravigliandosi che io osassi rivolgermi a lei. Fu per me un colpo terribile... Ciò che avvenne non lo ricordo' [I only remember that she responded badly, calling me a coward and marvelling that I dared to ask her this. It was a terrible blow for me... I don't remember what happened].[11] Olivo contended that he remembered only that he woke up the next morning to find 'quella donna' [that woman] dead and understood that he must have killed her. Olivo continued his account in sophisticated language and conducted a psychological analysis of himself and his actions, possibly in an attempt to indicate the gap between his own character, as he saw it – that is, a cultured individual, capable of self-reflection – and that of his wife, an ignorant and narrow-minded woman. Responsibility for his wife's death was thus translated, by Olivo, to Beccaro herself – who he went on calling 'that woman' – arguing in addition that she had made him a murderer:

> Constatato il delitto, compiuto senza volerlo, pensai a costituirmi. Ma il fatto che io non avevo voluto, non mi faceva sentire il pungolo dell'espiazione. Quella donna, dopo avermi dato il dolore di farmi ritrovare assassino, non mi faceva

---

10 *Corriere della Sera*, 27 May 1903, p. 2.

11 Ibid.

> sentire rimorsi. Pensai quindi alla mia salvezza, non per salvare me, ma piuttosto il mio nome dalla vergogna
>
> [Having realised the crime, committed involuntarily, I thought about turning myself in. But the fact that I had not wanted her death did not make me feel the sting of atonement. That woman, having given me the pain of making me find myself a murderer, did not make me feel remorse. I then thought about my salvation, not to save myself, but rather my name from shame].[12]

Olivo went on to insist that he and Beccaro were incompatible, with the *Corriere della Sera* reporting that 'mentre egli è un uomo assai colto, l'uccisa era analfabeta' [while he is a very cultured man, the murder victim was illiterate].[13] It went on to quote information it had discovered from the concierge of the couple's residence. Beccaro was described in the stereotypical terms of the female victim: that is, in terms of her looks:

> era una donnina di statura molto bassa, ma aveva belli i lineamenti del viso; capigliatura folta, castano-scura; vestiva con una eleganza moderata. Pareva insomma – dicono i portinai della casa – proprio una *pigottina* (una bambola), e nell'insieme era piacevole
>
> [she was a little woman of very short stature, but she had nice facial features and thick, dark brown hair; she dressed with moderate elegance. In short, she was – say the concierges of the building – just like a *pigottina* (a [little] doll), and overall, she was pleasant].[14]

The narrative then focused on the relationship between the couple, often insinuating that Beccaro did not behave as a typical wife should. Specifically, the *Corriere della Sera* reported that Olivo would often come home tired from work and not in the mood to talk, but rather than offering support, Beccaro would provoke him and then take his silence as an excuse to leave the house. In fact, 'senza ulteriori preamboli, si vestiva, metteva il cappellino, infilava le scale e usciva' [without another word, she would get dressed, put on her hat, go down the stairs, and leave the building].[15] The reportedly salient traits of Beccaro and Olivo, upon which the entire narrative of the case relied, began

12 Ibid.
13 Ibid.
14 Ibid.
15 Ibid.

to emerge. The newspaper lingered on details from the police officer's report suggesting that the most striking feature on entering the house was the great volume of books. Olivo, it noted, was 'molto colto e studioso, aveva in casa proprio una intera libreria. In questa figurano i classici tedeschi, e pure nella loro lingua originale molti altri classici stranieri' [very cultured and studious, with an entire library at home. This includes the German classics, as well as many other foreign classics in their original language].[16] The *Corriere della Sera* then went on to discuss Olivo's unsatisfactory relationships with colleagues at his place of work, a ceramics firm by the name of Richard-Ginori: he was said to be condescending, leading his colleagues to implement 'una specie di isolamento: un vero boycottaggio' [a kind of isolation of him: a true boycott].[17] Some, having been seated at a desk next to him, had asked to be moved. Even in the restaurant where he went to eat during his lunch break, he 'si era fatto notare per il più vivace e intollerante' [was notable for being the most animated and intolerant].[18]

A shorter article on similar lines came out in *La Stampa*, maintaining that 'lui è un brutto tipo; lei era bassa di statura, magra, dal colorito bruno; era piacevole e godeva le simpatie degli inquilini, coi quali spesso si fermava a chiacchierare' [he is an unpleasant sort of man; she was short and thin, with a dark complexion, pleasant, and enjoyed the sympathies of the other tenants, with whom she often stopped to chat].[19] *La Stampa* reported that Olivo had fallen desperately in love with Beccaro seven years previously, adding that 'la povera giovane era domestica ed era analfabeta' [the poor young woman was a maid and was illiterate], insinuating that one of the main reasons for their arguments was the disparity in their level of education.[20]

La Stampa concluded its article by stressing that Olivo had 'tutti i più palesi segni della degenerazione' [all the most obvious signs of degeneracy], and that Beccaro, 'benché buona massaia, [era] frivola, impetuosa e colle sue strane bizze, pare desse motivo a sospettare di sé' [although a good housewife, (was) frivolous, impetuous and with her peculiar tantrums, seems to

[16] Ibid.
[17] Ibid.
[18] Ibid.
[19] *La Stampa*, 27 May 1903, p. 2.
[20] Ibid.

Figure 1 *I grandi processi illustrati*, 6 (1904)

Image reproduced by kind permission of Ministry of Culture – Pinacoteca di Brera – Biblioteca Braidense, Milan. Further reproduction or duplication by any means is prohibited.

give a reason to suspect her].[21] The use of *benché* – 'although' – exposes some interesting expectations of women at the time. Beccaro conformed with one aspect of the typical wife: she was able to take care of the house, but this was overshadowed by her frivolity and moral ambiguity – behaviour unbecoming in a society that, according to anthropologist Antonino Buttitta, expected women to espouse values of purity and sexual fidelity.[22]

In an article dated 28 May 1903 under the byline of Augusto Guido Bianchi, a journalist who went on to co-author studies with Cesare Lombroso, the *Corriere della Sera* explained that the most contradictory rumours circulating around the terrible event concerned the victim's conduct.[23] In particular, one of the concierges of Beccaro's building was asked, in relation to Beccaro:

> – Che contegno teneva qui la ragazza? …
> – Punto biasimevole. Era buona, affabile, l'unico suo difetto era di essere alquanto ciarlona.
>
> ["What was the girl's attitude here?" …
> "Not blameworthy in the slightest. She was good, affable, her only flaw was that she was a bit chatty."[24]

Olivo was described as having a calm demeanour that he maintained even when arrested: 'lo si direbbe un fatalista' [he seems to be a fatalist].[25] Moreover, the newspaper wrote that

> come ha accettato il delitto, penetrato nella sua vita, senza premeditazioni – ciò sembra indubbio – dopo quarantasette anni di esistenza onesta, così ha accettato la prigionia, sopraggiunta dopo i suoi inefficaci sforzi per procurarsi l'impunità
>
> [just as he accepted the crime that entered into his life without premeditation – this seems beyond doubt – after forty-seven years of an honest existence, so he accepted imprisonment after his ineffective efforts to procure himself impunity].[26]

---

21 Ibid., p. 3.

22 Antonino Buttitta, *Semiotica e antropologia* (Palermo: Sellerio, 1979), p. 135.

23 *Corriere della Sera*, 28 May 1903, p. 2. Augusto Guido Bianchi (1868–1951) was a journalist who worked for the *Corriere della Sera* and other newspapers. He became very familiar with Lombroso's theories, and wrote *Il caso Olivo* with Lombroso. He also contributed to *Il mondo criminale italiano* (1893), alongside Guglielmo Ferrero and Scipio Sighele.

24 Ibid.

25 Ibid.

26 Ibid.

The journalist interviewed people who knew Olivo and Beccaro, concluding that Olivo considered his wife, who he had married for reasons of physical attraction alone, as below him.[27] The *Corriere della Sera* also inferred that this factor was behind the irremediable conflicts that gave rise to the crime.[28]

An article published in the *Corriere della Sera* on 18 July 1903 began by referring to the murder as 'il misfatto della donna tagliata a pezzi' [the crime of the woman chopped to pieces], announcing that the trial would be an interesting one since the defendant was no vulgar criminal and whose past was 'uno specchio di onestà, di integrità' [the very reflection of honesty and integrity]. After reporting on Olivo's dedication to study and culture and the fact that he was found to have no vices – 'era di una temperanza rara. Quasi completamente astemio, non usciva mai di casa, né frequentava i caffè' [he was of a rare temperament – almost completely abstemious, and never left the house or frequented cafés] – the newspaper characterised Beccaro as 'una misera domestica, analfabeta, piccola, e neppur bella' [a miserable housemaid, illiterate, small, and not even beautiful].[29] The *Corriere della Sera* also added that there were witnesses who would put beyond all doubt 'l'amore dell'Olivo per la moglie: per quanto si trattasse di un amore a scatto ed a contrasto' [Olivo's love for his wife: for all it was a hot-headed and quarrelsome love].[30] Poised between trying to offer a human-interest article and providing as much detail as possible, the *Corriere della Sera* seemed already to have drawn conclusions about the couple's incompatibility, thus making sense of the ending of their story. The contrast between the positive depiction of the murderer – a virtuous man of rare restraint – and the negative character of the victim – miserable and not even beautiful – invites the reader to empathise with Olivo, and to judge Beccaro for wasting the good fortune that life provided her.

At the end of November 1903, the preliminary cross-examination phase was over. Augusto Guido Bianchi, having set out in full the details of the murder itself and the effects on the body, suggested that Olivo was justifying his crime as the result of an impulse of anger resulting from serious and

27 Ibid.

28 Ibid.

29 *Corriere della Sera*, 18 July 1903, p. 2.

30 Ibid.

unjust provocation and was portraying himself as the victim of a wife who had caused serious distress in his life, ultimately driving him to the excess of desperation on that fatal night of 16 May.[31] The *Corriere della Sera* reported that the prosecution assumed premeditation and went on to analyse elements that suggested premeditation. Bianchi observed that a 'frigido pacatoque animo' [coldness and calmness of mind] was evident in Olivo's entire conduct after the murder,[32] to the extent that he even used particular expressions, such as a reference to a 'nube sanguigna e maledetta' [bloody and cursed cloud] that obscured his mind,[33] in an attempt to justify his behaviour, whilst simultaneously demonstrating his highly cultured status. According to Bianchi, the prosecution claimed that the murder was motivated by a very particular impulse to kill, a desire born of his psychology, which was 'così povera di correttivi morali, così abbondante di egotismi intellettuali e di istinti bassi e volgari' [so poor in moral correctives, so abundant in intellectual egotism and base and vulgar instincts].[34] The article also argued that, in this trial, the study of the moral characters of the defence and his victim might have more value in determining the nature of the crime than the criminal evidence itself.[35] In this way, from the very beginning, responsibility began to shift towards Beccaro, rather than framing Olivo's attitude within the boundaries of culpability.

---

31 *Corriere della Sera*, 25 November 1903, p. 3.

32 On premeditation, see also Carrara, *Programma del corso di diritto criminale*, I, pp. 120–21. *Frigido pacatoque animo* designates the psychological element of premeditation, which consists in the persistence of the criminal purpose for the time between the formation of the criminal idea and its practical implementation. This expression was used by jurist Giovanni Carmignani who, in his *Juris criminalis elementa*, explained that premeditation is defined as 'occidendi propositum frigido, pacatoque animo susceptum moram habens, atque occasionem quaerens, ut crimen veluti exoptatum finem perficiat' [the intention of killing undertaken with a cold and calm mind, having delayed and sought an opportunity to complete the crime as the desired end] (Carmignani, *Juris criminalis elementa*, II, p. 79).

33 *Corriere della Sera*, 25 November 1903, p. 3.

34 Ibid.

35 Ibid.

Figure 2 *I grandi processi illustrati*, 8 (1904)

Image reproduced by kind permission of Ministry of Culture – Pinacoteca di Brera – Biblioteca Braidense, Milan. Further reproduction or duplication by any means is prohibited.

CHAPTER 5

The trial and the account of the murder

The first day of the trial of Alberto Olivo was 31 May 1904. Newspapers briefly described the events leading up to the discovery of Ernestina Beccaro's death, highlighting the fact that initially the body was thought to be that of a young man and the huge mystery of its identity. However, it was reported that Milan's Chief of Police had connected the discovery of the body in Genoa with the report of Ernestina Beccaro as a missing person by neighbours of the couple who had heard the two arguing on the night of 16 May 1903. Noticing the disappearance of Beccaro, they had questioned Olivo, who had replied that his wife had suddenly had to visit relatives in the countryside. Articles reporting the first day of the trial, again, dwelt on descriptions of the couple, their life, their past histories, and their respective behaviour. According to *La Stampa*, the motive for the crime remained unclear; further, neither their respective pasts nor their characteristic behaviours were clear. *La Stampa* went on to suggest that the victim's reputation was somewhat ambiguous. Both before and during her marriage, the paper reported, Beccaro had had 'avventure' [affairs]. In particular, the newspaper noted the case of a 'famoso "gobbo misterioso"' [a famous mysterious hunchback], who 'protected' her, observing that Olivo had readily agreed to 'such kinds of protections'.[1] *La Stampa* offered details of the public attendees of the trial: alongside the many lawyers from both within and outside Milan, there was a large and varied crowd composed of the '*abitués* dei processi interessanti' [frequenters of interesting trials] and a number

---

1 *La Stampa*, 1 June 1904, p. 3.

of women.[2] Similar details were given by *Il Giornale d'Italia*, which wrote of 'pubblico enorme, tra cui molte signore' [enormous public, among which there were many ladies].[3] Since the first publication of articles concerning the murder, Alberto Olivo's depiction started to be constructed as that of a gallows hero, who, despite having committed a heinous crime, was capable of exuding a contagious charm.[4] Therefore, the description of his figure, along with that of the public, concurred both to satisfy people's curiosity and to heroise Olivo: through subtle and tacit manipulation of details, he emerged as an ordinary person, with some peculiarities, but ultimately similar to anyone else. And by situating the man within the realm of the ordinary, the press also reframed his crime as something inevitable that could have happened to anyone.

The first day of the trial was quickly concluded. Newspapers lingered on descriptive details. *La Stampa*, for example, wrote that, when Alberto Olivo entered the courtroom, he was calm, almost smiling; his physiognomy was 'intelligente, la fronte spaziosa, un po' calva sulle tempie; spazioso il mento; l'occhio aquilino, ma non truce' [intelligent, the forehead wide, a little bald at the temples; the chin is long; the eye is aquiline, but not grim].[5] Moreover, he was 'accuratamente sbarbato, veste di scuro, con cravatta nera. La sua statura è inferiore alla media' [cleanly shaven, dressed in sober colours, with a black tie. He is shorter than average].[6]

The President of the Court asked Alberto Olivo a few preliminary questions about his age and to confirm that he was the widower of Ernestina Beccaro. His answer was in the affirmative. Then, Clotilde Beccaro, Ernestina's sister, entered the courtroom. She was described as 'magrolina, dagli occhi neri e i capelli corvini; ha aspetto insignificante' [very thin, with black eyes and raven hair; she has an insignificant appearance].[7] The hearing was adjourned until the following day.

---

2 Ibid.

3 *Il Giornale d'Italia*, 1 June 1904, p. 3.

4 On this "heroicisation", see Alberto Natale, 'Paura mediatica e propaganda', *Griselda. Il portale di letteratura* (2016). <https://site.unibo.it/griseldaonline/it/approfondimenti/alberto-natale-paura-mediatica-propaganda> [accessed on 30 April 2024]; Alberto Natale, *Gli specchi della paura: il sensazionale e il prodigioso nella letteratura di consumo (secoli XVII-XVIII)* (Rome: Carocci, 2008).

5 *La Stampa*, 1 June 1904, p. 3.

6 Ibid.

7 Ibid.

Il Secolo reported that despite the suffocating heat, the hall was packed with members of the public and that there were several ladies sitting in the reserved seats. The paper's description of Olivo's appearance was not particularly flattering: it described his hair as cut very short, thick and bristly; he had a wide and protruding forehead; small, sunken eyes; a sloping aquiline nose and a brown moustache; he was thin and reasonably tall.[8] Upon being asked if he was Ernestina's widower, he very calmly answered, 'sissignore' [yes, sir].[9]

On the second day of the trial, the newspapers had all chosen similar headlines. *La Stampa* proclaimed: *Gruesome interrogation of Olivo, uxoricide butcher.*[10] *Il Giornale d'Italia* entitled its article *The husband who butchered his wife* and explained that 'Ernestina lo tradiva, lo indebitava, lo sprezzava rendendolo infelicissimo' [Ernestina cheated on him, put him in debt, despised him, making him very unhappy].[11] *Il Secolo*'s article, under the headline *Wife-butcherer*, picking up the case again, reported that there were fifty-eight witnesses, including thirty-two for the prosecution and twenty-six for the defence, adding that it was not clear why so many witnesses were necessary, given the confession of the accused and the irrefutable findings of the investigation.[12] Beneath the headline, *Trial of Alberto Olivo, wife-butcherer*,[13] the *Corriere della Sera* included two letters written by Olivo to a friend, written in poetic style, in which Olivo described his emotions and his experience in custody. The newspaper commented that from these letters, it could be inferred that Olivo, who observed the opening elements of the drama that encircled him with a detached curiosity amounting almost to indifference, had a brain that, albeit in its own way, was capable of feeling, suffering, and reason.[14] The analysis appeared to seek to instantiate a process of humanisation of the accused, a process that could lead to a perception of the murderer as victim, shifting responsibility for the crime onto the murder victim herself.

---

8 *Il Secolo*, 1–2 June 1904, p. 2.
9 Ibid.
10 *La Stampa*, 2 June 1904, p. 3.
11 *Il Giornale d'Italia*, 2 June 1904, p. 3.
12 *Il Secolo*, 3–4 June 1904, p. 2.
13 *Corriere della Sera*, 2 June 1904, p. 2.
14 Ibid.

Olivo was accused of premeditated uxoricide and of the crime established in Art. 144, paragraph 1, desecration of the body of the victim.[15] *La Stampa* reported that Olivo 'ascolta attentamente la lettura e scuote la testa, sorridendo quando sente chiamare affettuoso il carattere della moglie ed attribuire il delitto ad odio e avarizia' [listens attentively to the reading of the indictment and shakes his head, smiling when he hears his wife's character described as affectionate, and the crime attributed to hate and greed].[16] Olivo was then asked to describe his relationship with his wife and began to tell his story. He had first met Beccaro in a small restaurant on 1 January 1895; she was living at that time in the house of a dressmaker and would go to that same restaurant every day to eat. Olivo said that, because she was a lively young woman, 'facile agli scherzi e ad accettare bibite e vivande' [easy to joke with and happy to accept drinks and food],[17] he took a liking to her and invited her to go for a walk. Ernestina told him about herself: she had been born in Biella (a town not far from Milan); her father, a baker, had died when she was just ten years old. Her married sister had put her into service, but she had never found a situation that had suited her. One day, she met a travelling salesman, who invited her to travel with him. 'L'Ernestina annuì, ammaliata' [Ernestina nodded, enchanted], recounted Olivo; the *Corriere della Sera* adding that the description, 'with a flavour of literary research', was typical of Olivo's turn of phrase.[18] Meanwhile, Ernestina was initially seduced and then abandoned in Livorno:[19] the man she had met, it transpired, was married and had children. Following other vicissitudes, Ernestina eventually returned to Biella to stay with her sister, who accommodated her

---

15 Art. 44, par. 1, ruled that 'Chiunque commette atti di vilipendio sopra un cadavere umano o sopra le sue ceneri, ovvero, per fine d'ingiuria o per qualsiasi altro fine illecito, sottrae per intero o in parte il cadavere o le ceneri, o ne viola in qualsiasi modo il sepolcro o l'urna, è punito con la reclusione da sei a trenta mesi e con la multa sino a lire mille' [Whoever commits acts of contempt on a human corpse or its ashes, or, for the purpose of insult or for any other illicit purpose, removes the whole or part of the corpse or the ashes, or violates in any way either the tomb or the urn, is punished with imprisonment for between six and thirty months and a fine of up to one thousand lire]. See *Il codice penale per il Regno d'Italia*, ed. by Giulio Crivellari, p. 66.

16 *La Stampa*, 2 June 1904, p. 3.

17 *Il Secolo*, 3–4 June 1904, p. 2.

18 *Corriere della Sera*, 2 June 1904, p. 2.

19 *Il Secolo*, 3–4 June 1904, p. 2.

until the money ran out. Olivo continued that Ernestina then returned to Milan, where once again she took up with the travelling salesman. She lived with him for a further month,[20] but was once again abandoned, this time suffering with pneumonia. Olivo commented, 'vedremo poi ...che razza di polmonite fosse!' [We will see later ...what kind of pneumonia it was!].[21] It later emerged that Beccaro had been placed in a hospital for syphiliacs. This tactic of sowing small seeds of suspicion without offering full information emerged as a strategy on Olivo's part to instill doubts about Beccaro's moral character, in contrast with his own generosity.

Olivo went on to recount that, one evening during that time, Ernestina had wanted to take her own life, planning to throw herself from the top of the cathedral. She did not have the courage. She had no money, but at the same time, she did not have a deeply ingrained desire to die. Shortly afterwards, she met up with an individual named Antonio Colombo, who she claimed was her cousin. He took on the payment of her lodgings and provided her with four lire a week for sustenance.[22] *Il Secolo* reported that Colombo became her lover.[23] As we shall see, however, the relationship between Beccaro and Colombo in fact was never clearly defined as being a sexual one.

Ernestina told Alberto that she was not inclined to live as a servant and led him to understand that she would like to find a single gentleman to sustain her,[24] even if he was not prepared to actually marry her, since she understood that it would be hard to find a husband given what had befallen her in her past. Olivo replied that he was alone and that he earned 175 lire a month, suggesting that he might be that gentleman for her. He then asked Beccaro if she would comport herself as a 'brava donna' [good woman] if he were to permit her to live with him.[25] Beccaro answered in the affirmative, and the couple ended up living together. Once again, Olivo was careful to highlight the fact that Beccaro had deceived him, presenting herself at that point to be a victim of circumstance and a hard life.

---

20 *La Stampa*, 2 June 1904, p. 3.
21 *Il Secolo*, 3–4 June 1904, p. 2.
22 *La Stampa*, 2 June 1904, p. 3.
23 *Il Secolo*, 3–4 June 1904, p. 2.
24 *La Stampa*, 2 June 1904, p. 3.
25 *Corriere della Sera*, 2 June 1904, p. 2.

Olivo went on to recount how Colombo had invited Olivo for a conversation in order to find out more about him. Following a meeting, Colombo approved a marriage between Alberto and Ernestina, promising that, if she comported herself well, he would give her a hundred lire as a gift. It is worth noting the emphasis on 'comporting' well, which served to show that Beccaro was not a good person, but both Olivo and Colombo gave her an opportunity to redeem herself. Moreover, Colombo had no entitlement to approve or not approve Beccaro's marriage, but this expression helps understand how relations between sexes were understood. Olivo added that, since Beccaro had no appropriate clothes, Colombo gave her fifty lire in advance. Olivo was at pains to point out that there was no truth in the claim that he had married Beccaro because of Colombo's financial gift: on the contrary, before their marriage, he said, he himself had spent sixty lire on food and a further hundred lire on other unspecified expenses for her.

Olivo continued his account with the information that he had tried to find Beccaro a job. She began work in a clothing house, but after a month, on returning home one evening, she suffered a miscarriage. After that, he preferred not to send her out to work, adding that 'nel gennaio 1897, siccome la Beccaro aveva ben saputo abbindolarmi, il giorno 17 la sposai' [in January 1897, since Beccaro knew full well how to con me, I married her, on the seventeenth of the month].[26] *Il Secolo*, however, reported that during the interrogation, Olivo said that he had married Beccaro 'per riguardo ai colleghi e perché la posizione irregolare era imbarazzante' [out of consideration for my colleagues and because the irregular situation was embarrassing].[27] *Il Giornale d'Italia* explained that Olivo told about the frequent quarrels with 'la moglie "raccolta dalla miseria" e "sposata per pietà" pure conoscendo i "precedenti falli di lei"' [his wife 'raised from poverty' and 'married out of pity' despite knowing her 'previous faults'].[28] *I grandi processi illustrati* commented that between Olivo and Beccaro there was an abyss: 'quali sieno state le doti di questa donna, non bella e per soprammercato idiota nel vero senso della parola, che riuscirono a sedurre questo intellettuale, fanatico degli studi più astrusi,

26 *La Stampa*, 2 June 1904, p. 3. The *Corriere della Sera* wrote that the couple married on 17 January 1896.

27 *Il Secolo*, 3–4 June 1904, p. 2. *Il Secolo* reported the date of the marriage as 7 January 1896.

28 *Il Giornale d'Italia*, 3 June 1904, p. 3.

rimane inespicabile' [what were the qualities of this woman, not beautiful and above all an idiot in the true sense of the word, which managed to seduce this intellectual, fanatic of the most abstruse studies, remains indespicable].[29]

The description of the period of their meeting and the early days of their marriage served Olivo's reputation well, permitting him to portray himself as a victim of his own good faith and of Beccaro's cunning. The following day of the trial, 2 June 1904, Olivo set out their married life. *La Stampa*'s headline, 'Un inferno coniugale' [a marital hell], concisely conveyed the content of the cross-examination. Olivo said that one day, 'le dissi che i suoi modi non mi piacevano, e la minacciai di separarmi. A queste parole mi lanciò addosso la zuppiera piena di minestra e, siccome minacciai di reagire, impugnò un coltello' [I told her that I did not like her ways, and I threatened to leave her. At these words, she threw the full tureen of soup at me and because I threatened to act in response, she grabbed a knife].[30] Olivo lamented that they continued to quarrel because he was unable to 'contentare tutti i suoi vizi' [satisfy all her vices] with his 175-lira wage.[31]

Further, of their life, he recounted:

> Un giorno mi mostrò la stoffa per un vestito e mi disse che l'aveva comprata con denaro che aveva guadagnato. Siccome non seppe darmi una spiegazione convincente sul modo con cui aveva guadagnato quel danaro, io le manifestai un dubbio atroce. Essa mi rispose con l'insulto più terribile. Ci collutammo, e siccome era caduta, io tentai di tenerla al suolo finché si calmasse; ma essa urlava così che io dovetti lasciarla.
>
> [One day she showed me the fabric for a dress and told me that she had bought it with money she had earned. Since she was unable to give me a convincing explanation of how she had earned that money, I expressed grave doubt. She responded to me with the most terrible insult. We fought, and because she had fallen, I tried to hold her on the ground so that she would calm down; but she screamed so much that I had to get up and leave her].[32]

Moreover, he admitted that he had slapped her several times because 'lo svillaneggiava e lo minacciava atrocemente e furiosamente' [she insulted and

---

29 *I grandi processi illustrati*, 1904, I, p. 5.

30 *La Stampa*, 3 June 1904, p. 3.

31 Ibid.

32 Ibid.

threatened him abominably and relentlessly].[33] Olivo said that at a certain point, Beccaro made the acquaintance of a young woman with a dubious reputation. One day, Beccaro wanted to bring this woman to their home to stay the night, but Olivo refused, so the two women went out together, and his wife stayed away all night. He contended that Beccaro was a drinker: when he scolded her, she would smash items in the house or destroy furnishings. Their conjugal life continued with constant arguments.

Early in May 1903, the illiterate Beccaro said she wanted to take lessons to learn how to read and write. Olivo, with pride, remarked that he could teach her himself and that he had a particular method for teaching;[34] but Beccaro refused him.[35] Instead, she hired a teacher. Shortly afterwards, Olivo sacked the teacher because 'non valeva niente, e ciò esasperò l'Ernestina' [she was useless; and this infuriated Ernestina].[36] In one of his numerous attempts to demonstrate and underline the vast difference between himself and his wife, Olivo explained that the teacher had sought to instruct Beccaro that to write 'noi altri andiamo' [we go] was incorrect – but, knew Olivo, Dante and Manzoni had used these words.[37]

Il Giornale d'Italia reported that '[questo] licenziamento determinò nella signora un terribile scoppio d'ira che gratificò l'Olivo di ogni più triviale insulto con offesa anche alla memoria della di lui madre. I vicini di casa udivano' [[this] dismissal caused a terrible outburst of anger in the lady, who rewarded Olivo with every offence including insulting the memory of his mother. The neighbours heard].[38] Use of the word 'rewarded' ('gratificò') to describe Beccaro's response to Olivo in relation to the teacher's dismissal is noteworthy. As we shall see, there is an ironic, mocking tone that began subtly in articles in the early days of the trial but would go on to become increasingly intense. On the one hand, it served to infantilise and even trivialise Beccaro's mode of conducting herself; on the other, it lessened an appreciation of the crime of which she was the victim, shifting responsibility for the crime

---

33 *Il Secolo*, 3–4 June 1904, p. 2.
34 Ibid.
35 *La Stampa*, 3 June 1904, p. 3.
36 Ibid.
37 *Corriere della Sera*, 2 June 1904, p. 2. The term 'noi altri' is a strengthening and circumscribing form of the pronoun 'we'.
38 *Il Giornale d'Italia*, 3 June 1904, p. 3.

to her and fostering the notion that Olivo was a victim of circumstance. Moreover, the inclusion of the observation, 'the neighbours heard', further emphasises the deplorable situation in which Olivo found himself: not only was he living in hell in his own home, but his neighbours were aware of it, rendering the situation even more humiliating, since it impinged upon his honour and reputation.

Olivo identified the dismissal of the teacher as the event that escalated their fighting and would eventually trigger the murder: in the words of Olivo, pronounced with a touch of solemnity, 'fu così che cominciammo la lite fatale' [so we began the fatal argument].[39] At a particular point, he recounted, Beccaro attacked him with a knife; he was wounded, but they fell asleep. Olivo recalled that his wife:

> venne a coricarsi e presto si addormentò vicinissima a me come era solita fare perché freddolosa. Io leggevo il giornale ma senza attenzione: mi era venuto il sospetto che nel contegno di mia moglie ci fosse il dileggio della moglie che l'ha fatta al marito. Osservai che essa quando dormiva era molto bella: pareva impossibile che da quella bocca così graziosa uscissero parole così brutte
>
> [came to bed and soon fell asleep very close to me, as was her wont, because she was sensitive to cold. I read the newspaper but without much attention: I suspected that in my wife's behaviour there was the mockery of a woman traducing her husband. I observed that when she was asleep she was very beautiful. It seemed impossible that such ugly words could come from that pretty mouth].[40]

The *Corriere della Sera* reported this in slightly different terms, writing that Olivo said 'chi direbbe al vederla così, che essa è tanto cattiva?' [who would say, seeing her like this, that she could be so bad?].[41] The inclusion of Olivo's passing observations, such as Beccaro's sensitivity to cold and the fact that she went to sleep very close to him, again served to construct an image of Olivo as a good, attentive person who comported himself well and was deceived by the seemingly sweet demeanour and appearance of his wife.

Olivo woke up several times that night and at two o'clock in the morning, after a terrible nightmare, asked Beccaro to prepare him a drink of lemonade.

---

39 *La Stampa*, 3 June 1904, p. 3.

40 *Il Giornale d'Italia*, 3 June 1904, p. 3.

41 *Corriere della Sera*, 2 June 1904, p. 2.

It was at this point, he contended, that she insulted his honour and that of his mother. *Il Giornale d'Italia* wrote that Olivo described that 'una nube rossa mi coprì gli occhi: io non so che sia successo: come spinto da una molla mi trovai addosso a mia moglie che era in letto voltandomi la schiena' [a red mist came over me: I don't know what happened. As if I was being impelled by some elastic force, I found myself leaning over my wife, who was lying in bed with her back to me].[42] *La Stampa* reported that he said, 'non ci vidi più; afferrai un coltello, feci un salto, e colpii' [I saw red; I grabbed a knife, leapt at her, and stabbed her].[43] This triggered a powerful response in the listening public in the courtroom, and, at the President's invitation, Olivo replayed his action in the middle of the room: 'colle mani levate dà un gran balzo, che rimbomba cupamente' [with his hands uplifted, he gives a great leap, which reverberates hollowly].[44]

He subsequently fell asleep, waking up two hours later. The light in the kitchen that gave off a dull glow, the slippers that had fallen when he leapt at her, the water ready for the lemonade, 'tutto mi richiamò alla realtà… Bisognava togliere tutto quel sangue. Feci scaldare dell'acqua, perché calda è più solvente' [everything brought me back to reality… All that blood had to be cleaned up. I boiled some water, because hot water is more solvent].[45] Olivo dwelt on details and the description of the scene and his emotions, again tacitly underlining the difference between himself, a cultured man of reason, and Beccaro, an illiterate woman so rooted in instinct that she had not even been able to grasp the right way to behave to save her own life. Olivo explained that, having washed his wife's body, he left the apartment and wandered the city, torn between handing himself in and killing himself. But handing himself in 'bothered him'.[46] He thought about 'carcere preventivo, al processo, alle difficoltà di far emergere la verità su un fatto avvenuto di notte, alla perdita dell'impiego, alle conseguenze che la cosa avrebbe avuto per un uomo senza parenti e senza amici' [custody, the trial, the difficulties in eliciting the truth about an event that took place at night, the loss of his

---

42 *Il Giornale d'Italia*, 3 June 1904, p. 3.
43 *La Stampa*, 3 June 1904, p. 3.
44 *Corriere della Sera*, 2 June 1904, p. 2.
45 Ibid.
46 *La Stampa*, 3 June 1904, p. 3.

job, the consequences of this for a man without family or friends],[47] and decided instead to dispose of the corpse, pay off his debts, and then take his own life. So, after buying a bag and travelling to Monza to sell off his wife's goods, he began to dismember Beccaro's body, disposing of the soft parts.[48]

Afterwards, he went to the Trattoria del Formentone, where he ate a meal and then slept there overnight. The following day, he returned home, put Beccaro's remains into the bag, and returned to the Trattoria with his bag. At this point, the President of the Court asked Olivo if he had slept with that bag in the room, to which he answered 'Sì, ma non faceva nessun odore' [Yes, but it did not smell at all], which caused a ripple in the courtroom.[49] *Il Secolo* added that he smiled as he said this, noting the growing intensity of public interest in this very strange figure: many were nauseated by his behaviour, which they attributed to a frightening cynicism; others were simply amazed.[50] *I grandi processi illustrati*, published a drawing depicting Olivo in the act of dismembering Beccaro and added that Olivo, 'serbando immutato il suo ripugnante cinismo' [keeping his repugnant cynicism unchanged], posited that the bag with her remains was not that heavy.[51]

La Stampa reported that Olivo continued his story with the information that he had gotten up at 4 o'clock in the morning the following day and had begun his journey to Genoa. 'Alla sera mi recai in riva al mare, ove un barcaiuolo mi disse se volevo fare una gita. M'imbarcai colla valigia, e, dopo quattro ore di remata al largo, gettai l'involto in mare. Tornai a terra, tornai a Milano, o dormii ancora al Formentone' [In the evening I went down to the shore, where a boatman asked me if I wanted to go on a trip. I embarked with my bag, and, after four hours' rowing from the shore, I threw the bag into the sea. I returned to land, returned to Milan, and slept again at the Formentone].[52] *La Stampa* reported that the primary response by the audience in the courtroom was not to the events of the story per se, but to the cynical way in which Olivo recounted it, adding that at certain points, he had the satisfied air of a man who had recounted a feat or was happy to have

47 *Corriere della Sera*, 2 June 1904, p. 2.
48 *La Stampa*, 3 June 1904, p. 3.
49 Ibid.
50 *Il Secolo*, 3–4 June 1904, p. 2.
51 *I grandi processi illustrati*, 1904, II, p. 9.
52 *La Stampa*, 3 June 1904, p. 3.

succeeded in its performance. The newspaper also observed, throughout the cross-examination, a strange obsession in Olivo for recounting insignificant detail at great length.[53] All of a sudden in the dock, however, Olivo was 'colto da un improvviso accesso di pazzia' [struck by a sudden fit of madness], described in the following terms:

> il reo è preso da convulsioni spaventose, e la sua faccia diventa cadaverica, orribile. La sua forza si centuplica: otto carabinieri stentano a trattenerlo. È la prima volta dopo che l'Olivo ha commesso il delitto che avviene in lui un tale fenomeno.
>
> [the accused is overtaken by frightening convulsions, and his face becomes cadaverous, dreadful. His strength increases a hundredfold: eight carabinieri struggle to restrain him. It is the first time since Olivo has committed his crime that such a phenomenon has overtaken him].[54]

On the pages of *Il Secolo*, it was reported that Olivo grew increasingly emotional: his moans came louder, and three robust carabinieri were unable to restrain him as he screamed like a man possessed.[55] The onlookers were greatly shocked, and Olivo was removed from the courtroom. *La Stampa* commented that 'evidentemente questa convulsione è la conseguenza di tutta la fatica enorme che la forte volontà dell'Olivo ha sostenuto per dominarsi durante l'udienza [evidently this convulsion is the consequence of the enormous cost to Olivo's strength of will to control himself during the hearing].[56] In an article in the *Corriere della Sera*, Augusto Guido Bianchi added that 'l'individuo che passa nel gabbione della colpa ha lasciato il posto al caso che resta' [the individual who passes into the cage of guilt has given way to the case that remains].[57] Similar comments, often obscure and abstruse, also appeared in editorials reflecting the opinions of renowned journalists and scholars. *La Stampa* and *La Tribuna*, for example, included similar observations on the case and on criminal studies under the byline 'Rastignac', a pseudonym of Vincenzo Morello, a famous journalist of the time (see Appendix 1).[58]

---

53 Ibid.

54 Ibid.

55 *Il Secolo*, 3–4 June 1904, p. 2.

56 *La Stampa*, 3 June 1904, p. 3.

57 *Corriere della Sera*, 2 June 1904, p. 2.

58 On Vincenzo Morello, see, in the first instance: Mario Missiroli, 'Rastignac e il suo tempo', in *Uomini e giornali. I grandi giornalisti di ieri negli scritti dei giornalisti di oggi*,

Figure 3 *I grandi processi illustrati*, 9 (1904)

Image reproduced by kind permission of Ministry of Culture – Pinacoteca di Brera – Biblioteca Braidense, Milan. Further reproduction or duplication by any means is prohibited.

Il Giornale d'Italia, instead, published some letters written by Alberto Olivo to a friend, in which he described his life with a poetic tone and even using rhymes, and added that from these documents it was evident that in this man there was a mind that 'sente, soffre e ragiona' [feels, suffers and reasons].[59] These comments and editorials themselves formed part of the totality of the spectacle and added to the sensationalisation of the trial, contributing to a perception that it was an event about which every well-known individual of the time had to have a say.

On 4 June 1904, as the trial continued, *La Stampa* reported that 'la folla, s'è possibile, si è ancora accresciuta; nei posti riservati il numero delle signore è grandissimamente aumentato. Decisamente la curiosità è femmina!' [The crowd, if it's possible, has continued to grow; in the reserved seats, the number of ladies has greatly increased. Curiosity is definitively a female characteristic!].[60] After mentioning Maria Beccaro, sister of Ernestina, 'una vecchietta' [a little old woman] who participated as a private citizen, the newspaper went on to relate Olivo's interrogation. It reported that he spoke of Beccaro and Colombo, the man who had supported her before she met Olivo. The President of the Court performed an intense interrogation: 'Era quindi sua amante, e ve la siete fatta cedere. Trovate ciò bello?' [So, she was his lover, and you made him give her up to you. Was that a nice thing to do?].[61] Olivo reportedly answered: 'Io non presi con me la Beccaro per sposarla; intendevo soccorrerla; e non avendo nessuno, farmene un'amica, una compagna' [I didn't take Beccaro with me in order to marry her. I intended to help her; and having no one myself, I would make her a friend of mine, a companion].[62] The President of the Court asked Olivo why, when he knew that Colombo was not in fact a relative of Beccaro, he accepted the gift of a hundred lire when he and Beccaro married. Olivo contended that the hundred lire was a reward for Beccaro for her to remain honest, given that Colombo loved her

ed. by Silvio Negro and Andrea Lazzarini (Florence: Salani, 1947), pp. 165–73; and Lina Anzalone, *Storia di Rastignac. Un calabrese protagonista e testimone del suo tempo* (Soveria Mannelli: Rubbettino, 2005).

59 *Il Giornale d'Italia*, 3 June 1904, p. 3. These letters have also been published without further comments on *I grandi processi illustrati*, 1904, n. 2, pp. 11–16.

60 *La Stampa*, 4 June 1904, p. 3.

61 Ibid.

62 Ibid.

like a daughter. *La Stampa* highlighted that Olivo was concerned to distance himself from 'il sospetto che abbia preso con sé la Beccaro per le 100 lire promesse dal Colombo' [the suspicion that he had taken Beccaro for the sake of the hundred lire promised by Colombo],[63] and that he was insistent about Beccaro's poverty, but the President of the Court returned that Olivo knew that Beccaro was uneducated and had been involved in certain 'marachelle' [shenanigans], such as the relationship with Colombo.[64] Reportedly, he further added: 'Ma scusate, come mai permettevate che la donna diventata vostra moglie ricevesse un compenso dei suoi favori dal Colombo?' [Forgive me, but why on earth would you allow the woman who became your wife to receive a reward for her favours from Colombo?].[65] The continuous focus on Beccaro's culpable behaviour, which was relentlessly emphasised as very far from what might be expected of a respectable woman and wife of the time, served to indicate that Olivo knew full well what kind of woman (in their vernacular) she was and married her nonetheless out of sheer greed. For his part, Olivo insisted that nothing about receiving the money had been equivocal. The President of the Court sought to provoke Olivo by asking why he married Beccaro, 'a malgrado dei precedenti della morta' [despite the deceased's precedents],[66] and by demonstrating how different the two were, additionally accusing Olivo of being irascible and ill-humoured; this elicited the response that he had married her to 'salvare una digraziata' [save a disgraced],[67] and become so only because his wife made him so, even going so far as to water down the wine so that she could drink more of it.[68] These words were received with hilarity by the attendant public. Olivo, however, far from seeing this as a joke, as we shall later see, took the watering down of the wine as a major offence.

Olivo was then accused of being mean and replied by setting out his expenses. *Il Secolo* commented that the precision of his accounting brought surprise: 'il pubblico è trasecolato udendo quella selva di numeri' [the audience

---

63 Ibid.
64 *Il Secolo*, 3–4 June 1904, p. 2.
65 *La Stampa*, 4 June 1904, p. 3.
66 *Il Giornale d'Italia*, 4 June 1904, p. 4.
67 Ibid.
68 *Il Secolo*, 3–4 June 1904, p. 2.

was astonished to hear all those numbers].[69] *Il Secolo* continued to describe the cross-examination, adding that Olivo's manner of response was extravagant: 'sembra convintissimo di avere fatto la cosa più naturale e più giusta del mondo assassinando la moglie' [he seems absolutely convinced that he did the most natural and just thing in the world in murdering his wife].[70] He continued to describe his life with Beccaro: in the evenings, she would want to go out rather than stay at home with him; he would chide her, but she did not want to obey him. He would try to convince her by taking her lightly by the arm – showing how he did so by taking the arm of one of the carabinieri – but she would resist. Olivo commented that they were in the century of female emancipation and grew heated, describing how his wife had spat in his face at least a dozen times, crying to the courtroom: 'che cosa dovevo fare io? Strozzarla? Ha visto che cosa è successo poi per colpa sua!' [what was I supposed to do? Strangle her? You saw what happened in the end that was of her own making!].[71] Olivo was then asked if he knew that his wife had betrayed him. He answered that he had believed her to be honest and that he was peacefully at rest.[72] Then he went on to recount his efforts to educate Beccaro, arguing that she was resistant to learning anything 'per timore che, una volta, istruita, l'avesse [sic!] messa, a lavorare' [for fear that, once she was educated, he would put her to work].[73]

None of the newspapers reporting the trial commented on the fact that Olivo said that 'what happened' was Beccaro's own fault. The terminology of this dispute speaks volumes not only about the relationship between Olivo and Beccaro but also about how men saw themselves in relation to women. The use of the words, 'you made him give her up to you', 'I did not take Beccaro with me', 'he would put her to work' clearly indicate an imbalance in how they perceived themselves and how their roles were perceived in their society. Furthermore, the question of whether Beccaro betrayed Olivo again shifts the question of worthiness and reputation solely onto the woman in the couple. Indeed, from the outset, Olivo's sexual behaviour was never under question; rather, inquiries were made only as to why he had agreed to marry

69 Ibid.
70 Ibid.
71 Ibid.
72 Ibid.
73 *La Stampa*, 4 June 1904, p. 3.

a woman with a bad reputation who had already had sexual intercourse with other men.

The cross-examination of Olivo continued to dig deeper into the couple's life. The President of the Court asked if it was true that during the first years of their marriage, Beccaro was so weak from malnutrition that she was unable to climb their stairs. Olivo firmly denied this and added that these were all his wife's lies. *La Stampa* commented that 'a quest'accusa l'Olivo si agita di più di quello che non si fosse agitato quando descrisse la dissezione del cadavere' [Olivo is more agitated at this accusation than when he was describing the dismemberment of the corpse].[74] Olivo was then asked to tell about the knife with which he killed Beccaro. He explained that it was an extremely dangerous knife he bought because three years earlier Beccaro had asked him for a good knife to lard. Olivo added that, sometime later, Beccaro wanted to prepare a chicken and asked him to slaughter a hen they had: he reportedly said, 'tu sai bene che a me fa pena uccidere una povera bestia (ilarità). Mi fa senso veder del sangue scorrere (rumori). Allora mia moglie tirò il collo a quel povero pollo' [you know well that it pains me to kill a poor beast (laughter). It makes sense to me to see blood flowing (noises). Then my wife pulled that poor chicken's neck].[75] By recounting this story, Olivo might have grotesquely attempted to emphasise the paradox of his whole story: he wanted to show that he was a person who was extremely sensitive, but Beccaro distorted his nature to such a degree of making him commit not only her murder but also the dismembering of her body. When questioned about his personality, Olivo admitted to being 'un po' furioso' [a somewhat angry person], but 'smentisce di essersi mai mostrato sanguinario: anzi i suoi compagni di scuola lo chiamavano la femminetta' [he denies ever having had a thirst for blood: on the contrary, his schoolmates called him 'girly'].[76] *La Stampa* interrupted its speedy description of the trial to remark that:

> Aumenta sempre in modo straordinario, nelle tribune riservate, il numero delle signore: ve ne sono ora di elegantissime, afflitte da una morbosa curiosità. L'Olivo viene osservato col binocolo, come se si fosse a teatro; egli non si turba affatto pei quegli sguardi gentili

---

74 Ibid.

75 *I grandi processi illustrati*, 1904, n. 5, p. 40.

76 *La Stampa*, 4 June 1904, p. 3.

> [The number of ladies in the reserved stands continues to grow in an extraordinary fashion: there are now some very elegant ladies, afflicted by a morbid curiosity. They view Olivo through opera glasses, as if they were at the theatre; he is not at all disturbed by that genteel mode of observation.][77]

Far from being the cold interrogation of a murderer, the trial had become some kind of seductive game in which women, reportedly curious by nature, came to court elegantly dressed to observe with interest and politeness the accused, who, in turn, was undisturbed by such observation. The emphasis on these points says much about how masculinity and femininity were expected to be deployed: on the one hand, there was a man, able to sustain the gaze and curiosity of so many women; on the other, the women, somehow fascinated by such a person and still allegedly instinctive and weak-headed, who did not completely understand that he was perhaps to be understood but not to be admired.

Cross-examined on other details, Olivo's performance continued with his highlighting of 'una tale quantità di particolari da sembrare un professore intento a dare una lezione ad un uditorio di scolari' [such a quantity of detail that he seems a professor intent on giving a lesson to an audience of schoolchildren].[78] He went on to say that he would like to make an addition to Ernestina's grave, explaining that:

> Forse che, perché in un momento di atonia terribile, cagionata da un compendio di fatti più forte della mia ragione, io ho questa smarrita ed ho agito come un insensato, ravvedutomi nella calma della mia cella, non dovevo pensare alle conseguenze del mio misfatto e cercare di porre almeno un segno sulla tomba di quella disgraziata, vittima come me di una fatalità di eventi?
>
> [Perhaps because, in a moment of terrible weakness, caused by a compendium of deeds stronger than my reason, I was confused and acted like a fool, having come to my senses in the calm of my cell, was I not brought to think about the consequences of my misdeed, and to try to place at least some kind of sign on the tomb of that unfortunate woman, victim, like me, of a fatal sequence of events?].[79]

La Stampa commented on the fact that Olivo wanted to leave a compassionate mark on Beccaro's grave without mentioning that he considered himself and Beccaro both victims of circumstance and himself not guilty of her murder:

---

77 Ibid.
78 Ibid.
79 Ibid.

> Quale strano impasto è mai quest'uomo, che dopo aver narrato calmo, quasi senza dolore le sue gesta feroci, trova naturale, anzi doveroso il suo desiderio di porre una croce sulla tomba della vittima
>
> [What a strange mixture this man is, who, having calmly and almost without pain narrated his savage deeds, now finds his desire to place a cross on the victim's tomb not only natural, but dutiful].[80]

After a diversion in which Olivo asked if he could have newspapers delivered from Milan whilst he was in custody, since this would somewhat ease his burdened mind,[81] he talked about his youth. He had begun studying at the University of Padua, but was obliged to leave because he had run out of money. During his military service, he suffered sunstroke, which left him with incipient deafness and a perpetual ringing in his ears.[82] He also had to take care of an aunt and, following her death, found a job at Richard-Ginori, a company in Milan. There, he explained, his work skills and rapid and brilliant rise through the company caused him to be disliked by everyone – indeed hated – and not a day went by without some malice being done to him. Olivo 'ricambiava con sprezzo l'odio degli invidiosi, anche perché sapeva in quanta stima lo tenesse il suo principale' [returned the hatred of these envious people with contempt, because he knew the esteem in which his boss held him].[83]

On 4 June, the audience was not large; 'in compenso i posti riservati sono occupati da eleganti signore e signorine' [however, the reserved seats are occupied by elegant ladies and young ladies].[84] Clotilde Beccaro, one of Ernestina's sisters, was called to present her testimony. She was described as 'piccolina, bruna, con due occhioni neri, magrolina anzichenò. Si dice che assomigli alla morta' [small, dark-haired, with enormous dark eyes, very thin. They say she looks like the dead].[85] *La Stampa* reported that the two sisters were separated 'dal mare magnum della vita' [by the *mare magnum* of life] and had not seen each other until 1895, when Ernestina 'stava per maritarsi passando dal Colombo all'Olivo' [was about to get

80 Ibid.
81 Ibid.
82 Ibid.
83 Ibid.
84 *Il Giornale d'Italia*, 5 June 1904, p. 3.
85 *La Stampa*, 5 June 1904, p. 3.

married, passing from Colombo to Olivo].[86] The use of the term 'passing', carelessly included in the description, conveys how Beccaro's behaviour was interpreted at the time: far from being represented as a matter of feeling and emotion, her relations with Colombo and Olivo were depicted in the terms of an economic transaction.

Clotilde Beccaro continued her account of her sister and her relationship with Olivo, whom she depicted as very miserly. She ended her testimony by saying that her sister was 'di carattere un po' leggero, ma buono, molto buono' [a bit light-hearted, but of good, such good character].[87] *La Stampa* wrote that voices from the audience were heard to utter 'Oh! Oh!' and that at a certain point Olivo cried out, 'Già, le donne sono tutte uguali!' [Yes, all women are the same!],[88] reiterating the female stereotype depicting women as monotonal and devoid of originality.[89]

Alongside the stereotyped comments, it is worth noting how this testimony, by a woman saying positive things about Beccaro, was belittled by the press: first, by lingering on the physical characteristics of Clotilde; and second, by focusing on the disrespectful comments of the attendant public and Olivo. There is a similar approach evident in relation to the testimony of Ernestina's eldest sister, Maria. The part of the article describing Maria Beccaro's testimony bore the heading 'Un'altra sorella della squartata' [another sister of the butchered woman],[90] and Maria was described as 'una vecchietta piccola… Riuscendole ostico l'italiano, parla in piemontese schietto' [a little old lady… Since Italian is hard for her, she speaks in plain Piedmontese].[91] *La Stampa* reported her cross-examination and her answers, given in dialect. The court permitted Olivo to comment continuously on her answers, at times even laughing.

---

86 Ibid.

87 Ibid.

88 Ibid.

89 On this point Lombroso and Ferrero observed that women were monotonous, more susceptible to imitation, and had less originality than men; a fact that explained why 'le donne si rassomiglino tutte fra loro' [all women resemble one another], and the reason for their misoneism. See, Lombroso and Ferrero, *La donna delinquente, la prostituta e la donna normale*, pp. 160–63.

90 Ibid.

91 Ibid.

"Menzogne!" esclama di nuovo l'Olivo.
"*Ciuto chiel*!" grida la Maria, rivoltandosi come una furia verso l'Olivo, e con una faccia così rossa e furibonda che il pubblico pensa che se si fosse trovata lei al posto dell'Ernestina, l'Olivo non avrebbe potuto ridurla così a mal partito.
Il presidente mette la calma e l'Olivo ride.

["Lies!" Olivo exclaims again.
"Shut your face!" shouts Maria, turning to Olivo like a woman possessed, with a face so red and furious that the public gallery think that had Maria been in Ernestina's place, Olivo would not have been able to reduce her to such a poor state.
The President of the Court calms everyone down and Olivo laughs].[92]

In the cases of both Maria and Clotilde, in purporting to report facts of the events, *La Stampa* and other newspapers set off a process of devaluation of witness importance and credibility. Clotilde's great dark eyes or Maria's fury were characteristics that, together with the irony and mockery that littered the article, contributed to undermine the voices of these women, denoting them as less significant and of lesser value than the men. The same was true for Ernestina Beccaro herself: alongside being objectified ('she was about to get married, passing from Colombo to Olivo'), she was often mentioned by her first name alone, not her family name (as Olivo was), or was referred to simply through terms such as 'the deceased' or 'the butchered woman'.

The trial continued with the demonstration of evidence collected from the couple's home to the jurors. On hearing the description of the remains of the corpse and the doctors' report, Olivo was seen to nervously pat his forehead with a handkerchief.[93] As the medical report on his mental state was read out, suggesting him to be a selfish and greedy man, he responded with denials,[94] seeking to further promote the idea that he was provoked into the killing of Beccaro because of her behaviour and that the murder was not premeditated.

On 5 June, the weekly legal journal *I Tribunali* introduced its article by explaining that there was a strong curiosity among the general public before the beginning of the trial against Olivo. This curiosity was pushed by interests in the macabre operation of the butchering of Beccaro's corpse, and everyone

---

[92] Ibid.
[93] Ibid.
[94] Ibid.

agreed in qualifying Olivo as a bloodthirsty, human beast endowed with boundless ferocity.[95] But, after three days of trial, according to the journal, things had significantly changed, and the accused made an impression on the public:

> Donne d'ogni ceto, specialmente donnine... allegre, signore per bene, giovanette, vecchie, povere e ricche, si urtavano, si pigiavano, si sarebbero rotte anche l'osso del collo, pur d'entrare, e di vedere lo squartatore.
>
> Quando l'Olivo poté parlare e narrare tutta la sua storia, ora dolorosa, ora vergognosa, ora infame, il pubblico si sentì commosso
>
> [Women of all classes, especially women of... easy virtue, respectable ladies, young, old, poor and rich, bumped into each other, pressed each other, they would have even broken their necks, just to get in and see the butcherer.
>
> When Olivo was able to speak and tell his whole story, now painful, now shameful, now infamous, the public felt moved].[96]

In the *Corriere della Sera* of 7 June 1904, instead, Augusto Guido Bianchi reported on the expert witnesses' assessment of Olivo, concluding his article by saying that he had asked Lorenzo Ellero, a psychologist and one of the expert witnesses, 'Cos'è adunque l'Olivo?' [So, what is this Olivo character, then?], receiving the answer that the late Silvio Venturi would have termed him 'un "caratteristico"' [a 'singularity' (literally, a characteristic one)].[97] Bianchi explained that the term *caratteristico* here denoted a category Venturi placed 'tra il manicomio e la vita, a determinare individualità che sono eccezioni, fra le due grandi classifiche che la società ha stabilito per mettervi la ragione da una parte e dall'altra la pazzia [between the mental hospital and life, to denote individualities that are exceptions, located between the two great classifications society has established to put reason on one side and madness on the other].[98]

The trial continued. On 7 June, again, the court was filled with 'pubblico in prevalenza femminile, e quando l'accusato entra nella gabbia si ripete il movimento di curiosità morbosa: tutti si alzano in piedi. L'Olivo se ne

95 *I Tribunali*, 5 June 1904, p. 3.

96 Ibid.

97 *Corriere della Sera*, 7 June 1904, p. 3. Silvio Venturi (1851–1900) was a renowned Italian psychiatrist. Of particular interest in this context are his works *L'allucinazione a due e la pazzia a due* (1886) and *I discorsi dei pazzi* (1893).

98 *Corriere della Sera*, 7 June 1904, p. 3.

accorge e sorride beffardamente' [a predominantly female audience, and when the accused enters the dock, the movement of morbid curiosity is repeated: everyone stands. Olivo notices this and smiles mockingly].[99] A similar description appeared in *Il Secolo*: 'l'aula va sempre più affollandosi; moltissime sono le signore nei posti riservati; fuori, sotto al portico e nel cortile, rumoreggia la folla di coloro che non possono entrare' [the court is becoming ever more crowded; there are many ladies in the reserved seats; outside, under the portico and in the courtyard, the crowd of people unable to get in is noisy].[100]

On this day, Beccaro's youngest sister, Fortunata, was meant to present her testimony, but she did not arrive. The court moved on instead to question Francesco Vignolo, a salesman who lived on the same floor as the couple in their building.[101] He proposed that Olivo was a serious sort of person, but that Beccaro had many faults. However, he observed that she was very helpful, 'così che in occasione di una disgrazia famigliare accadutagli, malgrado il divieto fatto alla propria consorte di stringere relazione colla Beccaro, grazie alle prestazioni di questa, entrarono in intimità' [such that on the occasion of a misfortune that happened in his family, and despite the ban he placed on his wife having any kind of relationship with Beccaro, as a result of her kindnesses, the two women became intimate].[102]

Vignolo also observed that there was little peace in Olivo's and Beccaro's household, mentioning an event that had happened in February 1902:

> Venne l'Olivo a pregarmi di intromettermi; entrai in casa e vidi che aveva rotto dei vasi da fiori. La redarguii per le sue parole, e ricordo che essa era ferocissima e diceva di non temere il marito, e che aveva rotto i vasi perché così le era piaciuto.
>
> Liti…ne succedevano sempre, ma sempre per causa della moglie, che voleva fare spendere all'Olivo di più di quanto potesse. La Beccaro non aveva rispetto pel marito. L'Olivo, carattere irascibile, aveva trovato nella consorte un carattere identico al suo.
>
> [Olivo came over to ask me to intervene; I entered their home and saw that she had smashed some flower vases. I scolded her for her language, and I remember

99 *La Stampa*, 7 June 1904, p. 3.
100 *Il Secolo*, 7–8 June 1904, p. 2.
101 Ibid.
102 *La Stampa*, 7 June 1904, p. 3.

> she was really furious and said she wasn't scared of her husband, and that she had smashed the vases because she wanted to.
>
> Arguments... were always taking place, always started by the wife wanting to make Olivo spend more than he was able to. Beccaro had no respect for her husband. Olivo, an irascible character, had found in his wife a character identical to his own.][103]

The same event was described in *Il Secolo*, which reported that Vignolo went to their home and found Beccaro smashing vases and furniture like a woman possessed.[104] Vignolo also added: 'capiranno che con questi precedenti non si poteva a meno di venire a quello che è successo' [they [the public gallery] will understand that given these precedents, what came to pass was inevitable].[105] Vignolo was also asked whose fault it was when the couple argued. His answer gives us a clear indication of the expectations of the time: 'un po' di tutti e due: lei perché era una donna impossibile e lui perché pretendeva da una donna simile l'impossibile' [a bit of both: hers, because she was an impossible woman, and his, because he expected the impossible from such a woman].[106] *Il Giornale d'Italia* also added that Vignolo said that Olivo was irascible and 'qualche volta trascendeva ad atti violenti contro la moglie' [sometimes he escalated to violent acts against his wife].[107] Then, the witness was asked if he thought that Beccaro was an honest woman. He replied that he believed she was and that his wife believed the same.[108] It is worth noting that Olivo never said that he killed his wife out of jealousy, but the question of Beccaro's honesty was key in the trial and in the process of the construction of her as blameworthy, thus making her murder somehow acceptable.

Vignolo went on to describe how, on the day of her murder, Beccaro had come round to see Vignolo's wife. Ernestina was crying and very angry with her husband. She had indicated the drawer where she knew Vignolo kept his revolver and had said that, had she had a gun, she would have shot her husband in the face. Vignolo said he again reprimanded her for her words, and she went home. The following day, he did not see Beccaro at all and,

103 Ibid.
104 *Il Secolo*, 7–8 June 1904, p. 2.
105 Ibid.
106 Ibid.
107 *Il Giornale d'Italia*, 7 June 1904, p. 3.
108 *Il Secolo*, 7–8 June 1904, p. 2.

along with some others in the building, tried to find out about her disappearance. He reported that Olivo said that his wife had left, but the neighbours thought 'che fosse invece rimasta in casa per un fracco di botte pigliate' [that in fact she was staying inside because of the shed load of beatings she had received].[109] Further, he added, they also wondered if Beccaro had left early in the morning 'per non far vedere così le ammaccature avute nella notte dal marito' [so as not to show the bruises her husband had inflicted on her in the night].[110]

The cross-examination continued with Vignolo being asked about Beccaro. The President of the Court asked him if Beccaro had been a good housewife, in his view, and Vignolo answered that she was very good.[111] But again, Beccaro's character came under scrutiny:

> Il Vignolo conferma il particolare che la Beccaro, anziché placare il marito quando questi era irritato, faceva di tutto per aizzarlo. Dice anche che la Beccaro confessava d'aver minacciato parecchio volte col coltello il disgraziato marito.
>
> [Vignolo confirms the detail that, rather than appeasing her husband when he was irritated, Beccaro did everything she could to provoke him. He also says that Beccaro confessed to having threatened her unfortunate husband with a knife several times].[112]

The figure of Vignolo, and his testimony, provide us with a very interesting picture of the time. Vignolo precisely enacts the notion of the *paterfamilias* of the time: head of the household, it was he who decided with whom his wife could be friends, and he would forbid relations he did not think respectable for his family. Furthermore, so authoritative was he that other men, such as Olivo, would ask his opinion when they were in need, as Olivo had in asking him to intervene in a discussion with his own wife, and he even had the power to castigate others' wives. Moreover, Vignolo's casual report that it may have been the case that Beccaro had been beaten by Olivo suggests that such an act of violence was tolerated even when it left obvious marks. Indeed, the hierarchical structure of marriage and the unequal status of men

109 *La Stampa*, 7 June 1904, p. 3.
110 Ibid.
111 *Il Secolo*, 7–8 June 1904, p. 2.
112 *La Stampa*, 7 June 1904, p. 3.

and women made a certain degree of violence even legally acceptable and, not surprisingly, a matter pertaining to the privacy of the household, which, in the words of Claudia Passarella, was 'virtually invisible'.[113] In this context, it is easy to understand the naturalness with which such instances of violence were recounted and how the use of expressions such as 'bruises inflicted' or 'a shed load of beatings' contributed to normalise this. Furthermore, it is of note that the couple's neighbours did not think to go to the police to report the beating of Beccaro by her husband, since such behaviour was accepted as a tolerable component of a woman's life and within the bounds of the means of correction or discipline available to a man to make the members of his own family behave in an acceptable way.

Two further witnesses were called to answer questions about the relationship between Alberto and Ernestina, all of whom confirmed that the couple often argued. First was Luigi Spagnoli, a tenant who lived with his sister in the apartment below Olivo and Beccaro. *Il Secolo* observed that he was an assistant pharmacist and a sturdy young man who seemed to speak in a very low voice amidst the general hubbub of protest, but it subsequently became clear that in fact he was almost completely voiceless[114] – a phenomenon that highlighted, at a time when studies of the body aligned expected behaviours with particular body types, an alleged 'atypical' relation between a strong body and a weak voice. The second witness was Luigi's sister Maria, described variously as 'una bella signorina, vestita elegantemente di nero' [a beautiful young lady, elegantly dressed in black][115] and a 'giovane e simpatica signorina' [young and nice lady].[116]

On 8 June, the trial resumed, again drawing a large audience, including 'molte signore di ogni età e in svariate *toilettes*' [many ladies of all ages and variously *outfits*].[117] There were other witnesses for the defence to question, some of them concierges of the several buildings in which Beccaro and Olivo

---

113 Passarella, 'Between Leniency and Severity', p. 117. For violence and privacy, see, Reva B. Siegel's article, '"The Rule of Love': Wife Beating as Prerogative and Privacy', *The Yale Law Journal*, 105/8 (1996), 2117–207, in which the links between authority, privacy and violence are clearly exposed.

114 *Il Secolo*, 7–8 June 1904, p. 3.

115 *La Stampa*, 7 June 1904, p. 3.

116 *Il Secolo*, 7–8 June 1904, p. 3.

117 *Il Secolo*, 8–9 June 1904, p. 2.

had lived during their marriage – due, said Olivo, to the frequent moves the couple had had to make as a result of his wife's behaviour.[118] The testimonies were aimed at further staining Beccaro's reputation and demonstrating how unfortunate Olivo had been. One Rosa De Vecchi, for example, said that she considered Beccaro 'una donna grama' [a wretched woman], while Olivo was a good person.[119] Moreover, she reported that Beccaro received many visitors, but her husband knew about it. Asked about Beccaro's habits, Caterina Valsecchi, another concierge, replied that Beccaro was often out during the day and sometimes also in the evening, returning after the doors of the building had been shut for the night.[120] Giuditta Oldani, the concierge of a house where Beccaro had worked as a maid, was asked if Beccaro 'faceva dei torti a suo marito' [wronged her husband];[121] a leading question designed to be interpreted as meaning had Beccaro betrayed her husband. Answering no, Oldani was then asked if Beccaro kept a tidy house; her response was that Beccaro didn't leave so much as a solitary match lying around.[122] Next, the interrogation moved on to questions about the work Beccaro did at the house of a man by the name of Landriani, 'persona sola, dal quale la Beccaro si recava due volte alla settimana e a volte una volta al mese a prestare i suoi servizi...' [a single person, who Beccaro went to twice a week and sometimes once a month to offer her services...].[123] *La Stampa* included the three elliptical dots, suggesting that the 'services' carried out by Beccaro could be read in a particular way. *Il Secolo* reported that after Oldani said that Landriani was a bachelor, laughter had broken out in the courtroom.[124] This part of the article concluded by saying that the courtroom became disrupted and that an elegant lady moved to sit at the press table to inspect the defendant through opera glasses.[125]

Next, Cesare Landriani himself, a robust and pleasant managed forty-five and a railway employee,[126] was called to testify. He explained that he had fired

---

118 Ibid.
119 *Corriere della Sera*, 9 June 1904, p. 2.
120 Ibid.
121 *Il Secolo*, 8–9 June 1904, p. 2.
122 Ibid.
123 *La Stampa*, 8 June 1904, p. 3.
124 *Il Secolo*, 8–9 June 1904, p. 2.
125 Ibid.
126 Ibid.

Beccaro becuse he had heard that she had spoken badly of him.[127] Then, 'fra la soddisfazione generale' [to general satisfaction], came the teacher who had given Beccaro some literacy lessons; but, after reporting that Beccaro had been virtually illiterate, she confirmed only that Olivo had made her stop the lessons.[128] Then there was the testimony of Simone Pellignani, the husband of one of Beccaro's cousins. He 'definisce l'Ernestina un angelo e l'Olivo un boia' [defines Ernestina as an angel and Olivo as an executioner],[129] concluding by saying that whatever Ernestina did, Olivo always told her off.[130]

Finally, it was Antonio Colombo's turn. *La Stampa* introduced him as 'il vecchio gobbo da cui l'Olivo rilevò la Beccaro' [the old hunchback from whom Olivo had taken on Beccaro],[131] notably choosing to use the phrase 'taken on', as if it had been the passing of a chattel from one man to another, highlighting how a woman of Beccaro's behaviour was seen. The presence of Colombo in the court was described as triggering lively curiosity in the public gallery. Moreover, 'molte signore, tra cui alcune letterate, vengono ad invadere i banchi della stampa per meglio sentire' [many ladies, including the more educated, descend on the press tables so as to hear better].[132] *Il Secolo* described Colombo as 'un ometto d'anni 54; calvo, con un gran naso e i baffi grigi; di professione contabile' [a little man aged fifty-four; bald, with a big nose and a grey moustache; an accountant by profession].[133]

The 'gobbetto' [little hunchback][134] said he had met Beccaro at a party in the country in Magreglio, where she had been working as a waitress. The pair had met again in Milan, where Beccaro had tried to befriend him. Colombo had told her that if she needed anything, she could come to him. Before long, he had received a handwritten, ungrammatical note in which Beccaro had told him that she was a patient in a syphilis hospital and had begged him to help her, since she did not know how to get herself out of her troubles. She pleaded with him to have mercy on her. Ceding to her prayers, and despite

---

[127] *Corriere della Sera*, 9 June 1904, p. 2.
[128] *Il Secolo*, 8–9 June 1904, p. 3.
[129] *La Stampa*, 8 June 1904, p. 3.
[130] *Il Secolo*, 8–9 June 1904, p. 2.
[131] *La Stampa*, 8 June 1904, p. 3.
[132] Ibid.
[133] *Il Secolo*, 8–9 June 1904, p. 2.
[134] *La Stampa*, 8 June 1904, p. 3.

trying to protect himself with the excuse that he had a family of his own, Colombo agreed to take her on, finding her a room when she was discharged from the syphilis hospital and buying her clothes and shoes. The President of the Court jocularly suggested that the note Colombo had received had been 'lusinghiera' [flattering] – a comment greeted with laughter in the court – to which Colombo replied that it had not been flattering but instead had left him worried.[135] He explained that he had paid for a room, food, and clothes to help Beccaro. Asked if he had done so out of philanthropy, he replied in the affirmative, sparking more laughter.[136] Sometime later, Beccaro told Colombo that she had received a good offer and subsequently introduced Olivo to him. Olivo told Colombo that he intended to 'take' Beccaro as a companion, and 'quando avrebbe potuto l'avrebbe sposata, qualora avesse mantenuto un contegno degno d'una donna onesta' [when he was able to, he would marry her, providing she had behaved in a manner becoming of an honest woman].[137] Colombo added that he had once visited the home of Beccaro and Olivo with his son and had been really impressed by the kindness of the couple and was very happy that the good deed he had done had worked out so well. Challenged about the nature of his relationship with Beccaro, Colombo swore that he only wanted to do the right thing for such a young woman, adding that his wife had known what he was doing and had been happy and indeed proud of him for doing it.[138] *La Stampa* concluded its report with the observation that, following Colombo's testimony, the onlookers, 'che si attendeva da questo teste chissà quali rivelazioni, è rimasto deluso' [who were expecting who-knows-what revelations from this witness, were disappointed].[139]

---

[135] *Il Secolo*, 8–9 June 1904, p. 2.
[136] *La Stampa*, 8 June 1904, p. 3.
[137] Ibid.
[138] *Il Secolo*, 8–9 June 1904, p. 2.
[139] *La Stampa*, 8 June 1904, p. 3.

CHAPTER 6

The defence and the verdict

Next, the witnesses for the defence were called to testify. This part of the trial was designed specifically to sully Beccaro's reputation, emphasising behaviours and actions that made her appear unworthy of an upstanding citizen like Olivo, rendering his life with her difficult, almost intolerable, and her murder therefore understandable. Newspapers complied with this rhetoric, not always overtly, but through adoption of an ironic tone in reporting testimonies and by consistent allusions, such as a paragraph in an article in the *Corriere della Sera* of 9 June about the witnesses for the defence, entitled 'L'onestà della Beccaro' [The honesty of Beccaro].[1]

On 9 June 1904, the first witness called for the defence was Giuseppina Ciprelli, a teacher, who recounted how Beccaro had asked her to write letters to two men with whom she had been having affairs. This sparked 'ilarità vivissima' [great hilarity] among the audience.[2] Ciprelli concluded by saying that she hated Beccaro because she was a bad person, whilst Beccaro's husband, by contrast, was such a good man.[3] Other witnesses testified to Beccaro's behaviour: Enrico Ballerio, the owner of a house in which the couple had lived, said that Beccaro's reprehensible behaviour included showing herself off on the landing and at the window in her underwear. He even castigated her for this,[4] since the window looked out onto the street, and

1 *Corriere della Sera*, 9 June 1904, p. 2.
2 *Il Secolo*, 8–9 June 1904, p. 3.
3 *Corriere della Sera*, 9 June 1904, p. 2.
4 Ibid.

those who passed by could see her,[5] doing so because such behaviour could ruin not only her reputation but also that of the other families that lived there. Another witness was named Rometta Fresco. Described as 'una simpatica signorina vestita elegantemente di nero' [a nice young lady elegantly dressed in black],[6] she said that Beccaro had told her that she had a lover, and that had she been able to free herself from her husband, she could have had a rich protector.[7] Orfeo Chiodo-Grandi, a jeweller who knew the couple, reported that Beccaro had confided to him that she had a lover who gave her gifts; as a result, Chiodo-Grandi had forbidden her from visiting his family home to protect his reputation and that of his family from association with such a woman.[8] Fresco and Ciprelli were subsequently questioned further behind closed doors to prevent the public from hearing sensitive details. The *Corriere della Sera* reports that Beccaro emerged from this as being 'tutt'altro che un fior di moglie' [anything but a good wife].[9] *Il Secolo* noted that, whilst the public was curious to know what had been said behind closed doors, respect for its readers and indeed the law prevented it from satisfying this curiosity.[10] The newspaper did, however, mention that Fresco and Ciprelli had said that Beccaro had mixed something 'very intimate' with wine, adding that it was a 'sistema d'altronde altrettanto stupido e triviale quanto noto in certi ambienti' [a system as stupid and trivial as is known in certain circles], which, however, would still prove that she cared about her husband's affection.[11] This sentence is particularly interesting: on the one hand, the words suggest that this system had no scientific basis and was pointless; on the other, the term 'certain' bore a negative connotation, inferring that these were circles not frequented by respectable people. Beccaro was familiar with this system because she frequented, or had formerly frequented, such circles, and this meant she was not a respectable person.

Other witnesses continued to further tarnish Beccaro's reputation. Amalia Sella, a 'simpatica signorina' [nice young lady] who had known Beccaro for

---

5 *Il Secolo*, 8–9 June 1904, p. 3.

6 Ibid.

7 *Il Giornale d'Italia*, 8 June 1904, p. 3.

8 *Corriere della Sera*, 9 June 1904, p. 2.

9 Ibid.

10 *Il Secolo*, 9–10 June 1904, p. 2.

11 Ibid.

many years, testified that Beccaro had told her that she could not love her husband because she was in love with another man.[12] Maria Corbetta, a friend of Olivo's, characterised Beccaro as 'ignorante e sfacciata' [ignorant and brazen].[13] Giovanni Battista Del Fabbro described her as rude and said that she used to insult her husband.[14] Another, Adalgisa Nasoni, contended that Beccaro was not the right woman for Olivo: that whilst Olivo would go so far as to carry his wife up the stairs to the fourth floor when she was tired,[15] Beccaro, by contrast, was 'ignorante, superba, provocante a tal segno da trascinare un uomo a commettere anche un delitto' [ignorant, proud, provocative to the point even of dragging a man to commit a crime];[16] and, she added, when the couple quarrelled, it was always because of Beccaro.[17] Again, we can powerfully see the standards of the time laid bare, inherent also in the testimonies of other women. Beccaro is characterised not only as non-compliant with expected patterns of female behaviour, but also as someone who did not know when to stop, not only a contributor to her own murder but also taking an even more significant role: she 'dragged' a man to kill her, thereby entirely shifting all culpability onto herself.

The interrogation of the witnesses for the defence continued. It lingered on elements pertaining to the couple's lifestyle: the wine supplier reported that he had sold forty to forty-five litres of wine to the couple and that Olivo had told him that Beccaro watered down the wine.[18] Then there was the shoemaker, who said that Olivo made sure that Beccaro was always supplied with footwear.[19] Other merchants reported supplying dresses and hats. The interrogation of these witnesses served to show what a thoughtful person Olivo was, whilst Beccaro, in contrast, repaid such a good man only by treating him badly and betraying him.

Then one of Beccaro's former employers, Seregno Motta, took the stand. He testified that he had sacked her because she was lazy at work and generally

---

12 *Il Secolo*, 9–10 June 1904, p. 2.
13 *Corriere della Sera*, 9 June 1904, p. 2.
14 Ibid.
15 *Il Secolo*, 9–10 June 1904, p. 2.
16 *Corriere della Sera*, 9 June 1904, p. 3.
17 *Il Secolo*, 9–10 June 1904, p. 2.
18 *Corriere della Sera*, 9 June 1904, p. 3.
19 Ibid.

behaved badly: indeed, at night, instead of going to sleep, she would go out and about around town with certain young men.[20]

A former colleague of Olivo, Angelo Ferrara, said that Olivo was a good person but did note that his relations with colleagues were not good, as he was not very tolerant.[21]

Then another witness for the defence, Ismaele Del Grazia, a friend of Olivo's, defined Olivo variously as a gentleman, somewhat impetuous, and very badly matched with his wife.[22] He reported that one evening, Beccaro, despite observing that her husband was becoming angry as she talked about a love affair she had had before they married, nonetheless continued with her anecdote for some time, seeming almost to take pleasure in it, despite Olivo's pleas for her to stop. Olivo, he said, then slapped her wrist.[23] Olivo broke in at this point to explain that he had not physically slapped Beccaro, but had merely made the gesture.[24] Del Grazia concluded by saying that the couple were always complaining about how each treated the other.[25]

Next, the court turned to hearing the testimony of several people who had encountered Olivo as he was disposing of his wife's body, beginning with Edoardo Guerci, the boy who had carried the bag containing Beccaro's remains. Just fourteen years old, he was described as 'vispo birichino, di professione scalpellino, quando ha voglia di lavorare' [a lively and mischievous boy, a stonemason by trade, when he feels like working].[26] Edoardo and several others who had met Olivo testified that Olivo was clearly a miser who sought to spend as little money as possible. The boy also added that Olivo had shouted at him that he was greedy, triggering 'ilarità vivissima' [lively hilarity] in the courtroom.[27] Then it was the turn of Gerolamo Motti, the boatman who had taken Olivo for the boat tour. Although his testimony was barely comprehensible since he was giving it in a Genoese dialect, Motti noted that Olivo had had a bag with him on the boat and, on hearing a

20 Ibid.
21 Ibid.
22 *La Stampa*, 8 June 1904, p. 3.
23 *Il Secolo*, 8–9 June 1904, p. 2.
24 Ibid.
25 *La Stampa*, 8 June 1904, p. 3.
26 Ibid.
27 *Il Secolo*, 8–9 June 1904, p. 2.

splash, had asked Olivo what was going on. Olivo had answered that, since he did not want to pay extra taxes, he was getting rid of some stuff that he had. Motti went on to say that he then noticed a paper-wrapped package, tied with brand new rope, floating on the water. On their return to shore, Olivo was described as being a little pale but very calm.[28]

Then Domenico Traversi, a porter at the port, gave his testimony. He had been fishing near the port with two friends. They had seen a package in the sea, had picked it up, opened it, and, to their horror, had found it contained a human head. They had reported the matter to the customs officer, who had notified the port authority. The police were unable to ascertain the identity of the corpse but noted that it was wrapped in sheets of newspaper from Milan.[29]

Following all the witness testimonies and that of the medical experts who commented on Olivo and the crisis he had suffered a few days earlier in court, the trial came to a close with the final speech by the lawyer for Ernestina's sister Clotilde, positing that Olivo's murder of his wife was premeditated. He began by disputing some of the points Lombroso, the criminologist, had published the same day in an article in the *Corriere della Sera* (see Appendix 2) entitled 'L'Olivo criminaloide' [Olivo, the criminaloid].[30] Throughout the lawyer's lengthy speech, 'il presidente lo interrompe, fra le risate del pubblico; ma egli continua' [the President of the Court interrupts him, amidst laughter from the audience; but he continues].[31] *Il Secolo* also noted that this lawyer, as he was arguing that Beccaro's murder was premeditated, spoke with a distinctly Neapolitan accent and had been a resident in Milan for only six months;[32] in this way, the newspaper sought to undermine the authoritativeness and credibility of the lawyer's words by shifting attention to irrelevant detail.

Then it was the turn of the public prosecutor, whose claim was for Olivo to be judged as entirely responsible for premeditated murder. He went back

---

28 *La Stampa*, 8 June 1904, p. 3.

29 Ibid.

30 The term 'criminaloid' does not denote a 'born' criminal, but rather someone who is driven to commit crime by pressures of circumstance and environment; that is, a 'non-criminal' who has adopted criminal activity. It infers moral insensibility rather than an inherent impulsion towards evil.

31 *La Stampa*, 10 June 1904, p. 3.

32 *Il Secolo*, 10–11 June 1904, p. 3.

over certain key aspects of the trial, such as the important standing of the case, further evidenced in the throngs attending the courtroom even though it was the summer season. He highlighted that in murdering Beccaro, Olivo had given her as a burial site, or 'sepoltura': 'la latrina e il porto di Genova' [the latrine and the port of Genoa];[33] and, addressing Olivo directly, he said: 'ma quelle carni ti avevano pure appartenuto, ti avevano pure dato abbracci d'amore, e tu, digraziato, hai piantato in esse ancora una volta il coltello!' [but this flesh had also belonged to you, had given you embraces of love, and you, you wretched man, you sank your knife into it time and again!].[34] He then argued that Olivo had a habit of speculative behaviour, recalling that, in 'l'incontro dell'Olivo e della Ernesta' [the meeting of Olivo and Ernesta],[35] Olivo had considered that, 'procurandosi l'Ernestina' [by procuring Ernestina for himself],[36] he could make some money. With the audience murmuring and signalling their agreement, he continued that Olivo was a man who, even at his most animal, did not lose his intellectual nature; asked if he had shed tears, he replied that to do so would have been pointless, since there was no one there to see him.[37] The prosecutor posited that their marriage was odd, since there was no respect between the spouses, greed reigned, and Olivo's miserliness was evident in the fact that he did not even get rid of the mattress stuffing soaked in his wife's blood, because it could still be usable at some point.[38] Although the prosecutor was advocating for the victim, and despite intense and dramatic rhetoric designed to get the jurors on side, he nonetheless was complicit with the language and stereotyped conceits of the time. This was evident in, for example, the use of expressions such as 'the flesh that [...] belonged to him' or 'by procuring Ernestina', and, as before, in the way he persisted in identifying Olivo by his surname but Ernestina by her first name.

When it was the turn of Olivo's lawyer, he opened his speech with the observation that the public prosecutor had peppered his eloquent speech with lyrical colour designed to create a sense of horror in relation to the

---

[33] *La Stampa*, 10 June 1904, p. 3.
[34] *Il Secolo*, 10–11 June 1904, p. 3.
[35] Ibid.
[36] *La Stampa*, 10 June 1904, p. 3.
[37] *Corriere della Sera*, 10 June 1904, p. 3.
[38] *La Stampa*, 10 June 1904, p. 3.

defendant.[39] He noted that Olivo had always been a model employee, and 'se in un dato giorno apre una parentesi nella sua vita e uccide la moglie, ben grave deve essere stata la causa' [if, on a given day, he opens a parenthesis in his life and kills his wife, the motivation must have been very grave].[40] Olivo's lawyer then attempted to situate his client in a positive light. Allowing that Olivo was attentive to money, he reasoned that this was because he had always had to work hard for it. As a 'spenditore matematico' [an individual who calculates his expenses],[41] asked the lawyer, 'doveva lasciare che la moglie lo sperperasse?' [should he let his wife squander [his money]?].[42] He focused on a proposal that there were two Beccaros: one, the woman her husband had believed her to be; the other, the woman who had emerged from the trial.[43] Ernesta, the lawyer argued, enjoyed provoking her husband when he was irritated and had threatened him with a knife on more than one occasion.[44] Moreover, he believed there was no doubt the jurors would acknowledge that Olivo had been seriously provoked, 'perché l'ingiuria contro la madre dell'Olivo, atroce, sanguinosa che fu in quella sera per la prima volta pronunciata, fece traboccare il vaso già ricolmo' [because the insult to Olivo's mother, atrocious and bloody, and uttered for the first time that evening, was the straw that broke the camel's back].[45] Furthermore, he insisted that 'l'Ernesta si vendeva per depravazione' [Ernesta sold herself, out of depravity] without Olivo's knowledge.[46] He concluded that Olivo was not a sane man, but rather a madman, aberrant and a man in whom many scientists, such as Lombroso, took an interest, and that 'tutti hanno sentito un fremito di pietà per l'uomo a cui il ragionamento manca per un momento, per l'uomo che non può essere normale' [everyone felt a frisson of pity for the man who momentarily loses his reason, for the man who cannot be normal].[47] The audience applauded the 'calorosa ed efficace

---

39 *Il Secolo*, 10–11 June 1904, p. 3.

40 *La Stampa*, 11 June 1904, p. 3.

41 *Il Secolo*, 10–11 June 1904, p. 3.

42 *La Stampa*, 11 June 1904, p. 3.

43 *Il Secolo*, 10–11 June 1904, p. 3.

44 Ibid.

45 *La Stampa*, 11 June 1904, p. 3.

46 *Il Secolo*, 10–11 June 1904, p. 3.

47 *La Stampa*, 10 June 1904, p. 3. As we shall see, not only Cesare Lombroso, but other scientists of the time, like Scipio Sighele, commented on the case.

arringa' [heated and effective defence],[48] which, as well as imparting a final definitive stain to Beccaro's honour, invited consideration of Olivo as a madman worthy of pity.

11 June 1904 was the day of the verdict. *La Stampa* headlined its article, 'Lo scandalo giudiziario di Milano. L'assoluzione dell'Olivo, squartatore della moglie. L'enorme impressione in Italia – I commenti' [The judicial scandal of Milan. Acquittal of Olivo, the wife-butcher. Massive impression in Italy – Commentary].[49] Similar headlines appeared in other newspapers. *La Stampa*, consistent with other publications, began with descriptive detail: 'L'aula è gremita di pubblico femminile, elegante e gaio, che forma un singolare contrasto colla gravità del dramma che si svolge nell'aula' [the courtroom is packed with female spectators, elegantly dressed and cheerful, in marked contrast to the seriousness of the drama unfolding in the court].[50] Next was the description of Olivo: 'La calma da cui sembra dominato è evidentemente forzata. Un tremito nervoso tormenta le sue mani. Le rughe della sua fronte sono più profonde; gli occhi sono infossati' [his apparent calm is evidently forced. His hands are tormented by a nervous tremor. The lines on his forehead have deepened; his eyes are sunken].[51]

Il Secolo set out the eleven counts upon which the jurors were asked to make their judgements. Relating to the first charge, murder, there were seven counts: (1) the deed; (2) Article 46 (total irresponsibility); (3) culpability; (4) premeditation; (5) provocation; (6) seriousness of provocation; (7) partial infirmity. The other four counts related to the second charge (the butchering of the body): (8) the deed; (9) culpability; (10) full responsibility; (11) partial responsibility.[52] On the third question, culpability, the jurors responded 'No' – not guilty: they considered Olivo the material perpetrator of the murder but did not judge that he had meant to kill. According to this verdict, therefore, Olivo was considered not guilty of murder and was acquitted.

Il Secolo explained that '[a] quel monosillabo gli avvocati e i magistrati presenti scattano e si odono qua e là queste parole pronunciate come in atto di terrore: "Ma è assolto! È assolto!"' [At that monosyllable, the lawyers and

---

48 *Il Secolo*, 11–12 June 1904, p. 3.
49 *La Stampa*, 12 June 1904, p. 3.
50 Ibid.
51 Ibid.
52 *Il Secolo*, 11–12 June 1904, p. 3.

magistrates present snap into life, and we hear these words pronounced throughout the court as if in an act of terror: 'But he is acquitted! He is acquitted!'].[53] Whilst the experts immediately grasped the consequences of the verdict, '[i]l pubblico non ha capito nulla; anche i giurati sembrano sbalorditi' [the general public understood nothing; even the jurors seem stunned].[54]

The public gallery, astonished to learn that Olivo was acquitted, broke into a 'mormorio di ilarità, più applausi fragorosi e invincibili (!!!). Le signore, dai posti riservati, applaudono l'Olivo (!!!), come si applaudirebbe l'autore di una grande commedia' [murmur of hilarity, and thunderous and invincible applause (!!!). The ladies in the reserved seats applaud Olivo (!!!), as one would applaud the author of a great comedy].[55] *La Stampa* continued its account of the day, describing how Olivo had expected to be sentenced to six or seven years in jail and how, immediately after the sentence was pronounced, he said he meant to spend another night in jail that night to recover from the weight of emotion he had suffered – although he later changed his mind. Olivo also added that he wanted to 'far erigere un ricordo sulla tomba della povera Beccaro a Genova (!!!)' [have a memorial erected on the tomb of poor Beccaro in Genoa (!!!)].[56] The author of the article in *La Stampa* further added a personal appraisal, commenting that 'Ci sono dei delinquenti, è vero, i quali hanno messo qualche cosa di eroico e di grande nei loro delitti, che possono parere agli occhi del pubblico come i vendicatori, i giustizieri (terribili sia pure), di un sentimento, di un'idea... di un pregiudizio anche! Ma nel delitto dell'Olivo... [...] non c'è in esso che l'atto di un pazzo e una carneficina!' [There are criminals, it is true, who have put something heroic and great into their crimes, who can seem avengers in the eye of the public, pursuing (terrible though it is), a feeling, an idea... even a prejudice! But in Olivo's crime... [...] there is nothing more to it than the act of a madman and a carnage!].[57] The repeated use of exclamation marks and ellipses served to underline the journalist's indignation as he explained that the President of the Court bore responsibility for the unexpected verdict, since he had formulated the counts

53 *Il Secolo*, 12–13 June 1904, p. 3.
54 *La Stampa*, 12 June 1904, p. 3.
55 Ibid.
56 Ibid.
57 Ibid.

in such a way as to allow the possibility of manslaughter, thereby raising the option of non-intentional murder. Olivo was sentenced to twelve days for contempt of a corpse, but since he had already been incarcerated since 26 May 1903, he was immediately released. As we shall see in a moment, the subsequent appeal by the prosecution would also lead to a similar verdict.

PART 3

CHAPTER 7

After the first trial's verdict

After this verdict at the first trial, a crowd gathered in the courtyard and around the courthouse: 'una folle enorme, chiassosa, inquieta, che fa ressa alle varie porte d'accesso' [a huge, noisy, restless crowd, rushing at the various entrance doors].[1] To avoid a major commotion, Olivo was released via a back door leading to the cells. About two hundred people were awaiting him there. *Il Secolo* noted that when the crowd saw him, there was no applause.[2]

From the courthouse, Olivo went to stay at a friend's house, from where he was interviewed. The journalist from *Il Secolo* observed that Olivo sat on a sofa, surrounded by friends and acquaintances, smoking.[3] He spoke about his plans and, in particular, about going to work outside Milan. He had expected to be sentenced to several years in prison, adding that 'Dio mi ha protetto, allorché mi fece venire all'udienza dell'altro dì, quel terribile male' [God protected me, when he brought that dreadful evil to me during the hearing the other day].[4] He then lashed out against the alienists who 'si misero d'accordo per escludere quello che è la verità: che cioè io ho una *rotella* fuor di posto, quella vera e propria infermità di mente, che anche i giurati, prestando fede ai medici, non hanno voluto ammettere' [agreed to exclude what is the truth: that is, that I have a *cog* out of place, a genuine

1 *Il Secolo*, 12–13 June 1904, p. 3.
2 Ibid.
3 Ibid.
4 Ibid.

mental illness, which even the jurors, who put their faith in the doctors, did not want to acknowledge].[5]

Interviewed by *La Stampa*, the President of the Court of Assizes said he wanted to appeal to the Supreme Court, although he conceded that appeals against jury verdicts were rarely admitted. He argued, though, that since the jury had acquitted Olivo without understanding that this was actually what they were doing, the verdict did not reflect their true will.[6] Moreover:

> Dio lo volesse, per onore della giustizia nostra; ma poche speranze esprimono i giuristi che il ricorso inoltrato dal P.M. di Milano possa avere accoglienza favorevole a Roma, e che una riparazione morale solenne si possa attendere la società, oltraggiata nella sua coscienza da un verdetto pel quale corre voce che si prenderanno provvedimenti disciplinari a carico dei magistrati che ne ressero le sorti.
>
> [God willing, for the honour of our justice; but the jurists express little hope that the appeal forwarded by the Prosecutor of Milan will be favourably received in Rome, and that society, outraged in its conscience by a verdict for which there are rumours that disciplinary measures will be taken against the magistrates who ruled it, can expect a solemn moral reparation].[7]

In addition, the President of the Court of Assizes commented:

> La verità è che i giurati, per degli scrupoli inspiegabili e deplorevolissimi, hanno commesso uno sproposito enorme. Ora cercano di attenuare la triste impressione prodotta dal loro verdetto attaccandosi a pretese deficienze del questionario. Ma non hanno ragione di farlo
>
> [The truth is that the jurors, for reasons of inexplicable and highly deplorable scruples, committed an enormous blunder. Now they try to attenuate the tragedy of their verdict by attacking alleged deficiencies in the counts they were instructed to consider. But they have no reason to do so].[8]

In fact, many claimed that the counts submitted to the jury had not been formulated correctly.[9]

---

5 Ibid.
6 *La Stampa*, 13 June 1904, p. 3.
7 Ibid.
8 *La Stampa*, 14 June 1904, p. 3.
9 See, for example, Scipio Sighele in Appendix 9.

The Genovese newspaper *Caffaro* reported an interview with the physician Enrico Morselli, who maintained that Olivo was a criminaloid, a fact identifiable in the way he had kept his wife's corpse with him for several days. Morselli added that Lombroso had already defined Olivo as a criminaloid, as well as an epileptic. Morselli was also asked to comment on the instances of applause from the attendant public in the courtroom and contended that those who frequented such trials were latent criminals themselves and craved drama.[10]

There was also criticism from *La Tribuna*, which commented that these kinds of verdicts arouse amazement but also moral sadness.[11] The newspaper *Il Messaggero* wrote that jurors had been indulgent or reckless jurors and that 'nessuno, scienziato o ignorante che sia, ha approvato l'assoluzione dell'Olivo: e questo fa onore al buon senso comune' [no one, whether scientist or ignorant, approved Olivo's acquittal: and this does honour to common sense].[12] *Avanti!* published an article by the jurist Enrico Ferri, who proposed his opinion on the case (see Appendix 5).[13] *Il Secolo*, instead, suggested that Olivo should move away from Milan so as to be forgotten (see Appendix 6).[14]

Pasquino, a humour magazine, published a cartoon with a macabre joke about the sentence entitled *After the trial of Olivo* and saying 'bisogna che io *operi* con inaudita ferocia, con crudeltà raffinata. Al caso sarà applicabile… il massimo della pena, e i giurati – per reazione – mi assolveranno!' [I must *operate* with unprecedented ferocity, with refined cruelty. The maximum sentence… will be applicable to the case, and the jurors – in reaction – will acquit me!] (see Figure 4), with 'operate' in italics probably suggesting a double entendre.[15] *Il Secolo XX*, a monthly journal, proposed a drawing of the trial, adding that the verdict aroused 'dolorosa meraviglia' [painful amazement]

---

10 *Caffaro*, 14 June 1904, p. 2.

11 *La Tribuna*, 12 June 1904, p. 4.

12 *Il Messaggero*, 14 June 1904, p. 1.

13 *Avanti!*, 12 June 1904, p. 1. See also Lombroso's letter dated 13 June 1904 thanking Enrico Ferri for writing his opinion about the case on this newspaper. #LOMBROSOProject, Online resource, <https://lombrosoproject.unito.it/en/correspondence-results/>, source held in Turin, Museo di antropologia criminale "Cesare Lombroso", University of Turin, 13 June 1904 [accessed 30 April 2024]

14 *Il Secolo*, 14–15 June 1904, p. 3.

15 *Pasquino*, 19 June 1904, n. 25, p. 3.

Figure 4 *Pasquino*, 19 June 1904, n. 25, p. 3.

Image reproduced by permission of the University of Milan – Centro Apice (Archivi della Parola, dell'Immagine e della Comunicazione Editoriale). Further reproduction or duplication by any means is prohibited.

(Figure 5).[16] *L'illustrazione italiana*, a weekly journal, published an editorial by scientist Scipio Sighele explaining his perspective on the trial and on the murder (see Appendix 9).[17] *I Tribunali*, instead, after briefly telling about Olivo's acquittal, published a long misogynistic article explaining the reason for the presence of many women during the hearings (see Appendix 3) and pointing out that they were driven by 'quel sentimento insano nelle donnine di voler ficcare un po' troppo il loro gentile nasino nelle faccende altrui' [that insane feeling in little women of wanting to stick a little too much their kind little noses into other people's affairs].[18] *I grandi processi illustrati* wrote that thunderous applause welcomed this sentence, that offended human conscience and has had a sad and humiliating effect on people.[19]

If *La Civiltà Cattolica* only reported the news,[20] *Il Buon Cuore*, a weekly magazine for families, gave a longer comment reporting that 'una pagina disonorante è quella scritta la scorsa settimana dalla nostra povera giustizia' [a dishonourable page is the one written last week by our poor justice] and that the moral sense has been brutally outraged.[21] However, despite condemning the verdict, the article ironically described the murder. Indeed,

> le buone popolane, colpite dal fatto dell'assoluzione di un uomo che ha tagliato a pezzi la moglie ed è stato assolto e applaudito, hanno commentato il fatto disonorante con queste parole: 'Povero Olivo! Non aveva alcuna intenzione di uccidere la sua Ernestina! Quando la colpiva replicatamente col coltello, intendeva soltanto di salassarla e farle delle carezze'
>
> [the good women commoners, struck by the fact of the acquittal of a man who cut his wife into pieces and was acquitted and applauded, commented on the dishonourable fact with these words: 'Poor Olivo! He had no intention of killing his Ernestina! When he repeatedly hit her with the knife, he only intended to bleed her and caress her'].[22]

The journal went on focusing on Beccaro's reputation and explained that Olivo was far from being the ideal of the betrayed husband, because 'egli

---

16 *Il Secolo XX*, July 1904, p. 561.
17 *L'Illustrazione Italiana*, 19 June 1904, n. 25, p. 486.
18 *I Tribunali*, 12 June 1904, p. 3. The term "donnine" in this case is not only diminutive but derogatory.
19 *I grandi processi illustrati*, 1904, n. 13, p. 103.
20 *La Civiltà cattolica*, 55 (1904), pp. 360–61.
21 *Il Buon Cuore*, 1 (1904), pp. 217–18 (p. 217).
22 Ibid.

Figure 5 *Il Secolo XX*, July 1904, p. 561.

sapeva *chi* fosse la donna da lui sposata' [he knew *who* the woman he married was].[23]

A few days after the end of the trial, Alberto Olivo responded to Lombroso's article published in *Corriere della Sera* on 9 June 1904 (see Appendix 8). Then, Cesare Lombroso invited him to Turin for psychological analysis. On 24 June 1904, *La Stampa* reported that Olivo stayed in Turin for two days. The criminologist was subsequently interviewed by *La Stampa*, which wrote that 'le anomalie nervose dell'Olivo sono assai superiori e più caratteristiche di quanto egli credeva, stando alla lettura dei resoconti del processo' [Olivo's nervous anomalies are much greater and more characteristic than [Lombroso] was led to believe by the trial reports].[24] Moreover, *La Stampa* reported that

[23] Ibid., p. 218. The term 'chi' was written in italics to emphasise and allude.
[24] *La Stampa*, 24 June 1904, p. 3.

Olivo had immediately revealed himself to be conceited, very proud of his intellectual abilities, and seemingly not at all worried about the possibility of the Supreme Court admitting an appeal.[25]

Lombroso went on to study Olivo from many perspectives and suggested Olivo write a journal in which he described his life and how he ended up killing his wife.[26] Lombroso himself cowrote a book with Augusto Guido Bianchi,[27] *Il caso Olivo*, in which he started by explaining Olivo's genetic inheritance. He pointed out that, first of all, there was a great difference in the age and temperament of Olivo's mother and his father.[28] When Olivo was born, his mother was just a 'giovinetta di 17 anni, virile, violenta' [seventeen year-old girl, virile, violent],[29] while his father was a thirty-eight year-old shoemaker, 'dolce, femmineo' [sweet, feminine] and an alcoholic, who went on to die of liver disease at the age of fifty-five. Olivo's father was of Italian, Slavonic, and Spanish origin;[30] his mother was Albanian with some Greek heritage. '[G]eniale, erotica, esteta, impulsiva, soggetta a convulsioni [ingenious, erotic, an aesthete, impulsive, prone to convulsions], she died of uterine cancer at just thirty-eight.[31] Other relatives had genetic characteristics deemed to have affected Olivo's mind and behaviour: his maternal grandfather was 'un tipo spiccato albanese… scialacquatore,

---

25 Ibid.

26 Olivo wrote this diary over ten days, between 24 June and 4 July 1904. See: Cesare Lombroso and Augusto Guido Bianchi, *Il caso Olivo* (Milan: Libreria editrice nazionale, 1905). Lombroso authored the first part, 'Il caso scientifico'; Bianchi wrote the part concerning the trial; and the third part is the autobiographical diary written by Olivo himself. Olivo's autobiography is also available in an edition by Bollati Boringhieri, with additional information about the case supplied by Ermanno Cavazzoni. See: Alberto Olivo, *Ira fatale. Autobiografia di un* uxoricida, ed. by Ermanno Cavazzoni (Milan: Bollati Boringhieri, 1988), pp. 135–53. See also the exchange of letters between Lombroso and Bianchi, in #LOMBROSOProject, Online resource, <https://lombrosoproject.unito.it/en/correspondence-results/>, source held in Turin, Museo di antropologia criminale "Cesare Lombroso", University of Turin, 15 September 1904, 27 September 1904, 12 December 1904 [accessed 30 April 2024]

27 Lombroso and Bianchi, *Il caso Olivo*, p. 11.

28 Ibid., p. 11.

29 On virile traits and women, see Cesare Lombroso and Guglielmo Ferrero, *La donna delinquente, la prostituta e la donna normale* (Turin: Roux, 1893).

30 Lombroso and Bianchi, *Il caso Olivo*, p. 11.

31 Ibid.

bevitore, donnaiolo' [a strong Albanian type… a spendthrift, drinker, [and] womaniser]. His grandmother was reportedly irascible and jealous; certain uncles on his father's side were alcoholics, like their own father. One of them, Antonio, reportedly had 'strani e irascibili' [strange and irascible] children and was afflicted with a religious paranoia, to the extent that 'si era fissato di voler emulare il santo suo omonimo' [he was determined to emulate his saintly namesake].[32] An aunt of Olivo, a midwife, was said to have had strange obsessions: alongside a phobia of dirt (rupophobia), she had spent 4,600 lira playing the *lotto*, always betting on the same number (four).[33]

Olivo was born at just seven months' gestation and suffered with medical issues as a teenager. At the age of twenty, serving in the army, he suffered sunstroke.[34] He went on to claim that this event was the origin of the dizziness and headaches that tormented him in the following years.

The physical inspection undertaken by Lombroso was vitally important to the confirmation of his theories on crime and criminals. Specifically, he argued that 'a prima vista ti colpisce per una bella armonica fisionomia e per membra ben conformate, sicché ti par la negazione del carattere criminale' [what first strikes you is the attractive and harmonious physiognomy and well-formed limbs, such that he appears the very opposite of the criminal character]; but a more meticulous investigation revealed a lack of symmetry and other 'anomalies' – including an 'asimmetria pigmentaria dell'iride essendo l'iride sinistra più scura' [asymmetry in the pigmentation of the irises, the left being darker] – deemed important signs to consider.[35]

Lombroso detected in Olivo an early sexuality, manifest at thirteen years of age, and defined it as 'forse eccessiva' [perhaps excessive]. He added that, under the influence of small amounts of alcohol and recreational ether, he would hold conversations characterised by a crude eroticism with a woman who brought him meals and who almost went so far as to invite her to engage in a sex act in front of others.[36] His inclination towards an excessive sexuality

---

32 Ibid.

33 Ibid.

34 Ibid., p. 12.

35 Ibid., p. 18. Symmetry was a sign of mental and physical equilibrium. See, Cesare Lombroso, *L'uomo bianco e l'uomo di colore* (Padua: Sacchetto, 1871), p. 222.

36 Ibid., p. 21.

was also noted when Lombroso showed him an engraving of two women working outdoors: the image generated six ideas associations for Olivo, two of which were of an erotic nature.[37]

Lombroso and his team tested Olivo with the latest cutting-edge and improved diagnostic and measurement equipment of the times, including Patrizi's volumetric glove (see Figure 6), used on the plethysmograph (see Figure 7).[38] Blood pressure was taken simultaneously on both arms with two Riva-Rocci sphygmomanometers (see Figure 8).

Olivo's blood pressure was found to be much higher in his right arm,[39] leading Lombroso to conclude that Olivo had significant blood pressure asymmetry linked with 'esagerato destrismo' [exaggerated right-handedness]. This phenomenon had also been detected by Lombroso and his assistant, Edoardo Audenino, in others with epilepsy and in criminals.[40]

Lombroso also tested Olivo's reactions to specific stimuli and reported that they were strong, particularly when he was induced to think about the dismissed teacher 'che tanto fu causa del suo delitto' [who was a significant cause of his crime].[41] Lombroso also argued that whilst Olivo often quoted poets such as Dante and Manzoni, there was no originality in his citations,

---

37 Ibid., p. 32. On theory, criminology and images, see also Nicole Rafter, 'Introduction', *Theoretical Criminology*, 18/2 (2014), 128–33; Kate West, 'Visual Criminology and Lombroso: In Memory of Nicole Rafter (1939–2016)', *Theoretical Criminology*, 21/3 (2017), 271–87.

38 See Cesare Lombroso, *Criminal Man, according to the classification of Cesare Lombroso, briefly summarised by his daughter Gina Lombroso-Ferrero, with an introduction by Cesare Lombroso* (New York: Putnam, 1911), p. 224. Mariano Luigi Patrizi (1866–1935) was an Italian physician and academic. Among his many medical publications, the use of his volumetric glove was explained specifically in *Sensazione postuma e oscillazione vascolare conseguenti allo stimolo termico freddo. Nuove ricerche col guanto volumetrico* (Modena: Società Tipografica, 1905). On the use of the plethysmograph, see also David G. Horn, *The Criminal Body. Lombroso and the Anatomy of Deviance* (London: Routledge, 2003), pp. 128–32. See Patrizi's glove in Figure 6.

39 Scipione Riva Rocci's studies on blood measurements, and his sphygmomanometer (a type of blood pressure monitor), presented at Turin's Accademia Medica in 1897, marked significant advancements in the field of medicine. On Riva Rocci, see Giuseppe Mancia, 'Scipione Riva-Rocci', *Clinical Cardiology*, 20/5 (1997), 503–04.

40 Lombroso and Bianchi, *Il caso Olivo*, p. 22. Edoardo Audenino (1876–1944), a physician, worked with Cesare Lombroso, and wrote on epilepsy and corporeal asymmetry.

41 Lombroso and Bianchi, *Il caso Olivo*, p. 32.

Figure 6 Patrizi's glove

Reproduced by kind permission of the Fondazione Mario Tobino
ph. Sergio Fortuna
in: Franco Bellato, Gino Fornaciari, Marco Natalizi, Renzo Sabbatini, Valentina Giuffra, eds, *Catalogo degli strumenti medici e scientifici* (Lucca: Edizioni Fondazione Mario Tobino, 2009).

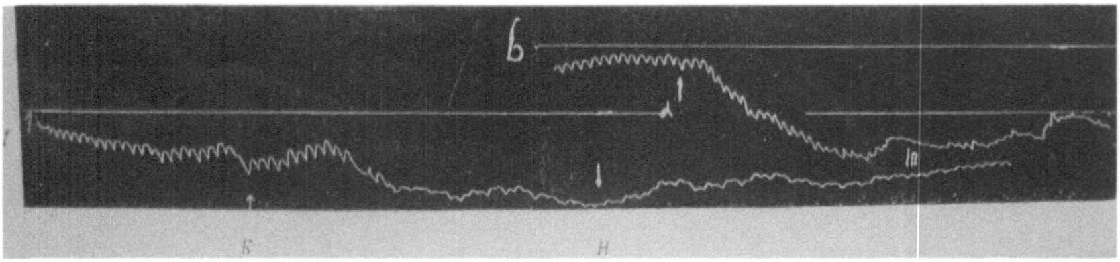

Figure 7 Alberto Olivo's Plethysmogram

In: Cesare Lombroso and Augusto Guido Bianchi, *Il caso Olivo* (Milan: Libreria editrice nazionale, 1905).

Figure 8 Riva-Rocci sphygmomanometer
Licence: Attribution 4.0 International (CC BY 4.0)
Credit: Riva-Rocci's spygmomanometer in use. Collection. Source: Wellcome Collection.

and he often did not understand that to introduce quotations to comment on tragic events sounded ridiculous.[42] According to Lombroso, Olivo was convinced that he was possessed of great ability, and it was this 'inutile parvenza e coscienza della genialità che forma il substrato di quello che io chiamo *mattoidismo*' [pointless semblance and awareness of genius that

[42] Ibid., p. 36.

forms the substratum of what I call *mattoidism*].[43] An egoist and ego-centred man, for Olivo, any disruption to his well-being was experienced as the fault of others:[44] this was a particularly important point for an understanding of his personality and his reaction on finding that his wife was watering down the wine, for example. Lombroso reported that Olivo wrote the following:

> Gli insulti [...] non lacerano le mani, né lascian traccia. Invece l'atto di annacquare, di battezzare il vino, così [in]significante e ridicolo in apparenza, era, all'opposto, più grave di quello che a tutta prima non sembri; grave pel movente e per le conseguenze.
>
> Infatti. Il movente: una sete, una passione morbosa per il vino; passione volgare e indegna di una donna che si rispetta; dannosa nei riguardi della salute e del carattere; pericolosa per la pace e la quiete domestica.
>
> [Insults [...] do not rent the hands, nor leave a trace. Instead, the act of watering down, christening the wine, seemingly so [in]significant and ridiculous, was, on the contrary, more serious than it might initially seem; serious both in terms of motive and consequences.
>
> Indeed. The motive: a thirst, a morbid passion for wine; the vulgar and undignified passion of a respectable woman; harmful to health and to character; dangerous for domestic peace and calm].[45]

Notwithstanding Olivo's focus on Beccaro's passion for wine and the related appraisal of the vulgarity and unsuitability of such a passion in a woman,[46] Lombroso's wider argument was that Olivo lacked a sense of morality. This was evident in multiple facts: the dismemberment and disposal of his wife's body without hesitation; his bragging to certain strangers that he was 'quell'Olivo omicida' [that Olivo, the murderer]; the 'facilità del suo matrimonio con donna posseduta da altri' [ease of his marriage to a woman already

---

43 Ibid., p. 37.

44 Ibid.

45 Ibid.

46 In antiquity, wine consumption was forbidden to women. The *ius osculi*, the right of kiss, was a right that allowed a man to kiss a member of his *familia* to ascertain that she had not drank. See, Eva Cantarella, *L'ambiguo malanno: condizione e immagine della donna nell'antichità greca e romana* (Rome: Editori riuniti, 1981), p. 146; Carla Fayer, *La familia romana: aspetti giuridici ed antiquari*, 3 vols (Rome: "L'Erma" di Bretschneider, 1994), II, pp. 394–95. This understanding of wine and its use by women could have been elaborated by Olivo for pretending to be an intellectual with a wide knowledge of the classics.

possessed by others].[47] The 'sense of morality' that Lombroso expected of Olivo, and that indeed was expected of any man of the time, was the shared confirmation of a masculinity inextricably linked with a concept of honour. As Pierre Bourdieu eloquently highlighted, 'the principle of the conservation and increase of honour, remains indissociable, tacitly at least, from physical virility, in particular through the attestation of sexual potency – deflowering of the bride, abundant male offspring, etc – which are expected of a "real" man'.[48] So, whilst 'a real man' could have sexual intercourse with a woman 'already possessed by others', a marriage to such a woman was unacceptable, or at least not without due consideration.

Overall, Lombroso was convinced that Olivo had killed his wife because he was epileptic. That is, he claimed epilepsy to be the endogenous cause of the crime, but he noted too that there was also an exogenous cause – namely, the victim herself, who was 'scioperata, libertina, bevona, litigiosa, impulsiva, con tutti i caratteri di una prostituta' [lazy, libertine, hard-drinking, quarrelsome, impulsive, with all the characteristics of a prostitute].[49] Essentially, this means that whilst being epileptic was a factor over which no control could be exerted, the victim's behaviour *could* have been different. In Lombroso's opinion, then, had Beccaro behaved in the correct and expected way for a respectable woman, she would not have been murdered; and since Olivo could not be considered responsible because of his epilepsy, Beccaro, instead, had full responsibility for her own death.

47 Ibid., pp. 38–39.

48 Bourdieu, *Masculine Domination*, p. 12.

49 Lombroso and Bianchi, *Il caso Olivo*, p. 53.

CHAPTER 8

The second trial

The public prosecutor appealed the verdict, and the Supreme Court ordered a new trial to be held. On 20 July 1904, Alberto Olivo was again arrested. *La Stampa*'s reporter recorded attending Olivo's home shortly before his arrest and found him smiling, albeit also rather worried. At six o'clock that evening, when the police arrived to arrest him, a small crowd of journalists and members of the public was already there. Olivo greeted them with a smile, murmuring 'con tono quasi beffardo: - Guarda quanta gente!' [almost mockingly: 'Look at all the people!'].[1] As soon as Olivo was taken away by the police, the crowd began shouting, '*Abbasso Olivo!*' [Down with Olivo!] and other animated comments.[2]

The new trial of Alberto Olivo began in Bergamo on 19 November 1904 and was even more of a spectacle than the first. Accompanying the testimony of Olivo and the multiple witnesses was irony, smiles, and laughter; there were insinuations and things provocatively left unsaid about Beccaro, endorsing the status of Olivo as victim and repeatedly shifting the blame onto Beccaro. The expert witnesses were also part of the performance: famous scientists like Cesare Lombroso presented their assessments, relishing the platform to display their knowledge and advance their theories. The reporting of the journalists played into this context, narrativising the trial's reports and resting heavily on stereotypes and gendered expectations.

1 *La Stampa*, 20 July 1904, p. 3.
2 Ibid.

The first day of the second trial was the preliminaries. Olivo was asked to confirm his identity, described thus in *La Stampa*:

> Il presidente domanda: – Voi siete Alberto Olivo?
> – Alberto Olivo – risponde l'accusato – fu Luigi e fu Luigia Teia, nato a Udine nel 1856.
> – Vedovo senza figli? – domanda il presidente.
> – Sissignore – risponde l'accusato e un sorriso malinconico sfiora le sue labbra.
>
> [The President of the Court asks: 'You are Alberto Olivo?'
> 'Alberto Olivo', replies the accused, 'of the late Luigi and the late Luigia Teia, born in Udine in 1856'.
> 'Widower, no children?' asks the president.
> 'Yes, sir', replies the accused, and a melancholy smile brushes his lips].[3]

In addition to the evocation of the melancholy smile, *La Stampa*'s reporter further humanised Olivo, preparing the ground for empathy, by noting that Olivo had recognised him in court and had asked him not to misrepresent him in his newspaper, observing that *La Stampa* had been harsh with him on the first verdict.[4] In this context, Olivo was depicted as a person with simple dreams (i.e., to have had children)[5] and the same simple desire as any other person to be represented fairly. The description of minor details served the same aim, rendering the defendant ordinary, just like anyone else, who had only extraordinarily become a murderer. *La Stampa* commented that in Bergamo, almost everyone was in favour of Olivo, adding a parenthetical question mark – '(?)' – after this sentence. Indeed, the newspaper explained that the ruling of the Supreme Court that reversed the judgement in Milan 'lo ha reso qui, purtroppo, simpatico!' [has unfortunately made him likeable here!].[6]

---

3 *La Stampa*, 20 November 1904, p. 3.

4 Ibid.

5 On this point, *I grandi processi illustrati* had commented that 'la sterilità dell'uno o dell'altro o di tutti due assieme non consentì loro il frutto che il matrimonio sancisce e cementa' [the sterility of one or of the other or of both together did not allow them to have the fruit that establishes and cements a marriage], *I grandi processi illustrati*, 1904, I, p. 5).

6 *La Stampa*, 20 November 1904, p. 3.

Figure 9 *I grandi processi illustrati*, 3 (1904)

Ernestina Beccaro

Image reproduced by kind permission of Ministry of Culture – Pinacoteca di Brera – Biblioteca Braidense, Milan. Further reproduction or duplication by any means is prohibited.

La Stampa's journalist reported that he had been informed by a reliable source that Olivo was convinced that he would be acquitted again, saying that, following this, 'nessuno più oserà tenergli rancore' [no one will dare hold a grudge against him anymore].[7] Furthermore, Olivo was reported to be maintaining a healthy appetite in prison and was complaining that he was not being given as much paper as he would like in order to do his writing. On his release, indeed, he had plans to publish a work of his own.[8] Furthermore, it was expected that the trial would arouse a great deal of interest, given that not only would there be experts of the calibre of Lombroso present, but also photographic evidence of Beccaro's remains, which had made a great impression on the jurors in Milan, was to be shown.[9] During the trial, *Il Secolo*'s journalist wrote that he had a seat near Olivo and took the opportunity to observe him closely:

> presenta spiccatissimi, anche agli occhi del profano, i pochi segni somatici del criminaloide, riscontrati dal Lombroso. Fronte altissima e sfuggente, con rughe profonde, e sproporzionata tra il cranio e la faccia. È abbastanza calmo, ma una leggera convulsione ne altera di quando in quando i lineamenti. Sembrano lampi di epilessia larvata
>
> [very distinctively, even to the eyes of a layman, he presents the key somatic signs of the criminaloid, discovered by Lombroso. Very high, receding forehead, deeply lined, and a disproportion between skull size and face. He is quite calm, but a slight convulsion occasionally alters his features. It looks like flashes of larval epilepsy].[10]

On 23 November 1904, Fortunata Beccaro, one of Ernestina's sisters, was present in court. The newspapers did not report her testimony; instead, they reported that she was 'una giovanetta bruna, con due occhietti vivi e piacenti. Veste modestamente senza cappello' [a young brunette, with lively and pleasant eyes. She dresses modestly, with no hat].[11]

The cross-examination of Olivo saw him pointing out minor details and seeking to defend himself not from the accusation of murder, which he readily admitted, but rather from the possession of characteristics such as

---

7 *La Stampa*, 20 November 1904, p. 3.
8 Ibid.
9 Ibid.
10 *Il Secolo*, 22–23 November 1904, p. 2.
11 *La Stampa*, 23 November 1904, p. 3.

'sordida avarizia' [sordid avarice], in order to contest accusations of premeditation: 'mi premeva – dice – sfatare quest'accusa per mostrare che io non ho ucciso mia moglie per avarizia, per liberarmi di un grave carico che pesava sul mio bilancio; e quindi non ho premeditato il delitto' ['I was keen', he says, 'to dispel this accusation, to show that I did not kill my wife out of greed, or to rid myself of a heavy burden on my budget; and therefore I did not premeditate the crime'].[12] He then described the night of the murder. Ernestina had fallen asleep next to him: 'La contemplai, pareva un angelo, dormendo… E sveglia così demonio. Feci per dormire, ma soffro un ronzio in seguito a congestione cerebrale' [I gazed at her; she looked like an angel as she slept… Yet such a devil when she was awake. I tried to sleep, but I was suffering from a ringing in the ears as a result of cerebral congestion].[13] Then he woke up and asked her to prepare him a lemonade. She refused and additionally insulted him. He saw 'una nube rossa, come un vento' [a red mist, like a wind], and killed her.[14]

He was then cross-examined on his past life. *Il Secolo* argued that 'dalla esposizione fatta risulta che lavorò sempre come un cane e risparmiò come la formica' [from the expositions given, it seems he always worked like a dog and saved like an ant].[15] This observation, along with other similar comments made by other newspapers, contributed to the construction of a positive image of Olivo as a hard worker and a careful saver with a precise view of how money should be spent, an image that contrasted with the picture of the victim as a spendthrift and ignorant of the effort by which the money she spent had been earned.

Olivo was also questioned by Lombroso. Lombroso asked him about mathematics. Olivo responded that he was unwilling to talk about his study, since it was possible he had made a mathematical breakthrough he did not yet want made public.[16] Later, there was a dispute over the reading by a court clerk of a sonnet Olivo had written, the 'burocratica lettura' [bureaucratic reading] causing him pain.[17] What may have seemed immaterial comments

---

12 Ibid.
13 *Il Secolo*, 22–23 November 1904, p. 3.
14 Ibid.
15 Ibid.
16 Ibid.
17 Ibid.

about Olivo's knowledge of mathematics, or the pain the clumsy reading of his sonnet provoked in him, contributed instead to an understanding and construction of the figures of both Beccaro and Olivo and the context of their cohabitation – Olivo, again, the cultured and sensitive soul; Beccaro, basic, rude, and instinctive.

The ensuing days of the second trial were similar to those of the first, as far as witness testimonies and topics of discussion were concerned. However, the cross-examinations and the newspaper reports were even more emphatic in their stance: namely, that Beccaro's behaviour was reprehensible in every way, and Olivo was therefore not culpable. For example, *Il Giornale d'Italia* opened one of its articles by claiming that every concierge of every building where Olivo and Beccaro had lived had confirmed that Beccaro secretly provided service to Cesare Landriani, who was believed to be her lover.[18] Moreover, without exception, everyone confirmed that 'la Beccaro era di carattere leggerissimo' [Beccaro was a very superficial character].[19]

Cesare Landriani once again served to tarnish Beccaro's reputation: *La Tribuna*, for example, entitled 'Un probabile amante della Beccaro' [A probable lover of Beccaro] the paragraph about his testimony.[20] His testimony, whilst not actually suggesting anything deplorable, nonetheless was presented as though there was something equivocal between them, and this was met with nudges and smiles. He said that he had met Beccaro when she was working as a maid for the Mottas, and she had told him that she was short of money as a result of expenses her husband had incurred in setting up their house. For this reason, Landriani took her on to do some cleaning for a few hours a day. Asked about Beccaro's behaviour, he denied 'che la Beccaro bevesse e bestemiasse. Ammette solo che era un po' pettegola' [that Beccaro drank and swore. He would say only that she was a bit of a gossip].[21] He was pressed to say if he had any romantic feelings for her, but he firmly denied this, adding that at certain points he had asked her to stop working for him, but she had elected to continue nonetheless. *La Stampa* reported that Olivo's lawyer continued to ask embarrassing questions of Landriani, who they described as 'un

18 *Il Giornale d'Italia*, 27 November 1904, p. 3.
19 Ibid.
20 *La Tribuna*, 27 November 1904, p. 4.
21 *La Stampa*, 27 November 1904, p. 3.

bell'uomo, dai capelli brizzolati, vestito correttamente in finanziera, elegante nel gesto e gaudente nell'aspetto' [a handsome man, with greying hair, well-dressed in a frock coat, elegant in manner and a bon viveur in appearance].[22] This focus on his appearance insinuated that a woman whose virtue was already greatly in doubt could plainly not be attending the house of such a man just for the sake of cleaning and that Landriani, 'a bon viveur' himself, undoubtedly would have enjoyed the pleasures that Beccaro could provide.

La Tribuna commented on his testimony by writing that he was so vague in his answers that 'i sospetti dell'antica relazione si mutano ormai per tutti in certezza' [the suspicions of the ancient relationship now turn into certainty for everyone].[23]

The concierges of the building where Landriani had his apartment were also questioned. They commented that, even when Beccaro was no longer employed by Landriani, she still went to his house at least once a month. Olivo's lawyer asked, with heavy irony, if Beccaro was going there to deliver a service, and one of the concierges said that she had not been in the apartment to see for herself. The interrogation ended 'fra i sorrisi ironici del pubblico' [amid mocking smiles from the audience].[24]

The cross-examination of Antonio Colombo, 'il famoso gobbo di cui s'è tanto parlato' [the famous hunchback about whom so much has been said],[25] was welcomed with equal curiosity and was described in similar detail in the newspapers, even though he merely provided the same account he had during the trial in Milan. *La Stampa* reported that the courtroom was silent and attentive during his testimony, adding that Colombo, like Olivo, was an accountant, and observing that 'decisamente la Ernestina era tenera per questa professione' [Ernestina definitely had a soft spot for this profession].[26]

The increasing intensity of such jokes and mockery contributed to an impression that the verdict had already been made, insofar as the trial had become about Beccaro's respectability rather than the trial of a man for a murder.

---

22 Ibid.
23 *La Tribuna*, 27 November 1904, p. 4.
24 *La Stampa*, 27 November 1904, p. 3.
25 Ibid.
26 Ibid.

The description of the trial continued with the testimony of Rosa De Vecchi, the concierge of one of the buildings where Olivo and Beccaro had lived. She said that the couple had been evicted because of Beccaro's poor behaviour and Olivo's anger. Specifically, there had been men coming back and forth to their home, to the extent that Beccaro's flat had virtually become a brothel; 'ben inteso' – she reckoned – 'ciò, quando non c'era il marito' [of course, this was when the husband was not there].[27] *La Stampa* reported that these words created a ripple through the audience, who were further impressed when the witness added that, when Olivo's wife brought home money, Olivo did not chastise her for her affairs, but when she came home empty-handed, he did.[28] Another witness, a neighbour of the couple, said that he himself had forbidden his sister to go out with Beccaro since her behaviour in the streets was not respectable, stating that 'L'Ernestina era una donna leggera, l'Olivo una buona persona' [Ernestina was a shallow woman, Olivo a good person].[29]

Newspaper reports in the following days continued to cover the couple's life and behaviour. For example, Ernesta Crasini, the teacher Beccaro had found for herself, recounted that Olivo had turned up at her house one day and, in a very imperious tone, had ordered her to cease the lessons she was giving Beccaro.[30] Other witnesses confirmed that Beccaro was a frivolous woman, including further detail that the court could only hear behind closed doors. *La Stampa* reported that one of these witnesses said things about Beccaro 'che qui è impossibile ripetere, ma che lasciano un'impressione enorme nell'animo di chi le ha udite' [that are impossible to repeat here, but which leave a great impression on the mind of those that hear them].[31] The same journalist concluded by noting that he had had the opportunity to read the poem Olivo had written in jail: entitled 'Il Natale del Re' [The King's Birth], the poem was dedicated to the Prince of Savoy and written in the style of Alessandro Manzoni's *The Fifth of May*.

Il Giornale d'Italia reported on the testimony of Francesco Vignolo, next-door neighbour, along with his wife, to Olivo and Beccaro. Vignolo said

27 Ibid.
28 Ibid.
29 Ibid.
30 Ibid.
31 Ibid.

that Beccaro complained that her husband, Olivo, had no passion for her, other than:

> quella brutale, al cui soddisfacimento pretendeva che la moglie si prestasse a tutte le ore. Una sera che il teste si ritirava dallo studio, salendo le scale di casa, udì la Beccaro che discorrendo con la sua signora si lamentava del marito in termini così turpi e volgari, che egli sentì il dovere di accompagnarla fino all'uscio della propria abitazione per significarle che le proibiva di tenere un linguaggio così sconveniente davanti alla propria moglie, ai bambini e alla domestica
>
> [the brutal [passion], to the satisfaction of which he expected his wife to give herself at any time of the day or night. One evening, when the witness was leaving his study, going up the stairs of his house, he heard Beccaro talking to his own wife, and complaining about her husband in such obscene and vulgar terms that he felt it was his duty to march her back to her own front door, to make it understood that he forbade her from using such inappropriate language in front of his wife, his children, and his maid].[32]

In the hearings that followed, attended by 'una folla enorme, composta in gran parte da signore' [an enormous crowd mainly composed of ladies],[33] other witnesses continued to testify on various matters, including a neighbour who said that she had seen Olivo watering his plants straight after the crime, another who maintained they had good reason to believe that Beccaro was a dishonest woman, and the shoemaker who explained that she wore out a lot of shoes.[34]

---

32 *Il Giornale d'Italia*, 29 November 1904, p. 3.

33 *La Tribuna*, 30 November 1904, p. 4.

34 *La Stampa*, 2 December 1904, p. 3.

CHAPTER 9

'Science'

On 2 December 1904, the trial was coming to an end, with experts called to give their opinion on Alberto Olivo.

Il Giornale d'Italia opened its article by asking who Alberto Olivo really was:

> Ha avuto finalmente la parola la scienza su Alberto Olivo, per portare i suoi lumi sopra un problema così oscuro quale è quello dell'esame di un uomo che pare circondato dal più strano mistero…è egli un uomo normale che ha agito sotto un impeto d'ira; è un semi irresponsabile cui la grave provocazione produce scatti assai più forti e pericolosi che non nei normali; oppure è un irresponsabile epilettico che ha agito sotto l'influenza di un accesso al quale egli non poteva sottrarsi?
>
> [Science has finally had its say on Alberto Olivo, shedding its light on as obscure a problem as that of the examination of a man who appears surrounded in the strangest mystery…. [I]s he a normal man who acted under an impulse of anger? [A] person of diminished responsibility in whom serious provocation produces a much stronger and more dangerous response than in normal people? [O]r is he an epileptic, without responsibility, who acted under the influence of an uncontrollable fit?].[1]

Experts for the prosecution explained why Olivo should be considered responsible for the murder he had committed.[2] The first to speak was a certain Professor Raggi, who excluded Olivo from having any mental illness or neuroses, including epilepsy; indeed, notwithstanding Olivo's assertion of having been a premature baby born at just seven months, and consequently of fragile constitution, Raggi observed that as an adult, Olivo had been able

1 *Il Giornale d'Italia*, 4 December 1904, p. 2.
2 *La Stampa*, 2 December 1904, p. 3.

to fulfil his military service, so he must not have any medical issues. Raggi further contended that the hereditary argument was also not reliable: there was no precise information about any supposed cerebral congestion, and this had only been mentioned in a letter of 1881, where Olivo had described an incipient congestion, but this was so long ago as to be scarcely linkable to the murder. Professor Raggi noted differences with the first trial, such as Olivo's greater facility to defend himself, and went on to declare that Olivo was entirely responsible for the murder he had committed, defining him as an egoist of mediocre intelligence, mean, and presumptuous.[3] *La Stampa* reported that Olivo 'ride ironicamente scrollando il capo. Di tanto in tanto chiude gli occhi e appoggia la testa ai ferri della gabbia; sembra cercare nel freddo del metallo un refrigerio all'ardere della sua mente' [laughs ironically and shakes his head. From time to time, he closes his eyes and rests his head on the bars of the dock; he seems to be searching for relief in the coldness of the metal from the burning of his mind].[4]

A second assessment was provided by a certain Doctor Venanzio. *Il Giornale d'Italia* pointed out that this expert claimed that Olivo's marriage proposal had not in fact been the base speculative act described during the trial in Milan, but rather had been an act of generosity inspired by passion.[5] Venanzio considered Olivo's crime an impulsive crime, committed in the throes of impassionment due to intense provocation. He concluded that Olivo was responsible for his crime, even though many cruel circumstances had contributed to its context.[6]

Then it was the turn of the third prosecution expert witness, a Professor Binda, director of Milan's Institute for Forensic Medicine. He spoke extensively about Olivo's physical and psychological characteristics, recognising certain degenerative traits and a number of functional disorders of limited importance. He also suggested that it was an error to consider Olivo impulsive. On the contrary, his inhibitory powers were neither lacking nor significantly weakened; he was inherently reactive, but he was able to weigh his actions. As far as his crime was concerned, specifically, this could not be linked to epilepsy, since Olivo lacked multiple features of this condition.[7]

---

3 Ibid.

4 *La Stampa*, 2 December 1904, p. 3.

5 *Il Giornale d'Italia*, 4 December 1904, p. 2.

6 *La Stampa*, 2 December 1904, p. 3.

7 Ibid.

Binda defended Olivo's moral sense, and, given what Olivo had managed to tolerate of his wife's constant provocations, Binda was drawn to conclude that in fact Olivo was not at all impulsive by nature: 'anche l'uomo il più regolare e normale ha una data forza di resistenza oltre la quale scatta' [even the most regular normative man has a given level of tolerance beyond which he snaps].[8] He agreed that Olivo acted only after sustained and serious provocation and argued that, under existing law, acting in the heat of anger, as Olivo had, was considered action within mitigating circumstances. Such a circumstance clouded the balance of the mind, and the effect of this state of passion should not be confused with insanity.[9] He also added that at first he thought that the marriage between Olivo and Beccaro was a 'vile mercato' [vile trade], while he was then convinced that it was an act of generosity and love by Olivo towards a disgraced person.[10] It is easy to infer, again, the shifting of the blame to Beccaro, who emerges as a completely negative figure; by contrast with Olivo, who is commended for managing to resist the pressure of her provocations for so long.

After the prosecution's expert witnesses, attention turned to the experts for the defence: it was 'una battaglia poderosa tra la vecchia scuola psichiatrica e la nuova scuola positivista dell'antropologia criminale' [a powerful battle between the old psychiatric school and the new positivist school of criminal anthropology].[11] These were Cesare Lombroso and two of his colleagues, Giuseppe Antonini and Edoardo Audenino.[12]

Lombroso took the stand and began by noting his amazement at seeing the previous speakers presenting evidence established using methods and instruments from fifty years earlier, observing that they could not be

8 *Il Giornale d'Italia*, 4 December 1904, p. 2.

9 *La Stampa*, 2 December 1904, p. 3.

10 *Corriere della Sera*, 2 December 1904, p. 3.

11 *Avanti!*, 3 December 1904, p. 3. For an interesting overview of new sciences in courts, see, Simone Baral, 'Il frenologo in tribunale. Nota per una ricerca sul caso italiano', *Criminocorpus, Folie et justice de l'Antiquité à l'époque contemporaine* (2016) [accessed 30 April 2024].

12 Giuseppe Antonini (1864–1938) was an Italian psychiatrist. Born in Milan, he graduated in Turin, where he went on to work with Cesare Lombroso. He subsequently practiced as a psychiatrist in other locations in Italy, including, amongst others, Udine, Voghera, and Bergamo. His publications include *I precursori di Cesare Lombroso* (Turin: Bocca, 1900).

interested in establishing the true psychic physiognomy of the accused.[13] He then explained that his assessment would be divided into three parts: the first presented by Professor Antonini, the second by Doctor Audenino, and the third, he would present himself.

Antonini began by explaining that Olivo was not a fraud but rather worthy of belief. This could be seen from the fact that everything he said was confirmed by witnesses. Antonini went on to maintain that Olivo committed the crime in a moment of blackout: 'la sua condotta, il suo contegno ce lo mostrano come colui che non si sente responsabile' [his conduct, his behaviour shows us as someone who doesn't feel himself to be responsible [for what he has done]].[14]

Where Olivo's alcoholic father was concerned, Antonini believed that it was 'lodevole amor filiale' [laudable filial love] that had made Olivo try to hide his father's condition;[15] but Antonini was convinced, because of research he had conducted in Udine, that Olivo's father genuinely had been an alcoholic.[16] 'La nube rossa, il soffio di vento, la ispecie di incoscienza' [the red cloud, the breath of wind, the particular type of unconsciousness], under which Olivo had acted and by which he had felt himself overwhelmed,[17] were all due to the taint of genetic inheritance, since 'l'alcolismo degli ascendenti… è quasi sempre causa di nervosismo nei discendenti' [alcoholism in ancestors… almost always causes neuroticism in descendants].[18] Furthermore, the fact that he was born at just seven months gestation would have contributed to his neuroticism, making him more fragile.[19] There was evidence of material consequences throughout his life: for example, as a child, after a dark dream at night, he would sometimes wake up to find himself lying outside in the soil.[20] Even the instance of his sunstroke was a manifestation of his epileptic tendency; indeed, he had related that on the morning of that attack he had been unable to wake up. All this contributed to a circumstance in which, at

---

13 *La Stampa*, 2 December 1904, p. 3.
14 *Il Giornale d'Italia*, 4 December 1904, p. 2.
15 *La Stampa*, 2 December 1904, p. 3.
16 *Il Giornale d'Italia*, 4 December 1904, p. 2.
17 *La Stampa*, 2 December 1904, p. 3.
18 *Il Giornale d'Italia*, 4 December 1904, p. 2.
19 Ibid.
20 *La Stampa*, 2 December 1904, p. 3.

the time of his crime, Olivo was not aware of what was happening. On the night of the crime, Olivo had been under pressure from constant irritation and was consequently in a state of greater emotional arousal than usual. This was demonstrated by the fact that Olivo had fallen asleep in the kitchen from seven to nine o'clock that evening.[21] 'Non emerse forse che quando si svegliò egli non ricordava più il primo litigio?' [Did it not emerge that when he woke up, he no longer remembered the first argument?], reiterated Antonini.[22]

The second report was presented by Doctor Audenino, who aimed to demonstrate 'con le tecniche della scienza, che l'Olivo è un degenerato' [with the techniques of science, that Olivo is a degenerate].[23] Audenino set out how, in the study he had undertaken with Lombroso, they had not limited the investigation to Olivo's profile and cranial contouring but had sought to deepen the analysis to include the interior of the organism.[24] Olivo presented with some degenerative anomalies: he was prematurely bald; he had exaggerated frontal wrinkles; and the somatic measurements reported by Professor Raggi were inconsistent with those found by Professor Lombroso and his team.[25] Rather, reported Audenino:

> il cranio dell'Olivo è di capacità quasi normale, il lato destro però prevale sul sinistro, e nella parte superiore del cranio v'è asimmetria; lo stesso dicasi del volto. Questa è caratteristica degli epilettici. L'occhio destro è più largo che il sinistro. Anche gli orecchi dell'Olivo sono asimmetrici, paiono appartenenti a due individui diversi. Nel collo si osservano contrazioni vivissime come nei cavalli e questo è appunto un carattere degenerativo.
>
> Il torace è asimmetrico; l'arto sinistro prevale sul destro.
>
> Vi sono poi altre caratteristiche, fra cui la grandissima agilità, ciò dimostra proprio come l'Olivo abbia tutti i requisiti dell'epilettico.
>
> Il campo visivo è asimmetrico, con lacune che vennero riscontrate dal prof. Ottolenghi di Roma, negli epilettici.
>
> [Olivo's skull is almost normal in capacity; however the right side is dominant over the left, and in the upper part of the skull there is asymmetry; the face has the same characteristics. This is characteristic of an epileptic. The right eye is larger than the left. Olivo's ears are also asymmetrical; they appear to belong to two different

---

21 Ibid.

22 Ibid.

23 *Il Giornale d'Italia*, 4 December 1904, p. 2.

24 *La Stampa*, 2 December 1904, p. 3.

25 Ibid.

> individuals. Very lively contractions can be seen in the neck, as we see in horses, and this is indeed a degenerative characteristic.
>
> The chest is asymmetrical; the left limb is dominant over the right.
>
> Then there are other characteristics, including great agility, which demonstrates how the Olivo has all the requisites of an epileptic.
>
> The field of vision is asymmetrical, with evidence of the gaps found in epileptics by Professor Ottolenghi of Rome].[26]

The following day, it was Cesare Lombroso's turn to speak. He prefaced his analysis with the information that the term 'anomalous' referred to a person who was formed differently from others, and that 'alienated' referred to someone who acted in a way contrary to the way others act.[27] According to Lombroso, Olivo was 'anomalo ed epilettico insieme' [both anomalous and epileptic].[28] He asserted that 'l'eredità morbosa in lui non solo è diretta da madre isterica, e da padre beone, ma ha lunghi sprazzi che si estendono ai nonni, agli zii, alle sorelle, e a cui si aggiunge l'innesto isterico, così ricco fattore di genio, di delitto o di pazzia' [the morbid hereditariness in him derives not only from a mother who was a hysteric and a drunkard father, but exists in long glimpses that extend to his grandparents, uncles, sisters, and to which is joined the hysterical connection, such a rich factor of genius, crime or madness].[29]

As for the organic anomalies, Lombroso contended that there were so many of these that it was hard to know where to start. They corresponded to atavism and would have been enough to characterise not one but ten epileptics.[30] The eye alone, for example, contained no fewer than eight anomalies. But the most complete and exaggerated anomaly was the double asymmetry due to the unbalanced development of the right and left sides of the head, chest, face, eyes, and jaw.[31]

As far as Olivo's intelligence was concerned, the criminologist considered his great knowledge of languages, literature, mathematics, and his eloquence to be astonishing and impressive. However, for all this facility, Olivo had

---

26 *La Stampa*, 2 December 1904, p. 3.
27 *Il Giornale d'Italia*, 4 December 1904, p. 2.
28 Ibid.
29 *La Stampa*, 3 December 1904, p. 3.
30 Ibid.
31 Ibid.

failed to pass his exams at school, and in his work had only managed to gain a low-status role with a negligible wage.[32] Lombroso suggested that the appearance of genius but without substance behind it in fact forms the basis of the mattoid, even more emphatically when coupled with a boundless sense of one's own merit.[33]

Il Giornale d'Italia also reported that Lombroso proposed that there was also a tendency in the mattoid to write poetry and obsessively study mathematics. The newspaper wrote that his mattoidism was also evident in the fact that Olivo ended his account of the murder by quoting Dante: 'e caddi come l'uom cui sonno piglia' [and I fell like a man whom sleep has seized].[34] *Il Giornale d'Italia* argues that with this quotation, 'ci sta come Pilato col Credo' [he is there like Pilate with the Creed], another verse, 'e caddi come corpo morto cade' [and then I fell as a dead body falls], would have been more appropriate.[35]

At one point in Lombroso's speech, Olivo intervened by saying that the date of a poem he had written had been wrongly stated and that Lombroso was uttering a series of 'corbellerie e falsità' [nonsense and falsehoods]. Lombroso smiled at this intervention and commented: 'ecco un'altra prova della sua pazzia!' [here is further proof of his madness!].[36]

Amidst the report of Lombroso's evaluation, *Il Giornale d'Italia* added that Olivo had '[una] straordinaria eccitabilità ed irascibilità' [[an] extraordinary excitability and irascibility], and that this had been confirmed by Olivo's employer, Chevalier Richard, who said that he was so aggressive in his business communications as to have had to be reprimanded.[37]

Olivo was also deemed to be 'morbosamente ottuso' [morbidly obtuse], evidenced by his marriage to a prostitute, his excessive tolerance of her exploits, and his declarations of himself as an honest man.[38] The use of the word 'prostitute' here marked the definitive point of no return in the judgement of Beccaro and her life. Further, it encapsulated the perceptions of society, and

32 *Il Giornale d'Italia*, 4 December 1904, p. 2.
33 *La Stampa*, 3 December 1904, p. 3.
34 Dante, *The Divine Comedy*: Inferno III, 136.
35 *Il Giornale d'Italia*, 4 December 1904, p. 2.
36 Ibid.
37 *Il Giornale d'Italia*, 4 December 1904, p. 2.
38 *La Stampa*, 3 December 1904, p. 3.

its scientists, about marriage with an individual without a good reputation: it was inconceivable, unless there was some sort of morbidity to explain it, as, for example, in the case of Olivo, possessed of morbid thick-headedness and all the other characteristics just enumerated by Lombroso.

The criminologist continued with a claim that vanity was in fact the predominant characteristic in Olivo, to the extent that during both trials, in Milan and Bergamo, he had been more concerned about his reputation as a man of letters than the possibility of being judged a murderer. This was particularly in evidence in the epigraph in his autobiography, where he again quotes Dante from the *Divine Comedy*: 'e se 'l mondo sapesse il cor ch'elli ebbe | [...] | assai lo loda, e più lo loderebbe' [and if the world knew the heart he had | [...] | it would praise him much, and would praise him more].[39] But the most salient characteristic of all was his contradictoriness: in Olivo, found Lombroso, lyricism contrasted with unaccountable baseness, having killed and butchered his wife, he had fond memories of her and dedicated ugly and passionate verses to her.[40] Moreover, in him, highly tenacious memory contrasted with frequent amnesia, lively intelligence with mattoid absurdity, and sincerity – one of his most notable characteristics – with the dissimulation of his illicit loves.[41]

Professor Lombroso concluded that Olivo did not show any sign of repentance, and was not even conscious of the evil he had brought.[42] He was driven to the crime by a combination of 'eredità etnica e morbosa' [ethnic and morbid inheritance],[43] resulting from an 'incrocio che è in lui di tre razze: italiana, albanese e greca' [crossbreed which is in him three races: Italian, Albanian and Greek],[44] and serious provocation due to the sustained insults from a 'moglie viziosa' [vicious wife]:[45] and therefore was acting under a state of mental ill health that deprived him of the awareness of his actions. During Lombro's presentation, Olivo suffered a sudden outburst. Addressing the jurors, he said, 'Mi mandino in galera, ma non permetto che mi si faccia

---

39 Dante, *The Divine Comedy*: Paradiso VI, 140–42.

40 *La Stampa*, 3 December 1904, p. 3.

41 Ibid.

42 *Il Giornale d'Italia*, 4 December 1904, p. 2.

43 *La Stampa*, 3 December 1904, p. 3.

44 *Il Giornale d'Italia*, 4 December 1904, p. 2.

45 Ibid.

passare per bugiardo' [They can send me to prison, but I will not allow myself to be made out to be a liar].[46]

The morning session ended with a declaration by all the experts that Olivo, despite everything, was not sufficiently dangerous that he should be detained in a mental hospital.[47]

During this session, the reporter for *La Stampa* obtained a five-minute interview with Olivo. In it, Olivo said he never would have believed a scientist like Lombroso could speak so much nonsense. He contested Lombroso's right to comment on his poetry, since Lombroso 'in materia è assolutamente ignorante' [is absolutely ignorant on that subject],[48] and further added that, in his opinion, Lombroso had not been completely in his right mind the day before.[49]

Then it was the turn of the lawyers for the civil party to argue that, when he committed the murder, Olivo was in full possession of his own will. Olivo lacked affectivity, had a desire for solitude, and also lacked moral sense: he was fully aware of Beccaro's behaviour and permitted this behaviour to continue. The lawyer concluded by saying that the judgement in fact required consideration not only of the poor victim herself, but also 'di tutta la società, dell'istituto della famiglia, del rispetto alle più sante tradizioni, dall'Olivo calpestate' [of the whole of society, the institution of the family, respect for the most holy traditions, all trampled over by Olivo].[50]

The Deputy Prosecutor believed that Olivo was not a run-of-the-mill individual. He again retraced a version of Olivo's history, demonstrating how, after being a good student, Olivo had become an excellent employee until, unfortunately for him, he found himself with Beccaro, herself 'naufraga della vita e pronta a darsi al primo venuto' [shipwrecked in life and ready to give herself to the first comer].[51] He outlined the union of these two very different individuals: the one cultured, albeit with an exaggerated opinion of himself, and the other ignorant and accustomed since childhood to doing

46 *La Stampa*, 3 December 1904, p. 3.
47 Ibid.
48 *La Stampa*, 4 December 1904, p. 3.
49 Ibid.
50 *La Stampa*, 6 December 1904, p. 3.
51 Ibid.

the bidding of others.[52] Olivo married Beccaro after living with her for a year, and 'dovette cedere ad un falso fascino, forse carnale, forse platonico' [had to give in to a false charm, perhaps carnal, perhaps platonic];[53] resigned to the life he had made, he just wanted to prevent his home from turning into a hell. The prosecutor believed that 'l'ira, da tanto tempo accumulata nel cuore dell'Olivo, divampò, ed egli uccise' [the anger, pooling for so long in Olivo's heart, flared up, and he killed].[54] He asked the jury to consider Olivo to be fully responsible, to exclude premeditation, but to consider serious provocation.[55]

After this speech, in a courtroom crowded as never before,[56] the lawyer for the defence made his statement. He claimed that public opinion had turned against the Milan verdict because the trial had not been followed carefully, or only through newspaper reports, which had not always been accurate:[57] 'tutti conoscevano gli atti d'accusa, ma non tutti avevano assistito alle testimonianze e alle prove dell'inferno in cui viveva l'Olivo' [everyone knew the indictments, but not everyone had witnessed the testimonies and the evidence of the hell in which Olivo lived].[58] *La Stampa* reported that the lawyer for the defence went on to applaud the Milanese jury: composed of the cream of Milan's citizens, he said, they had issued a fair verdict. By contrast, he found the acts of the Attorney General to have been illicit

52 Ibid.
53 Ibid.
54 Ibid.
55 Ibid.
56 *La Tribuna*, 6 December 1904, p. 3.
57 The notion of 'public opinion' started to emerge in the late seventeenth century. Its conceptualisation was further structured throughout time. In general terms, public opinion refers to attitudes, ideas, viewpoints, and reflects the prevalent sentiments and consensus that a segment of a community or society holds regarding specific topics, issues, events, people hold at a given time. For an analysis of public opinion, see the groundbreaking studies by Walter Lippmann, *L'opinione pubblica* (Rome: Donzelli, 2004 [1922]); Jürgen Habermas, *Storia e critica dell'opinione pubblica* (Rome: Laterza, 2000 [1962]). For a study on public opinion and the press in Italy, see Valerio Castronovo, ed., *La nascita dell'opinione pubblica in Italia. La stampa nella Torino del Risorgimento e capitale d'Italia (1848–1864)* (Rome-Bari: Laterza, 2004); Massimo M. Augello, Marco E. L. Guidi, Giovanni Pavanelli, eds, *Economia e opinione pubblica nell'Italia liberale: gli economisti e la stampa quotidiana* (Milan: FrancoAngeli, 2016).
58 *La Stampa*, 6 December 1904, p. 3.

and illegal.[59] He then set out Olivo's life, a man who married a woman not 'perduta, ma una tradita' [lost, but betrayed] by life,[60] saying it had helped to inspire the Milan verdict. Finally, he claimed that the Supreme Court's ruling had trampled on the law of nations and asked the jurors to rebel not against the law but to reinstate that rule of law that had been violated by the first ruling.[61] Olivo's behaviour following his first acquittal was also examined: 'preghiera e lavoro' [prayer and work],[62] he summarised, and concluded by asking the jurors to return a blank vote in protest against the Supreme Court's ruling, given that Olivo acted in a state of mental illness and was therefore not responsible for his actions.[63]

On 7 December 1904, it was the turn of the civil party to present its final conclusion. The lawyers went over the whole story again. *La Stampa* reported that Olivo listened attentively, 'con un sorrisetto sardonico, quasi di compatimento' [with a sardonic smile, almost of pity], and spoke every now and then in a low voice with his lawyers to provide them with arguments in response.[64] The lawyer concluded by claiming that Olivo had premeditated his wife's murder and was equipped with full responsibility at the time, although this responsibility could be attenuated by taking into account serious provocation. He ended by calling on the jurors for 'giustizia, e non verdetto' [justice, not a verdict].[65]

7 December was also the day of the verdict. *La Stampa* recorded the moment as follows:

> L'attesa nell'aula è enorme. Non vi è un posto vuoto; il pubblico è così stipato che il caldo è soffocante...Il presidente legge i quesiti. Sono le 10.15: nell'aula vi è un silenzio religioso.
>
> [The air of expectation in the room is enormous. No seat is unfilled; the audience is so packed in that the heat is suffocating.... The President reads out the counts. It is 10.15 a.m.: in the room there is a godly silence].[66]

---

59 Ibid.
60 *Corriere della Sera*, 7 December 1904, p. 3.
61 *La Stampa*, 6 December 1904, p. 3.
62 Ibid.
63 *La Stampa*, 6 December 1904, p. 3.
64 *La Stampa*, 7 December 1904, p. 3.
65 Ibid.
66 Ibid.

The President of the Court greeted all parties involved, who 'hanno scritto una bella pagina nella storia del Foro italiano, lottando nei diversi campi con tanta tenacia e tanto interesse pel trionfo della giustizia' [have inscribed a beautiful page into Italian Court history, battling through the diverse fields with such tenacity and so much interest in the triumph of justice].[67]

The President of the Court summarised the 'mattanza' [slaughter] of the case very clearly and, at 10.40 a.m., moved to explain the counts on which the jury were to pronounce. There were seven counts, compiled as follows:

> il 1° riguarda il fatto materiale; il 2° riguarda la irresponsabilità; il 3° riguarda se il colpevole ha ucciso a scopo di uccidere; il 4° se è colpevole d'aver invece semplicemente ferito; il 5° riguarda la premeditazione; il 6° la grave provocazione; il 7° la semi-infermità di mente.
>
> [the 1st concerns the material fact; the 2nd concerns irresponsibility; the 3rd concerns whether the perpetrator killed with the intent to kill; the 4th, if he is guilty instead of simply injury; the 5th concerns premeditation; the 6th, serious provocation; the 7th, partial insanity].[68]

The description of Olivo and of the wait to hear the verdict was described in such a way as to increase the tension: Olivo was 'nervosissimo, assiste a tutta la scena coll'aspetto di un uomo affranto, stanco; e quando, alle 10,45, il presidente lo fa ritirare, egli se ne va svelto, quasi anelasse di andarsene' [very nervous, he watches the whole scene with the appearance of a broken, tired man; and when, at 10.45 a.m., the President orders him to withdraw, he leaves quickly, almost as though he was longing to leave].[69]

Immediately afterwards, the jury withdrew to deliberate; meanwhile, 'nell'aula i commenti sono infiniti, l'ansia è dipinta sul volto di tutti' [in the room, the comments are endless, the anxiety is painted on everyone's faces].[70] Then the jurors re-entered the room. The nominated spokesperson for the jurors declared, his hand on his heart, that on the first count, material fact, the jurors had voted 'no' by majority, thereby excluding the possibility that Olivo had committed the material act, with a split of ten votes to two.[71]

---

67 Ibid.
68 Ibid.
69 Ibid.
70 Ibid.
71 Ibid.

Alberto Olivo was consequently ruled not guilty, and *La Stampa* commented that 'la Giurìa bergamasca ha voluto così protestare contro la sentenza della Cassazione, e il suo verdetto è accolto da frenetici applausi, che neanche il presidente, che scampanella a distesa, riesce a frenare' [the Bergamo jury wanted in this way to protest against the ruling of the Supreme Court, and its verdict was greeted by wild applause, which not even the President, ringing the bell, was able to stop].[72]

Olivo was readmitted into the room. *La Stampa* wrote:

> è pallidissimo. Tra il silenzio religioso, gli si legge il verdetto. Il presidente quindi pronunzia le sacramentali parole di assoluzione. L'Olivo ha uno scatto nervoso; sorride un po'; poi cade sulla panca, scoppiando in singhiozzi.
>
> Gli avvocati lo circondano, e tutti applaudono al verdetto dei giurati bergamaschi e dicono che questa lezione alla Cassazione è meritata.
>
> Gli avvocati difensori fanno uscire l'Olivo, che partirà alle 12,40 per Milano, libero, questa volta completamente.
>
> [he is very pale. Amid the religious silence, the verdict is read to him. The President then pronounces the sacramental words of absolution. Olivo has a nervous outburst; he smiles a little; then he falls onto the bench, bursting into sobs.
>
> The lawyers gather around him, all applauding the verdict of the Bergamo jury, and saying the Supreme Court deserved this lesson.
>
> The defence lawyers usher Olivo outside. He will leave at 12.40 p.m. for Milan, free, this time completely so].[73]

La Stampa also remarked on 'un fatto inaudito o incomprensibile' [an unheard of or incomprehensible event] that took place outside the Court: 'la folla segue la carrozza dove è salito l'Olivo, applaudendola; egli ringrazia!' [the crowd follows the coach that Olivo has got into, clapping it; he thanks them!].[74]

The day after, 8 December, *Avanti!* applauded unreservedly Olivo's acquittal, saying that 'la ragione di questa assoluzione è evidente non solo per le anormalità che presenta l'Olivo, ma perché i giurati di Bergamo sentirono l'anormalità del verdetto della Cassazione di Roma' [the reason for this acquittal is obvious not only because of the abnormalities Olivo presents, but because the Bergamo jurors felt the abnormality of the verdict of the

72 Ibid.
73 Ibid.
74 Ibid.

Supreme Court of Rome];[75] *Il Giornale d'Italia* reported that the verdict of the Bergamo jurors was 'la risposta allo svisamento della legge fatto dalla Cassazione di Roma' [the response to the distortion of the law effected by the Supreme Court of Rome];[76] *Corriere della Sera* commented that the verdict was due to the 'ingiustizia latente del provvedimento' [latent injustice of the measure] taken by the Supreme Court;[77] and *La Tribuna* wrote about a 'coraggiosa protesta contro la sentenza della Cassazione' [courageous protest against the Supreme Court ruling].[78] *L'illustrazione italiana* contended that

> A Milano è stato uno sproposito; ma a Bergamo è stato un falso. Giacché ai signori giurati si domandava: ha l'Olivo ucciso la moglie? Ed essi hanno risposto... non un no propriamente, ché sarebbe stato un falso giuramento... ma con tante schede bianche, che equivalgono. Infatti l'assassino, lo squartatore, fu subito liberato, e anche applaudito, e perfino portato in trionfo!
>
> [In Milan it was a blunder; but in Bergamo it was a forgery. The jurors were asked: did Olivo kill his wife? And they replied... not exactly a no, which would have been a false oath... but with many blank ballots, which are equivalent. In fact, the murderer, the butcher, was immediately freed, and even applauded, and even carried in triumph!].[79]

L'illustrazione italiana concluded that jurors were asked to pronounce a verdict and they 'hanno detto il falso. Ciò è a dirittura mostruoso' [they told a lie. This is downright monstrous].[80]

The legal journal *La Giustizia penale* commented that after Milan's trial and Olivo's acquittal, public opinion was alarmed and that the Supreme Court, 'in nome della moralità' [in the name of morality], believed it was necessary to annul the verdict, even if legally issued, in the erroneous assumption that it is permissible to silence any reason of formal legality when it comes to repairing a substantial injustice.[81]

---

75 *Avanti!*, 8 December 1904, p. 3.
76 *Il Giornale d'Italia*, 8 December 1904, p. 2.
77 *Corriere della Sera*, 8 December 1904, p. 3.
78 *La Tribuna*, 8 December 1904, p. 3.
79 *L'Illustrazione italiana*, 11 December 1904, p. 474.
80 Ibid.
81 *La Giustizia penale*, 10 (1904), 1065–70 (p. 1065).

Figure 10 *I grandi processi illustrati*, 12–13 (1904)

Image reproduced by kind permission of Ministry of Culture – Pinacoteca di Brera – Biblioteca Braidense, Milan. Further reproduction or duplication by any means is prohibited.

Conclusion

'Perché allora – io domando – levare alte grida di meraviglia
se quando il male assume le forme estreme e
quindi interessantissime del delitto,
esso esercita su di noi tanto fascino?'

[Why then – I ask – raise loud cries of wonder
if when evil takes the extreme and therefore
very interesting forms of crime,
it exerts such fascination on us?]

Scipio Sighele, *Letteratura tragica* (Milan: Treves, 1906), p. 251.

Alberto Olivo went on conducting an ordinary life and even published an autobiographical drama, *Dal culmine all'abisso*, in which he fictionally related his story.[1]

Throughout the trials against him, the perception of his murder morphed from something horrifying and incomprehensible into something predictable and acceptable. From the bloodthirsty man who butchered his wife, his image evolved into that of a person who, 'on a given day, [...] opens a parenthesis in his life and kills his wife'. This 'parenthesis' was deemed to have been caused by all the vicissitudes he experienced from Beccaro's conduct. At first considered a criminal, Olivo then became what the historian Anne-Claude Ambroise-Rendu defined as 'un être normal et moral' [a normal and moral being], who is not a danger for society and whose acts, as we saw in Chapter 3, are perceived as crime without criminality.[2]

What I attempted to do with this work is to show how a peculiar representation affected perception and interpretation of facts and circumstances and made this transition foreseeable. Two main layers were conjured to make

1 See, Alberto Olivo, *Dal culmine all'abisso: dramma in tre atti e un epilogo* (Milan: Grassi, 1906). See also, Alberto Olivo, *La mia difesa contro il professor Cesare Lombroso* (Milan: Società Editoriale Milanese, 1905).

2 Ambroise-Rendu, 'Le Chroniqueur, la justice et l'opinion publique', p. 77.

this transition possible: one was formed by societal values and moral norms, and the other related to the delivery of these accepted values and norms to ordinary people. The first layer was built up by scientists and jurists, who contributed with their works to give ground to inequality and discrimination. By analysing physical and non-physical features and characteristics and by manipulating their understanding to comply with their prejudicial ideas, they justified the different treatment of men and women. Other than creating hierarchies between men and women, they also designed various degrees of authority and authoritativeness within sexes in order to conform to ideal models and to create and maintain a stratified and static society. Since the social and the legal are tightly linked and evolve together, the number of works addressing women's status – not only those limited to legal status – flourished from the mid-nineteenth century onwards: indeed, the many changes in the economic and social framework (i.e. industrialisation, the rise of the bourgeoisie, urbanisation, new ideals, new movements…) made women question their status and redefine the boundaries between the male and female realms. The bulk of these works contributed to creating a solid ground on which society could rely to perpetuate its centuries-old conceptual building blocks. Besides the first layer, there was a second one composed of journalists and professionals of the cultural industry who, through their works – written and visual – addressed the general public by reducing these concepts to everyday contexts. Thanks to the increase in literacy rate,[3] newspapers, magazines and journals were able to reach a vast audience, which made journalists spread these ideas and propound, overtly or hiddenly, their own vision and that of the intelligentsia of the time, grounding their words on the authoritativeness of scientists' and jurists' works. Therefore, if the first layer targeted experts or highly educated people, the second one addressed the general public in an entangled system of representation and reinforcement of the praised status quo. These two main layers had the formative goal of

---

3 On literacy, see Simonetta Soldani, eds, *L'educazione delle donne. Scuole e modelli di vita femminile nell'Italia dell'Ottocento* (Milan: Franco Angeli, 1989); Simonetta Soldani, *Nascita della maestra elementare*, in *Fare gli italiani. Scuola e cultura nell'Italia contemporanea*, ed. by Simonetta Soldani e Gabriele Turi, 2 vols (Bologna: Il Mulino, 1993), I, pp. 67–130; Ester De Fort, *Scuola e analfabetismo nell'Italia del '900* (Bologna: Il Mulino, 1995); Monica Galfré, *Tutti a scuola! L'istruzione nell'Italia del Novecento* (Rome: Carocci, 2017).

defining, justifying and pointing out values and determined the characteristics of those who could include themselves among the good ones, i.e., those worthy individuals enjoying society's praise and protection. At the same time, they also contributed to outlining the characteristics of the bad ones, i.e., the marginalised and despised members of society.

In the specific case analysed in this book, it is precisely from the analysis of these two layers and from the way their contents were delivered that it could be inferred and understood how people's perception was moulded and Beccaro's murder changed from an inhumane and dreadful act into something predictable and acceptable. As we saw, Beccaro's failure to meet the standards for a respectable woman and a good wife, that is, being obedient and honest with a clear reputation, mitigated the feelings towards her murder. If, on the one hand, the verdict surprised almost everyone – people expected a lenient sentence but not Olivo's absolution – on the other hand, Beccaro rapidly started to be considered an accomplice and, at the end, the real culprit of her own murder, because she was deemed to have provoked her husband so strongly that she triggered her own assassination. And it was precisely her behaviour that aroused anger in Olivo and deprived him of reason at the moment of her killing: her provocation was beyond endurance, and, in the thought of the people of the time, any man would have reacted the same way, should he be so hardly provoked. Since the very beginning of the case, newspapers focused their inquiries and articles on Beccaro's reputation – one of the first questions asked by journalists to the couple's neighbours they interviewed was about the victim's behaviour and respectability – thus setting the direction the case would take from the very beginning. If, at the time of the discovery of her corpse, Beccaro's murder was considered despicable and had to be punished, throughout the two trials Beccaro underwent a process of depersonalisation and objectification. Her blameworthy behaviour and her insubordinate attitude reduced the societal protection she would have deserved by being a compliant woman. In most of the newspapers dealing with the case, she rapidly started to be mentioned by her first name only or, even worse, by the use of terms such as 'the butchered' or 'the deceased'; often expressions such as 'give her up' or 'passing from Colombo to Olivo' were employed to describe her actions and what she experienced.

Moreover, journalists employed sensationalising narratives, boosted by an easy-fruible style, language and tone and by a masterly use of punctuation and intonation marks, to emphasise what might seem negligible details in order to induce emotional responses. The attention was shifted from a trial for murder to a spectacle in which the many characters performed a role. The courtroom hosting the trials, too, was part of the show and soon became overcrowded by women and men of every social class allegedly driven by that 'misterioso potere pervertitore' [mysterious perverting power],[4] that is, the irresistible 'fascino del male' [allure of evil].[5] The days of the trials and the many testimonies were reported by using comments, ironies, and allusions in order to minimise and ridiculise behaviours, situations, circumstances, and actions concerning Beccaro, who was constantly infantilised and reduced to a naive, naughty, and uneducated woman doing shenanigans and coming from a context of social disease. Her female relatives who testified were described in a similar way to comply with this vision. From this depiction, the figure of Olivo eventually emerged as that of a saviour. Despite being a '*caratteristico*', Olivo was seen as a hard-working and respectable man who had the bad fate to meet such a woman. The way he told his story and the way the press related it to the audience were highly spectacularised and invited empathy. In this arena, in which everyone showed off their virtuosity and ability to conquer the scene, Beccaro's murder became marginal and started to be understood as an inevitable and accepted consequence of unruly behaviour and misunderstanding of her place in society.

The 'case Olivo', as has been defined by Lombroso and Bianchi, demonstrated how perceptions were, and are, strongly affected by the insinuating and devious oblique power of a peculiar representation. Reality could be interpreted and manipulated, and a certain kind of representation contributes to enforcing and reinforcing stereotypes and prejudices: day after day, the wave of indignation that emerged after the discovery of Beccaro's butchered corpse gave way to a process of construction of a different morally compliant interpretation. At the end, Olivo was considered a victim of an adverse fate, his acquittal was welcomed with frenetic applause, and Beccaro became the agent of her own murder, that is, a culprit.

---

4 Scipio Sighele, *Letteratura tragica* (Milan: Treves, 1906), p. 251.

5 The expression was used by the early nineteenth-century Italian writer Dora Melegari (1849–1924) in her works *Il sonno delle anime* (Milan: Treves, 1903), pp. 28–63 and *Il destarsi delle anime* (Milan: Treves, 1915), p. 61.

Appendix

1

La Stampa, 5 June 1904, p. 1,
Idee, persone e cose. L'uomo che squarta

La tribuna, 5 June 1904, p. 3,
Nell'arte e nella vita. L'uomo che squarta[1]

Alle Assise di Milano si discute in questo momento il processo di quell'Olivo che l'anno scorso uccise la moglie, poi la squartò, la chiuse in una valigia, e, dopo quattro giorni, andò a seppellirla nel mare di Genova. Chi è questo Olivo? Quando un gran delitto inonda di sangue la cronaca giudiziaria, quando un gran delinquente squarcia con la punta del suo coltello, non solo il ventre di una vittima, ma anche la barriera della morale, dietro la quale sta in riparo l'umanità, il pubblico si domanda sempre ansioso se l'uno e l'altro, il delitto e il delinquente, costituiscano un fenomeno degno di attenzione e di studio: se il delitto sia il frutto dell'albero del male o dell'albero del bene, se il delinquente sia un tipo normale o un tipo degenerato. Perché, ormai, è vano negare e dissimulare: il problema della delinquenza non si pone più alla coscienza generale come un problema giuridico, ma come un problema patologico: di fronte al sangue e al coltello si discute, non più col criterio della scienza morale, ma con quelli della scienza della natura.

Chi è Olivo? D'onde viene? Da quali preistoriche caverne ha mosso il suo viaggio? quali sono le dimensioni del suo piede o del suo cranio? quale è il

[1] The same editorial was published in both newspapers.

peso del suo corpo? quale la tensione del suo spirito? quale la funzione del suo sistema muscolare e del suo sistema nervoso? quale il processo di ideazione del suo cervello? quale la forma di attività della sua psiche? Interrogativi di profonda curiosità scientifica che dimostrano il radicale mutamento che la Scuola penale positiva ha prodotto nel mondo contemporaneo intorno al modo d'intendere e di pensare, di concepire e di sentire il problema della delinquenza.

Olivo, del resto, è uno di quei tipi *rappresentativi* così pieni o così completi in tutte le loro parti che basterà interrogarli perché rispondano esaurientemente a tutte le curiosità del pubblico e diano la riprova di tutte le esperienze della scienza.

Responsabile, dunque, o irresponsabile l'Olivo? – ecco oggi la questione.

Leggo nel resoconto di uno dei giornali di Milano: 'Non vi sono al dibattimento periti alienisti: è noto che la perizia assunta in istruttoria ha affermata la responsabilità dell'accusato'. Ha affermato, dunque, che l'accusato è un essere normale come voi, come me, come gli autori della perizia? Affermazione in verità che nessuno può negare sia sufficientemente disinvolta dopo il *fatto* dello squartamento. Perché esso solo, infine, valutato e considerato qual fatto, è rivelatore di uno dei caratteri più incontestabili della degenerazione criminale: insensibilità fisica e morale; e per questo, nella classificazione dei delinquenti, lo squartatore rimane come il tipo sintetico per eccellenza: il tipo che racchiude in sé tutti gli elementi essenziali dell'attività criminale. Guardate, infatti, come quegli elementi si sono manifestati in tutta la loro violenza e la loro intensità; nell'interrogatorio – nel quale, rivivendo tutto il suo delitto, l'imputato pareva agitato da una perpetua aura epilettica – dopo caduta la sua parola cadde egli stesso siccome fulminato in una tempesta patologica, nella quale disparve, tra le urla ed i singhiozzi, la memoria dell'uomo e il coraggio della bestia!

La stessa crisi, del resto, che ebbe dopo l'interrogatorio, egli l'aveva avuta dopo il delitto.

Egli commise il delitto così come ne fece il racconto nell'interrogatorio: in un turbine: nell'interrogatorio, di parole; nell'atto, di coltellate.

'Mi svegliai alle due, e mi sentivo male; il cuore palpitava forte e la fronte era arsa'.

Ricordate le febbri di Jacopo Lantier descritte da Zola nella *Bête humaine*? È il *virus* del delitto che possiede il sangue e lo riscalda e gli dà le alte temperature tropicali che distruggono le radici morali dell'essere.

'Alle prime contestazioni una nube rossa mi coprì gli occhi; io non so che cosa sia successo; come spinto da una molla, mi trovai addosso a mia moglie, che era in letto voltandomi la schiena. Quante volte colpii? Non posso dire né quante né dove. Poi fui preso da torpore, e per parecchie ore rimasi assopito; quando mi svegliai, mi trovai in un lago di sangue. E dovetti fare un grande sforzo per ricordarmi che cosa era avvenuto e per ricostruire la scena in tutti i suoi particolari'.

Terribile; ma vero. Lo sforzo del delitto esaurisce ordinariamente l'attività nervosa del delinquente, come lo sforzo dell'amore; e un profondo sonno catalettico sopravviene; e sullo stesso cuscino due sonni si incontrano in una sola pace: il sonno della morte e il sonno del delitto. Anche l'altro giorno, alle Assise di Troyes, nel processo per l'assassinio del cieco Langfelder, il quindicenne giovinetto che aveva commesso il delitto narrava candidamente che, dopo sgozzata la sua vittima, le si addormentò per parecchie ore al fianco, e dormì un profondo sonno riparatore; 'perché ci è voluto un grande sforzo, signori giurati, – ragiona l'*enfant terrible* – a vincere il vecchio, che anche sotto il laccio si dibatteva violentemente e tentava di sfuggire!' E dormì tutta una notte, dopo commesso il parricidio, accanto al cadavere della madre, prima di squartarla, quel contadino dell'Eure che passa, attraverso i trattati di antropologia, come uno degli esempi solenni della degenerazione criminale.

'Qualche volta, affaticato dalla lotta, *brisé par l'émotion,* l'assassino si riposa e *dort d'un profond sommeil*. Al risveglio, trovando quel cadavere ingombrante accanto a sé, concepisce il progetto di disfarsene, e *c'est alors que surgit l'idée de le mettre en morceau*'.

E così nacque anche l'idea nell'Olivo al suo risveglio dopo l'uxoricidio.

'Qualche volta lo squartatore è brutale; il tempo urge, la collera lo prende, una specie di furore invade l'assassino quando i pezzi di carne della vittima *ne peuvent passer dans les latrines...*'

E lo stesso furore invase l'Olivo quando vide che *les latrines* non erano sufficienti per contenere tutto il cadavere. E allora, abbandonate soltanto le parti molli alle fogne, chiuse il resto del cadavere nella valigia, e lo affidò al mare.

Come vedete, io intermezzo di citazioni di autori il racconto dello squartatore per dimostrare che nessun movimento, nessun atto, nessuna forma dell'attività criminale dell'Olivo è nuova; tutte si trovano minutamente descritte, registrate, commentate nei libri di antropologia criminale, specie in quelli del Lacassagne, del Raboux, del Rodriguez, che si occupano dello *squartamento* dal punto di vista patologico e psicologico; e quindi per dimostrare quanto strana e fantastica sia la perizia dell'istruttoria, che dichiara un tipo normale l'Olivo, che, viceversa, è il tipo classico, indiscusso, indiscutibile del degenerato criminale, quale la scienza lo ha oramai fissato e determinato per sempre, per tutti i tempi e per tutti i paesi. Uccidere è un bisogno organico per tutti gli esseri dello stampo dell'Olivo, così come è un bisogno organico dell'idrofobo mordere, e del tisico fare del male, senza ragione.

E non si lotta contro le forze della natura che hanno bisogno per la loro violenza di espandersi, per la loro pace di esaurirsi.

Uccidere i vivi – sia pure! – ma perché squartare i morti?

Perché?

Perché non vi è limite, evidentemente, al furore della bestia. Oggi lo squartamento è un'opera di difesa – e quindi di paura – del delinquente di contro alla giustizia; e far sparire il cadavere significa, far sparire la prova del delitto; ma una volta, nella tradizione guerriera come nella tradizione mistica e religiosa, il significato era diverso. Comunque, poiché nulla si perde nell'umanità, anche dopo svanito il sentimento guerriero e religioso che lo tennero in onore, rimane nel fondo degli organi l'istinto feroce dello squartare, che rendeva crudeli i nostri padri nell'atto del sacrifizio o nell'esecuzione della vendetta sociale. E quando e dove quell'istinto rigermoglia, un lampo di preistoria riappare sanguigno all'orizzonte della civiltà. Sono forse delinquenti ordinari i Wainwright, i Mestag, i Billoir, i Borré, i Menesclou, i Pell, gli Avinaia, i Visgueiro, gli Olivo, tutti celebri squartatori, che anche per paura e per difesa squartano la loro vittima, e dopo un'ora, dopo un giorno, dopo una settimana, dopo un anno – il Wainwright appunto dopo un anno – tagliuzzano, dispolpano, disarticolano le membra delle vittime che essi stessi hanno dato alla morte e alla putrefazione?

Ed anche nel modo di soddisfare all'istinto della difesa non vi è una scusa di soddisfare alla loro maggiore ferocia e alla loro maggiore crudeltà? Non vi è, nell'azione dello squartare, quasi un prolungamento del loro odio, della loro collera – e insieme della loro voluttà – nel maltrattare le carni umane? Non vi è anche quella suprema ebbrezza del sangue che alle volte li spinge all'antropofagia nel momento stesso dello squartamento?

E che cosa resta dell'uomo, dell'umanità, della civiltà in quell'essere che noi chiamiamo nostro simile e nostro prossimo, che, curvo sul cadavere, come la belva curva sulla carogna del deserto, ne strappa le carni, ne beve gli umori, ne assimila i veleni della putrefazione?

Che cosa resta?

Io lo domando ai redattori della perizia del processo di Milano.

Rastignac

[*La Stampa*, 5 June 1904, p. 1,
Ideas, people and things. The Butcherer

and *La Tribuna*, 5 June 1904, p. 3,
In art and in life. The Butcherer

At the Court of Assizes of Milan, the trial of the notorious Alberto Olivo, who, last year, killed his wife, butchered her, stuffed her into a suitcase, and then four days later, threw her into the sea of Genoa, is now underway. Who is this Olivo character? When a great crime floods the judicial news with blood, when a grand criminal slashes not only the belly of his victim with the tip of his knife but also the very boundaries of morality behind which humanity itself shelters, the public always anxiously questions whether both the crime and the criminal are phenomena needing attention and study: whether the crime is the fruit of the tree of evil or of the tree of good, whether the criminal is normal in typology or a degenerate. Because now we deny and dissimulate in vain: the problem of delinquency is no longer presented as a legal matter for the general conscience but as a pathological problem. In the face of blood and the knife, our discussions no longer consider criteria of moral science but those of natural science.

Who is Olivo? From where does he come? In which prehistoric cave did his journey begin? What are the measurements of his foot and his skull? What is his bodyweight? What is the gauge of his spirit? How do his muscular and nervous systems function? What processes does his brain use in the construction of thought? What is the activity of his psyche? These questions of profound scientific curiosity demonstrate the radical change the Positive Penal School has brought about in the way the contemporary world understands, thinks about, conceives of, or experiences the problem of delinquency.

After all, Olivo is one of those *representative* types so entire and so complete in all their parts that it is enough to question them such that they satisfy exhaustively all public curiosity and deliver proof of all scientific experience.

Is Olivo responsible for his actions, then, or not? – this is the question today.

I read in a report in one of the Milanese newspapers, 'There are no alienist experts at the trial: it is known that the expert report submitted during the investigation affirmed the responsibility of the accused'. Has it affirmed, then, that the accused is a normal being, like you and me, like the authors of the expert report? A statement, in truth, that no one could deny as sufficiently casual after the *fact* of the butchering. Because this alone, finally, evaluated and considered as a fact, reveals one of the most indisputable characteristics of criminal degeneracy, namely physical and moral insensitivity; and for this reason, in the classification of criminality, the butcherer remains the synthetic type par excellence: the type that contains within itself all essential elements of criminal activity. Indeed, look at how those elements manifested themselves in all their violence and intensity: in the interrogation – in which, reliving his full crime, the accused appeared agitated as if by a perpetual epileptic state – the words having fallen from his lips, he himself fell, as if electrocuted in a pathological storm wherein both human memory and animal courage disappeared, lost amongst his screams and sobs!

And this such crisis he experienced following the interrogation was the same such crisis he experienced after the crime.

He had committed the crime in the same fashion he later related the story in the interrogation: in a whirlwind – in the interrogation, a whirlwind of words; in the act, a whirlwind of stab wounds.

'I woke up at two in the morning, and I felt unwell; my heart was pounding and my forehead was burning.'

Do you remember Jacopo Lantier's fevers as Zola describes them in *La bête humaine*? It is the *virus* of crime that takes root in the blood and heats it up, giving it the baking tropical temperatures that destroy the moral roots of the self.

'At the first protests, a red mist came over my eyes; I don't know what happened; as if I was being pushed by something, I found myself on top of my wife, who had been lying in the bed with her back to me. How many times did I hit her? I can't say; or where I hit her. Then I was overcome by torpor, and for several hours I remained asleep; when I woke up, I found I was lying in a pool of blood. And I had to make a great effort to remember what had happened and to reconstruct the scene in all its details.'

Terrible, but true. The effort involved in committing a crime ordinarily is neurally exhausting for the criminal, like the effort of lovemaking; and a deep cataleptic sleep occurs, and on the same pillow, two instances of sleep meet in a single instance of peace: the sleep of death and the sleep of crime. Just the other day, at the Assizes of Troyes, in the trial for the murder of the blind man Langfelder, the fifteen-year-old boy who had committed the crime candidly related that, on slaughtering his victim, he then fell asleep for several hours next to the body and slept a deep restorative sleep 'because, gentlemen of the jury, it had taken a great effort' – so the *enfant terrible* reasons – 'to defeat the old man, who even under the noose struggled violently and tried to escape!' And he slept all night, after committing the parricide, next to his mother's corpse, before butchering her to pieces, that young peasant from Eure who now stands, through anthropological treatises, as one of the solemn examples of criminal degeneration.

'Sometimes, tired from the fight, *broken by emotion*, the murderer rests and *sleeps in a deep sleep*. Upon waking, and finding that cumbersome corpse next to him, he conceives a plan to rid himself of it, and *it is then that the idea of reducing it into pieces arises*.'

And so, the same idea was born in Olivo when he awoke after the uxoricide.

'Sometimes the butcherer is brutal; time is pressing, anger grips him, a kind of fury invades the murderer when the pieces of flesh of the victim *don't fit through the latrine…*'

And the same fury invaded Olivo when he saw that *the latrine* was not capable of holding the entire corpse. And then, abandoning only the soft parts to the latrine, he shut the rest of the corpse in the suitcase and entrusted it to the sea.

As you can see, I intersperse the story of the butcherer with quotes from authors to demonstrate that no gesture, no action, no form of Olivo's criminal activity is new; all of it has been minutely described, recorded and commented on in books of criminal anthropology, especially books by Lacassagne, Raboux and Rodriguez, which deal with *butchering* from a pathological and psychological point of view; and therefore, to demonstrate the strange and fantastical nature of the investigation's report that declares Olivo a normal character type – which, vice versa, is the classic, undisputed, indisputable type of the criminal degenerate, as science has now fixed and determined it always to be, across all time and for all nations. Killing is an organic need for all creatures of Olivo's type, just as the rabid creature has the organic need to bite and the consumptive to harm, without cause.

And we don't fight against the forces of nature, which need to expand to contain their violence, to exhaust themselves for their own peace.

Murder the living – if you must! – but why butcher the dead?

Why?

Because there is evidently no limit to the fury of the beast. Today, butchering is an act of defence – and therefore fear – by the criminal against the justice system, and getting rid of the corpse means getting rid of the evidence, but once upon a time, in the warrior tradition, as in the mystical and religious tradition, the meaning was different. However, since nothing is lost in humanity, even after the warrior and religious sentiment that once held it in honour has gone, the fierce instinct to butcher, which made our fathers cruel in the act of sacrifice or in the execution of social revenge, remains deep within the organs. And whenever and wherever that instinct resurges, we see a flash of the prehistoric again, sanguine, on the horizon of civilisation. Should we perhaps consider as ordinary criminals the Wainwrights, the Mestags, the Billoirs, the Borrés, the Menesclous, the Pells, the Avinaias, the Visgueiros, the Olivos: famous butcherers all, who butchered their victims from fear and defensiveness, and, an hour afterwards, a day, a week, a year later – Wainwright after precisely one year – shredded and stripped down the flesh, jointed the limbs of those victims that they themselves had handed over to death and putrefaction?

And even in satisfying an instinct for defence, is there not an excuse for satisfying their greater ferocity and their greater cruelty? Is there not, in the act of butchering, almost an extension of their hatred, their anger – at the same time, their pleasure – in abusing the human flesh? Is there not, too, the supreme intoxication of bloodletting that sometimes drives them to anthropophagy at the very instant of their butchery?

And what remains of man, of humanity, of civilisation in that being we call our fellow man, our neighbour, who, bent over the corpse, like the beast bent over the desert carcass, rips into its flesh, drinks its humours, ingests the poisons of its putrefaction?

What remains?

I ask this question of the authors of the report on the Milan trial.

Rastignac]

2

Corriere della sera, 9 giugno 1904, p. 1,
Olivo criminaloide

Molti mi chiedono, sorridendo sottecchi, se il caso Olivo non contraddica completamente le conclusioni della mia scuola, perché l'Olivo, sebbene abbia commesso un delitto gravissimo, non presenta alcuna anomalia.

Potrei, invero, rispondere che un solo caso non basta ad intaccare conclusioni basate su migliaia; ma son lieto invece di poter dimostrare che esso assai bene le conferma.

Certo né i tratti fisionomici, né la condotta anteriore dell'Olivo sono da delinquente nato. Infatti, salvo la sproporzione tra il cranio e la faccia, la profondità delle rughe, e la fronte troppo ampia e sfuggente, egli non ha veri caratteri degenerativi, e lungi dall'avere, come i rei nati, mostrato precocità nel delitto, trascorse, senza mancare all'onestà, una gioventù tempestosa, in cui non son solo da notare scoppì d'ira furibonda per cause levissime.

Ma, se a prima vista può parere ch'egli manchi completamente di anomalie psichiche, in realtà egli ci porge l'esempio delle più strane contraddizioni che si possano trovare riunite in un uomo. Dotato di ingegno acutissimo (e basterebbe a provarlo la lezione che improvvisò in risposta al Pubblico Ministero sulla possibilità di una gelosia ereditaria), provvisto inoltre di profonda cultura tecnica e letteraria, egli finiva tuttavia dopo inutili tentativi, col darsi ad una carriera mediocre. Anche alle Assise si perde in minuziosi conteggi, anno per anno, mese per mese, sulle spese d'affitto, sul vitto, pei traslochi ed anche sugli sputi ricevuti dalla moglie (dodici di numero). Tutto questo, mentre poco lo giustifica e indispone il pubblico, contrasta stranamente con le facoltà poetiche di cui diede non ispregevoli saggi e con la turbolente irrequietezza per cui sembra che non possa parlare e rispondere se non correndo a gran passi entro la gabbia.

Vanitoso e superbo co' suoi compagni, è anche preoccupato più del pensiero della sua fama di contabile, di letterato e persino di purista, che dall'idea d'essere colpevole d'un assassinio e di essere stato marito disonorato, diremmo, volontariamente. Diciamo così perché non è possibile che con quel suo acume egli non comprendesse la ragione delle troppe assenze diurne e notturne della moglie; e del resto egli aveva già saputo che ella era stata posseduta da molti, ed ella glielo ripeteva in musica. Né si concilia con la sua fierezza la quiescenza con cui si adatta ad accettare, appunto da questi ex protettori della moglie, somme troppo scarse per dare un sollievo anche momentaneo, ma pur sempre disonoranti.

Gli è che sempre difettava di senso morale. Fra tutti gli altri istinti predominava in lui quello dell'avarizia ribadita dalla stentata giovinezza e mal contrastata dall'orgoglio dell'*arrivato*. Da ciò forse il matrimonio prima, e poi la mancata separazione dalla moglie per non passarle un assegno; da ciò le contese per 6 o per 10 lire colle cognate, i cibi e i vestiti legati alla moglie, e le altre infinite piccinerie.

Ma la maggiore anomalia (come ben notò A. G. Bianchi in questo giornale) era quella del senso morale. Questo individuo che aveva avuto palpiti veri d'amore per la Beccaro, ed era giunto a sollevarla sulle braccia per risparmiarle le scale, la taglia poi a pezzi colla massima freddezza; e quando il Presidente gli chiede se avesse dormito all'osteria nella stessa camera ove ne erano gli avanzi, risponde di sì, ed aggiunge: *perché non puzzavano*. Così nello squartamento come nel trasporto di quei tristi frammenti umani, egli mostrò la massima indifferenza, avaro sempre al punto di servirsi di un tram anziché di una carrozza, di questionare a Genova per il prezzo della vettura, e di dare due soldi di mancia ai ragazzi che gli portano la pesante valigia.

Nel descrivere tutti gli strazi fatti sul cadavere si perde in una freddezza di minuzie che mostra la completa mancanza di rimorso e di affetto. Eppure anche qui non manca la contraddizione, nel pensiero più volte espresso di raccogliere in una tomba gli avanzi, quegli avanzi da lui così profanati!

Ed è pure strano il vedere un uomo così fiero dar la stessa importanza agli insulti di *mezzano* e di *stupido* ed agli sputi lanciatigli al viso dalla moglie, e al fatto che la moglie stessa gli aveva annacquato il vino!

Soprattutto va in lui notata l'irascibilità e la litigiosità che, accentuate fin dall'infanzia, quando giungeva a ferire un compagno per un pisello, si estendono e perpetuano coi compagni, coi vicini, coi parenti della moglie, e infine con questa stessa, fino a creare scandali che lo costringono a cambiare più volte l'alloggio. Ed è curioso come egli sembri lodare questa litigiosità nei suoi versi *Furor savio* pur ammettendo che questo *furore* può portare alla strage. Ora questa irascibilità eccessiva, come i contrasti del carattere, sono propri dell'epilettico.

Qui va notato come egli, nato gracilissimo, abbia sofferto di iperemie cerebrali che s'acuirono, pare, al momento del reato e che egli pretende derivino da un'insolazione. Esse s'accompagnano a sordità, ronzio, smemoratezza, fenomeni che diventano gravissimi se si collegano colla sopra accennata irascibilità e coll'anestesia completa che ebbe durante il reato, sicché con la mano ferita continuò per molte ore una faticosa e lunga operazione senza avvertire dolore.

Deve infine osservarsi che egli fu spinto al delitto da una serie di minacce, di insulti e di scenate che duravano da parecchi mesi. Ma 'solo un punto fu quel che lo vinse' e fu quando a tutto ciò s'aggiunse l'offesa che a lui, come letterato e come avaro, doveva suonare più grave, il vedersi preferita dalla moglie, nelle lezioni d'italiano, una maestra che sbagliava nei gerundi; il caso – dice lui – d'un calzolaio che si volesse costringere a comperare da altri gli stivaletti della moglie.

V'era qui (senza dire del supremo insulto che sarebbe stato pronunciato da quella femmina contro sua madre), v'era di che suscitare anche in animo meno irascibile la classicamente nota *iracondia morbosa epilettica*. Ed io credo veramente che l'Olivo abbia avuto un accesso di epilessia psichica forse anche motoria, per cui, appena eseguito, con straordinaria violenza e con oscura crepuscolare coscienza, il reato, cadde d'un colpo sul letto, restando per qualche ora in uno stupore profondo da cui si risvegliò quasi dimentico di ogni cosa. Il verso che egli in proposito citava: – *E cadde come corpo morto cade* – esprime esattamente quel sintomo cui nessuno assistette e di cui nessuno può dare notizia, ma la cui verità viene appurata da quanto gli accadde alle Assise l'altro giorno, quando, eccitato dall'ira repressa e dal ridestarsi dei ricordi, vinto d'esaurimento per lungo dibattito, egli, che non aveva pianto all'arresto, ad un tratto si diede a lagrimare, urlando e agitandosi in convulsioni, che sei carabinieri non riescivano a dominare. E ce ne dà la prova anche egli stesso, quando asserisce – egli che nessuno sospetta di mentire – che non può ricordare come la tragedia si svolse, tanto che si meravigliò di veder la moglie colla mano tagliata e col coltello sotto il ventre e sospetta di averla strangolata prima di ferirla. Questo è il punto saliente dell'anomalia. Certo, egli non è un delinquente nato, perché non commise il male senza cagione, per il piacere del male, né ebbe precocità al delitto. Ma oltre i delinquenti nati – triste varietà clinica degli epilettici – la mia scuola ha descritto un gruppo di uomini in cui l'*ictus* epilettico, molto più mite e molto più raro, non spinge che nelle grandi occasioni al delitto e in cui non mancano, se non tutti, molti caratteri degenerativi. In tutti costoro, o almeno in quasi tutti (come ho notato nel mio

Uomo delinquente, II vol. pag. 522), si ha perfetta proporzionalità tra la causa che spinse al delitto e il delitto medesimo, con una certa analogia, dunque, coi delinquenti di impeto; invece di una scarsa e torbida intelligenza, voi vedete menti lucide; e quasi tutti hanno facile e sincera la confessione.

Un altro loro carattere (trovato questo dal Sighele) è il lungo tempo che occorre a deciderli all'atto criminoso, il quale invece nei delinquenti nati viene subito accettato come quello più semplice e naturale. 'Tagliare la testa ad un uomo – diceva Lacenaire – è come tagliare una fetta di cioccolato o del velluto'. Invece il Garnier, il Meille, la Noblia resistono a lungo alla causa che li spinge al delitto. È una ripetuta e grande serie di attriti che ve li precipita. E come non premeditano il reato, così non hanno mai complici, tanto frequenti invece tra i delinquenti nati.

Un ultimo carattere è la gravità della causa che li spinge al reato. Cito la Kleinroth, divenuta delinquente pei martirii che a lei ed ai figli infliggeva il marito, il quale pure profondeva ricchezze a serve e bastardi; e l'Ankermann che, onestissimo, incontra un debito con un servitore, non può pagarlo, chiede invano dappertutto dei prestiti, e quando, pochi giorni prima della scadenza, vede il servo installarsi nella sua casa, dormire nel suo letto, insultarlo per giunta, prende un bastone e l'uccide. Non mancano in essi le amnesie epilettoidi. Così nel *Delitto e pena* del Dostojewski, il Raskolnikoff – che aveva diviso il cibo con un compagno malato, che aveva salvato due ragazzini dal fuoco e che non presentava anomalie speciali, salvo negli occhi un ceruleo e nei capelli un biondo più esagerato del comune – divenuto povero, dovette interrompere gli studi, non essendo bastati sacrifici di una sorella per aiutarlo. Sente parlare di una malvagia usuraia odiata da tutti e a poco a poco è preso dal desiderio di ucciderla. Si prepara l'alibi, s'arma, e l'uccide non visto da alcuno; ma poi ne resta così turbato che nasconde il denaro rubato sotto una pietra, e non ne gode e alle prime arti di un poliziotto fa la più ampia confessione. Ma anch'egli ebbe accessi amnesici epilettici, e più volte presentì che perdeva la coscienza di sé stesso.

A questi infelici che formano l'anello di congiunzione tra i rei nati, quelli d'occasione e di passione, e l'uomo normale assillato da un fondo epilettico, ma che non sarebbe senza una grave causa caduto nel crimine, appartiene certo l'Olivo.

6 giugno 1904
C. Lombroso

[*Corriere della sera*, 9 June 1904, p. 1,
Olivo, criminaloid

Many ask me, secretly smiling, if the Olivo case does not completely contradict the conclusions of my School since Olivo, although he committed a very serious crime, does not present any anomaly.

I could naturally reply that a single case is not enough to undermine conclusions based on thousands of cases; but I am happy to be able to demonstrate that on the contrary it confirms them very well.

Of course, neither Olivo's physiognomic features nor his previous conduct are those of a born criminal. Indeed, other than the disproportion between skull and face, the depth of his facial lines, and the overly broad and receding forehead, he has no true visible characteristics of the degenerate; and, far from having shown a precocity in his crime, as born criminals do, in unfailing honesty, he had a turbulent youth, where explosions into furious anger at the slightest cause were not the only things of note.

But if at first glance it may seem that he is completely devoid of psychic anomalies, in reality he offers us an example of the strangest contradictions that can be found in a man. Possessed of a very sharp intellect (and the lesson he expounded in his response to the public prosecutor on the possibility of hereditary jealousy alone would be enough to prove this) and also equipped with a profound technical and literary cultural understanding, he nevertheless ended up giving himself to a mediocre career after several attempts otherwise. At the Assizes, he still gets lost in detailed numbers, the annual tally, the monthly tally, of rent, food, of transportation expenses; even of the occasions upon which his wife spat at him (twelve in number). All this, while it does little to justify his case and irritates the public, contrasts strangely with the poetic faculties through which he gave his not inconsiderable essays and with his turbulent restlessness, because of which it seems he cannot speak and respond unless he is running around in the dock.

Vain and proud with his companions, he is also more worried about his fame as an accountant, a man of letters, even as a purist, than about the idea of being found guilty of a murder and of, we might say, voluntarily having been a cuckolded husband. We say this because it is not possible that a man of his acumen could not have understood the reason for his wife's manifold daytime and nighttime absences; moreover, he had already been aware that she had been possessed by many; she had crowed about it to him. Nor can we reconcile with his pride the quiescence with which he came to accept, from precisely these former protectors of his wife, sums [of money] too small to provide even temporary financial relief but extending the dishonouring.

The fact is that he always lacked a moral compass. Amongst all other instincts, it was avarice that predominated in him, reinforced by his stunted youth and poorly countered by the pride of the successful man. Hence, perhaps, the marriage first, then the failure to separate from his wife, so as not to have to pay her off; hence the disputes over just six or ten liras with his sisters-in-law, for the food and clothes related to his wife, and the other endless pettinesses.

But the greatest anomaly (as A. G. Bianchi has noted in this newspaper) was that of the moral sense. This individual, who had experienced genuine heartbeats of love for Beccaro, and had gone as far as to carry her in his arms to spare her the stairs, had cut her to pieces with the utmost coldness; and then, when the President of the Court asks him, if he had slept at the inn in the same room as her remains, he replies yes and adds, *because they did not smell*. Both in the butchering and the transportation of those sad human fragments, he showed the utmost indifference, always parsimonious, to the point of taking a tram rather than a carriage, quarrelling over the price of the carriage in Genoa, and giving tips of just two cents to the lads who carried the heavy suitcase for him.

In describing all the tortures inflicted on the corpse, he gets lost in a froideur of minutiae that shows a complete lack of remorse and affection. Yet even here there is no lack of contradiction in the thought expressed several times of collecting the remains in a tomb, those remains so desecrated by him!

And it is also strange to see a man of such pride accord the same importance to insults such as *pimp* and *stupid*, and to his wife's spitting in his face and to the fact of his wife's watering down of his wine!

Above all, we should note in him the irascibility and quarrelsomeness that, evident since childhood when he would injure a companion at the slightest cause, grew and was perpetuated when he was with his peers, his neighbours, his wife's relatives, and finally his wife herself, until they created such scandals as forced him to relocate several times. And it is curious how he seems to praise this quarrelsomeness in his poem *Furor savio* [*Saviour Fury*] while admitting that this fury could lead to slaughter. Now, such excessive irascibility, much like internal conflict, is typical of the epileptic.

Here it should be noted that, born very frail, he suffered from cerebral hyperaemia, which apparently had worsened at the time of the crime and which he claims was the result of sunstroke. It is accompanied by deafness, ringing in the ears, forgetfulness: phenomena that become very serious when linked with the aforementioned irascibility and with the complete anaesthesia he experienced during the crime, such that he was able to undergo a tiring and long operation for many hours with his injured hand without feeling any pain.

Finally, it must be noted that he was driven to the crime by a series of threats, insults and scenes that had gone on for several months. But 'it was one point alone that overcame him', and it was when, on top of all this, was added the offence that must have seemed more serious to him, as a man of letters and also as a miser: to see his wife prefer, above him, an Italian teacher who made mistakes in gerunds, as if – he says – a shoemaker were forced to buy his wife's boots from another shoemaker.

This in itself (without mentioning the supreme insult that would have been uttered by that woman against his mother) would be enough to arouse even in a less irascible soul that which is classically known as *morbid epileptic anger*. And I truly believe that Olivo suffered an attack of psychical epilepsy, perhaps even motoral epilepsy, whereby, as soon as the crime was carried out, with extraordinary violence and with the dark consciousness of twilight, he suddenly fell on the bed, remaining there for several hours in a profound stupor, from which he woke forgetful of almost everything. The verse he quoted in this regard – *And he fell as a dead body falls* – expresses exactly that symptom that none has witnessed and of which no one can give news, but whose truth is ascertained by what happened to him in the Assizes the other day, when, enervated by repressed anger and by the reawakening of memories, and overcome by exhaustion due to a lengthy debate, this man, who had not wept at his arrest, suddenly began to cry, screaming and writhing with convulsions such that six carabinieri were not sufficient to control him. And he himself offers us more proof of this when he states – he, whom no one can suspect of lying – that he cannot remember how the tragedy unfolded, so much so that he was amazed to see his wife with her hand sliced off and the knife under her belly, and suspects he strangled her before slashing her. This is the salient point of the anomaly. Of course, he is not a born criminal, because he did not commit evil without cause and for the pure pleasure of evil; nor was he a precocious criminal. But beyond born criminals – that sad clinical genus of epileptics – my School has described a group of men in whom the epileptic attack, much milder and much rarer, pushes them to crime only in extraordinary cases, and that covers many, if not quite all, degenerate characters. In all of these, or at least in almost all (as I noted in my *Criminal Man*, II vol., p. 522), there is perfect proportionality between the cause that led to the crime and the crime itself, with a certain analogy, therefore, with the impetuous criminal: instead of a feeble and cloudy intelligence, you see clear minds; and almost all confess easily and sincerely.

Another characteristic of this group (this was found by Sighele) is the extended length of time it takes them to decide to carry out the criminal act, by contrast with born criminals, where the crime is immediately accepted as the simplest and most natural choice. 'Cutting off a man's head', said Lacenaire, 'is like slicing a piece of chocolate or velvet'; whereas Garnier, Meille, Noblia long resisted the motive that drove them to crime. For them, it takes a recurrent and grand series of irritations to precipitate them. And just as they do not premeditate the crime, so too they never have accomplices, which are so commonplace among the born criminals.

A final characteristic is the seriousness of the motive that impels them to commit the crime. I mention here Kleinroth, who became a criminal because of the martyrdom inflicted on her and her children by her husband, who also lavished wealth on his female servants and illegitimate children; and Ankermann, a very honest man who contracts a debt with a servant, cannot pay it, asks for loans everywhere in vain, and when, a few days before the debt is due, sees the servant making himself comfortable in his house, sleeping in his bed, even insulting him, grabs a stick and kills him. There is no shortage of epileptoid amnesia in these individuals. So too, in Dostoevsky's *Crime and Punishment*, Raskolnikov – who had shared food with a sick companion, saved two boys from a fire, and was possessed of no special anomalies other than a cerulean colour in his eyes and a more-exaggerated-than-usual blondness in his hair – on becoming poor, was forced to interrupt his studies, since the sacrifices of a sister were not sufficient to help him. He hears about an evil usuress hated by everyone and is gradually overcome by the desire to kill her. He prepares an alibi, arms himself, and, unseen by anyone, kills her; but then becomes so distraught that he hides the stolen money under a stone, takes no pleasure from it, and in response to the first unskilled efforts by a policeman, offers the most extensive confession.

But he too had an epileptic amnesic attack and several times felt he was losing consciousness of himself.

To these unfortunates, who constitute the link between the born criminals, those driven by opportunity and passion, and the normal man, tormented by an epileptic background and who would not have fallen into crime without serious cause, belongs, I am sure, Olivo.

6 June 1904
C. Lombroso]

3

I Tribunali, 12 giugno 1904, p. 3,
Una settimana al processo Olivo

[...] La curiosità morbosa suscitata, specialmente nel campo femminile dall'Olivo, ha ragioni varie; ma più sicuramente crediamo che essa sia originata da quel sentimento insano nelle donnine di voler ficcare un po' troppo il loro gentile nasino nelle faccende altrui.

Poiché non si potrà con serietà sostenere che tutte quelle signore, signorine, vecchie e giovani, che hanno seguito le varie fasi del processo (senza forse capire gran che!) siano venute, a prezzo di urtoni e di spinte, nell'aula della Giustizia per istudiare il *fenomeno criminale Olivo*, né per criticare i sistemi procedurali del Presidente, del P. M. o della difesa!

E nemmeno, è sperabile, si può supporre che tutte quelle signore abbiano seguito il processo Olivo per imparare da lui o dalla moglie di costui, i principi della morale famigliare.

E allora?

Allora non v'ha dubbio: nell'interesse che l'elemento femminile ha mostrato di avere per il processo di colui che ha smembrato il cadavere della moglie, c'entra anche la curiosità, il desiderio di sapere, il bisogno di conoscere cose delle quali, a molti, non importa un bel niente.

Bisognava vedere per credere!

Nel cortile del Tribunale – e precisamente accanto al cancello che dà accesso alla Corte d'Assise – tutto il santo giorno si poteva notare un vero e proprio accampamento femminile.

C'erano delle signore che, dopo aver aspettato tre o quattro ore di seguito per poter entrare, non si scoraggiavano ancora, ma anzi attendevano per curiosità intensificata, il desiato momento di vedere appagato il loro desiderio.

Quando qualche giornalista – per ragioni d'ufficio – doveva attraversare quel gajo sciame, veniva subito assediato da occhiate espressive... provocanti, da paroline dolci e melliflue, che avvolgevano il disgraziato come in una spira.

– Non posso! non si può!

– Sia buono, lei che scrive sui giornali! guardi se può farmi passare, un momento, un momento solo; tanto da dare un'occhiata e vedere l'Olivo.

– Ma non capite che nella sala non ci sta più nessuno?

– Ma io mi fermo un minuto solo...

Il disgraziato non sapeva come fare a liberarsi. Quando poteva sfuggire, però, ed il cancello si rinchiudeva dietro di lui, dalle signore partiva un coro d'imprecazioni e di proteste abbastanza… salate.

– Ah! quelli li lasciano passare, quelli!

– Già. La solita giustizia: noi chi siamo?

– Perché la colpa è tutta di quell'imbecille di carabiniere…

– … e di quegli imbecilli della stampa che occupano tutti i posti…

E così via, di seguito, la storia si è rinnovata per otto giorni!

Se però le donne al processo Olivo non erano scusabili, un pochino di più, lo furono gli uomini.

Ad eccezione dei professionisti e del pubblico della tribuna pubblica – composto di teppisti e di farabutti – gli uomini che seguirono il processo Olivo erano per lo più… ammogliati.

Indizio sicuro di questa loro… qualità, era il giudizio ch'essi davano dell'Olivo.

Per un ammogliato l'Olivo fu una vittima, e l'uccisione non fu che l'esplicazione della sua giusta ira. D'altra parte però gli uomini erano più desiderosi nel manifestare il desiderio di voler entrare nell'aula: non facevano, per lo meno, capire che se non vi fossero entrati sarebbero morti di curiosità.

A mano a mano che il processo volgeva al suo termine la curiosità di tutti era volta alla sentenza.

Le donne non davano mai il loro giudizio, ma lo chiedevano a tutti: al vicino, ad uno che transitava per un corridojo, al carabiniere di servizio, e a l'usciere.

– Quanto, dice che prenderà l'Olivo?

– Mah! – rispondeva l'interpellato – È un affar serio! Credo una ventina d'anni!

– La forca ci vorrebbe! son troppo pochi venti anni.

Gli uomini invece – infarinati di una superficiale coltura legale, facevano spesso dei discorsi di questo genere.

– La giurisprudenza non ammette lo scempio, se non vi è l'intenzione di offendere.

– Ma quello, scusi, è il Codice che dice così.

– Bravo! Codice e giurisprudenza non è forse la stessa cosa?

Solitamente però – e per fortuna anche del Ministero della Pubblica Istruzione d'Italia, le discussioni si troncavano quasi sempre qui.

[*I Tribunali*, 12 June 1904, p. 3,
A week at the Olivo trial

[...] The morbid curiosity aroused by Olivo, especially among women, has various causes, but we most surely believe that it originates from that unhealthy sentiment in little misses of wanting to stick their gentle little noses rather too much into other people's affairs.

Since it cannot be seriously maintained that all those ladies and little misses, the old and the young, who followed the various phases of the trial (perhaps without understanding much!) came to the courtroom – at a price of bumps and bargings – to study the Olivo criminal phenomenon, nor to critique the procedural systems of the President of the Court, the Public Prosecutor, or the defence!

Nor, it must be hoped, could it be imagined that all these ladies followed the Olivo trial to learn, from either him or his wife, the principles of family morality.

So what, then?

So, then there is no doubt: the interest that the female contingent has shown in the trial of the man who dismembered his wife's body is also driven by curiosity, the desire to know, and the need to know things that many people don't care about at all.

You had to see it to believe it!

All day long, in the courtyard of the Tribunal – and particularly right next to the gate that gives access to the Court of Assizes – you could see a true female encampment.

There were some ladies who, even after having to wait three or four hours straight to be let in, were still not put off but rather waited with even greater curiosity for the desired moment to see their wish fulfilled.

When some journalist had to make his way, for official reasons, through that cheerful swarm, he was immediately besieged by expressive... provocative glances and by sweet and mellifluous words, which encircled the unfortunate man like a coil.

– I can't! It's not possible!

– Be a dear, you write for the papers! See if you can get me in, for a moment, just for a moment, just to take a look and see that Olivo.

– Don't you understand? There's just no space.

– But I'm only stopping for a minute…

The poor man didn't know how to break free. When he did finally manage to escape, however, and the gate closed behind him, the ladies started a chorus of curses and protests that were quite… salty.

– Ah! They let those ones through!

– Yes. The usual justice: who are we?

– Well, it's all that idiot of a carabiniere's fault…

– … and those idiots in the press who take all the seats…

And so on, repeatedly: the same story every day for eight days!

But if the women at Olivo's trial were not excusable, the men were a little more so.

With the exception of the professionals at the trial and the public gallery – consisting of hooligans and scoundrels – the men who followed the Olivo trial were largely… married.

A sure sign of this… quality was their judgement of Olivo.

To the married man, Olivo was a victim, and the killing was merely the expression of his righteous anger. On the other hand, however, the men were keener in the manifestation of their desire to enter the courtroom: they did not make it clear, at least, that if they did not enter, they would die of curiosity.

As the trial drew to a close, everyone's curiosity was focused on the verdict.

The women never gave their own judgement, but asked everyone else theirs: their neighbour, a man walking down a corridor, the carabiniere on duty, and the usher.

– How long do you think Olivo will get?

– Huh! – the person being questioned would reply. – It's a serious business! I think about twenty years!

– The death sentence! Twenty years is too little.

The men, on the other hand – smeared with a superficial sense of the law – often made speeches of this kind:

– Jurisprudence does not admit slaughter if there was no intention to commit an offence.

– But excuse me, it's the Code that says that.

– Bravo! Aren't the Code and jurisprudence the same thing?

As a matter of course, however – and fortunately for the Ministry of Public Education of Italy, too – the discussions always ended there.]

4

La Stampa, 12 giugno 1904,
Lo scandalo giudiziario di Milano

[...] Prima questione – Siete convinti che l'accusato Alberto Olivo abbia la notte dal 16 al 17 maggio 1903, in Milano, con colpi di coltello e di corpo contundente, o con altre violenze, cagionato la morte di Ernesta Beccaro? Sì

Seconda questione – Siete convinti che l'accusato Olivo Alberto abbia commesso il fatto di cui la questione prima, in tale stato di mente che gli toglieva la coscienza o la libertà dei suoi atti? No

Terza questione – L'accusato Alberto Olivo è *colpevole* di avere nelle circostanze esposte alla questione prima, inferti a Ernesta Beccaro i colpi di coltello e di corpo contundente e le altre violenze ivi indicate che ne cagionarono la morte, al fine di uccidere? No

[i giurati non risposero alle seguenti quattro domande perché escluse dalla risposta negativa al terzo quesito]

Quarta questione – L'accusato Olivo Alberto ha commesso il fatto di cui la questione prima con premeditazione?

Quinta questione – L'accusato Olivo Alberto ha commesso il fatto di cui la questione prima nell'impeto d'ira o di intenso dolore determinato da ingiusta provocazione?

Sesta questione – La provocazione affermata colla risposta data alla questione quinta deve intendersi che sia stata grave?

Settima questione – L'accusato Olivo Alberto ha commesso il fatto di cui la questione prima in istato di infermità di mente non già tale da togliergli la coscienza o la libertà dei suoi atti, ma tale però da scemare grandemente la sua imputabilità senza escluderla?

[...]

Ottava questione – Siete convinti che l'accusato Olivo Alberto abbia, fra il 17 e 24 maggio 1903, sottratto il cadavere di Ernestina Beccaro, sua moglie, col gettarlo ridotto in pezzi:

a) parte nella latrina della propria, casa in Milano? Sì.
b) parto nelle acque del porto di Genova? Sì.

Nona questione – Siete convinti che l'accusato Olivo Alberto abbia commesso il fatto, di cui la questione ottava, in tale stato d'infermità di mente che gli toglieva la coscienza o la libertà dei suoi atti? No.

Decima questione – L'accusato Olivo Alberto è colpevole di avere commesso il fatto ritenuto colla risposta affermativa data ad entrambe o all'una o all'altra delle domande di cui la questione ottava? Sì.

Undicesima questione – L'accusato Olivo Alberto ha commesso il fatto ritenuto alla risposta affermativa data ad entrambe od all'una o all'altra delle domande di cui la questione ottava, in istato d'infermità di mente non già tale da togliergli la coscienza o la libertà dei suoi atti, ma tale però di scemare grandemente, la sua imputabilità, senza escluderla? Sì.

[*La Stampa*, 12 June 1904,
The judicial scandal of Milan

First question – Are you convinced that the accused, Alberto Olivo, caused the death of Ernesta Beccaro on the night between 16 and 17 May 1903, in Milan, with a knife and blunt blows of force, or with other violence? Yes.

Second question – Are you convinced that the accused, Olivo Alberto, committed the act referred to on the first count in a state of mind that took away his conscience or the freedom of his acts? No.

Third question – Is the accused, Alberto Olivo, guilty of inflicting knife and blunt blows of force and other violence indicated therein on Ernesta Beccaro in the circumstances set out in the previous count, with the intention to kill? No

[The jurors did not answer the following four counts as these were excluded due to the negative response to the third count above.]

Fourth question – Did the accused, Olivo Alberto, commit the act referred to in the first count with premeditation?

Fifth question – Did the accused, Olivo Alberto, commit the act referred to in the first count in a fit of anger or intense pain caused by unjust provocation?

Sixth question – Must the provocation stated in the response to the fifth count be understood as serious?

Seventh question – Did the accused, Olivo Alberto, commit the act referred to in the first count in a state of mental illness not such as to take away his conscience or the freedom of his acts, but such as to greatly diminish his imputability, without excluding it?

Eighth question – Are you convinced that the accused, Olivo Alberto, between 17 and 24 May 1903, stole the body of Ernestina Beccaro, his wife, by disposing of it in pieces?

a) partly in the latrine of his own house in Milan? Yes.
b) partly in the waters of the port of Genoa? Yes.

Ninth question – Are you convinced that the accused, Olivo Alberto, committed the act referred to in the eighth count in a state of mental illness such that it took away his conscience or the freedom of his acts? No.

Tenth question – Is the accused, Olivo Alberto, guilty of having committed the crime alleged with the affirmative response given to both, or to one or the other of, the questions referred to in the eighth count? Yes.

Eleventh question – Has the accused, Olivo Alberto, committed the act deemed to have an affirmative response to both, or to one or the other of, the questions referred to in the eighth count, in a state of mental illness not such as to take away his conscience or freedom of his acts, but to greatly diminish his imputability, without excluding it? Yes.]

5

Avanti!, 13 giugno 1904,
Lo squartatore di Milano e la giustizia penale

Il processo Dreyfus ha messo come sotto una lente di ingrandimento gli *errori giudiziari* in danno degli innocenti, di cui è intessuta l'opera quotidiana della giustizia penale, anche quando non è inquinata dalle influenze politiche.

Il verdetto assolutorio dello squartatore alle Assise di Milano ne mette ora sotto la stessa lente d'ingrandimento le *assurdità sistematiche*, determinate dagli antiquati concetti della metafisica punitiva.

***

Sarebbe puerile ed ingiusto pigliarsela con i giurati milanesi per il verdetto inaspettato e per la sua ridicola conseguenza di 12 giorni di carcere per... sottrazione di cadavere.

Da gran tempo io sono contrario al giurì per i delitti comuni – poiché credo che la giustizia penale sia o debba essere una *funzione tecnica*, per cui occorrono speciali cognizioni non tanto giuridiche quanto psicologiche, psichiatriche, antropologiche, eccetera. Ma è pure grande tempo che, a proposito del giurì, io sostenni non potersi esso abolire se prima non sia organizzata una magistratura tecnica, che abbia i due requisiti essenziali della *capacità* e della *indipendenza*. Anche perché, dicevo, frattanto i verdetti dei giurati servono spesso a mettere in luce il contrasto tra il giudizio della pubblica coscienza e le norme astratte della metafisica penale. Contrasto che sfugge nei trecentomila processi, che ogni anno si 'celebrano' in Italia (per delitti e contravvenzioni) senza che la pubblica attenzione se ne occupi: ma contrasto, che balza fuori, vivo e stridente, appena un processo si tolga, per la ferocia o la stranezza del fatto, dalla monotonia assonnata dei quotidiani giudizi.

***

E il verdetto milanese è una conferma eloquente di queste affermazioni della scuola criminale positiva.

Che l'Olivo fosse un 'anormale' – e più specialmente un tipo di criminaloide pazzesco e nevrotico – è ormai evidente. Basta aver letto il suo interrogatorio alle Assise, terminato con una crisi epilettica o nervosa, certo non simulata, per trovare nello squartatore Olivo un tipo come quelli, che, a dozzine, io descrissi (a base delle perizie medico-legali) nella parte psicopatologica dell'*Omicidio nell'antropologia criminale*.

Ora di fronte ad un omicida-squartatore di cui il misfatto tanto ribrezzo aveva suscitato nella pubblica coscienza, quale è la preoccupazione della giustizia penale inspirata ai vecchi concetti?

è una sola: trovare il numero dell'articolo di codice penale che è meglio risponde ai termini del *fatto materiale* e che porti *la pena più severa*... resistendo accanitamente a qualsiasi tentativo di mettere in luce *la personalità del delinquente*.

E questo, perché se si ammette che l'omicida-squartatore è un pazzo o uno squilibrato, secondo le vecchie idee, non si può più punire o lo si deve colpire con una dose assai meno forte di pena!

Di qui la lotta accanita ed irragionevole e scandalosa fra i magistrati (pubblico ministero e presidente d'Assise) e la difesa, per vedere a chi strapperà dai giurati una maggiore o minore dose di castigo!

Il presidente si rifiuta di mettere la subordinata del 'ferimento seguito da morte' – sol perché la pena ne sarebbe stata di qualche anno più breve – e tratta la giustizia come fosse un giuoco d'azzardo: o tutto o niente.

E i giurati – che in Italia non hanno come in Inghilterra, la facoltà di affermare le ipotesi subordinate, di loro iniziativa – sentendo, nella loro coscienza, che quel Olivo non era un delinquente nato, ma uno squilibrato, resistono alla coartazione della loro coscienza e ammettono il fatto materiale dell'uxoricidio, ma affermano che l'Olivo non era completamente irresponsabile (affermandone la semi-responsabilità nella parte relativa alla sottrazione del cadavere) e soggiungono che però non inferse i colpi con positiva intenzione di uccidere. Avrebbero – se avessero potuto, se il presidente avesse messo il quesito subordinato – affermato che però dai colpi dati a scopo di ferimento era derivata la morte.

E il verdetto, in sé, è perfettamente logico e, dirò anche, in accordo coi caratteri personali dell'accusato e le circostanze del fatto.

La conseguenza del verdetto è stata però grottescamente assurda.

***

E si noti. Se i giurati avessero affermata la pazzia completa dell'Olivo, la Corte avrebbe potuto ordinarne la consegna all'autorità di pubblica sicurezza per farlo rinchiudere in un manicomio, come 'pazzo pericoloso'. Avendo invece negata la completa pazzia ma anche la intenzione omicida, l'Olivo deve essere messo in libertà; anche perché nel caso di semi-responsabilità (riconosciuta nell'Olivo) la Corte potrebbe farne scontare la pena di... 12 giorni in una 'casa di custodia': ma viceversa avendo già scontato ben più di 12 giorni col carcere preventivo, l'Olivo deve essere messo in libertà.

Di qui l'impressione acuta nel pubblico che vede un contrasto così mefistofelico fra il delitto raccapricciante e la ridicola conseguenza del solenne giudizio!

***

La colpa però, come ho dimostrato, non è questa volta dei giurati. Essi non hanno fatto che mettere ancora una volta in piena luce le assurdità sistematiche della vecchia e metafisica giustizia penale, che vede il delitto e non il delinquente.

Infatti quali sono i cardini morali e legali delle vecchia giustizia penale?

Questi: I, si deve misurare la *colpa morale* del delinquente, perché dalla sua morale responsabilità dipende la sua responsabilità legale e penale – II, la pena deve essere *commisurata* in termini fini alla colpa morale.

Ora l'una e l'altra di queste norme sono due menzogne convenzionali, perché nessun giudice, nato di donna, può misurare "la colpa morale" di una creatura umana, di cui esso ignora o non valuta la miriade di condizioni organiche e psichiche, di precedenti famigliari e di circostanze della vita sociale, che l'hanno spinta al delitto.

Gli stessi periti psichiatri sono appena *tollerati* nelle aule della giustizia penale, che vede solo il delitto o non il delinquente. E gli stessi periti, esautorati e a disagio, troppo spesso cedono anche inconsciamente alle suggestioni delle impressioni giudiziarie nel segreto dell'istruttoria o delle impressioni della folla nei casi più clamorosi.

Passanante fu dichiarato sano di mente dai periti psichiatri! Olivo fu dichiarato sano di mente dai periti psichiatri!

***

E non solo il giudice, che è un uomo, non può avere l'onniscienza per conoscere e pesare "la colpa morale" del delinquente – e tutt'al più acqueterà la sua coscienza colla transazione delle circostanze attenuanti –; ma poi viene la seconda preoccupazione, ed è quella che io chiamai della *dosimetria* penale.

La grande preoccupazione del giudice è che il reo abbia venti anni e non 15 – dieci e non 5!

E il nostro codice ha portato fino al grottesco della chineseria – onde le leggi cinesi contano i centimetri di lunghezza e grossezza dei *bambù*, che servono alla bastonatura dei condannati! – il sistema di calcolare la responsabilità morale e legale dei delinquenti colle frazioni aritmetiche! E secondo le varie circostanze aggravanti e scusanti il giudice si trasforma in contabile e aggiunge 1/3 e poi 1/4 ma poi toglie 1/4 e poi 1/6 e salta fuori, in ultimo, con la stupefacente conclusione, che tutto ben pesato e conteggiato 'castigo' proporzionato alla "colpa" del reo è questo, per esempio: 8 anni, 5 mesi, 13 giorni! Non uno di più, non uno di meno!

E novanta volte per cento il 'castigo' è il carcere, più o meno cellulare – panacea per tutti i delitti, dall'ingiuria verbale allo stupro, dal falso all'assassinio!

E se il condannato a 8 anni, 5 mesi, 13 giorni – dopo tre, quattro anni di segregazione fosse già riadattabile alla vita sociale, non importa: deve stare sino alla scadenza della dose penale! La libertà condizionale è scritta nel codice, ma quasi non si applica, appunto perché tutto il sistema è imperniato della dosimetria penale.

E se il condannato alla scadenza della pena non è ancora riadatto alla vita sociale, non importa: deve uscire in libertà, perché così vuole la dosimetria!

Figuratevi un medico alla porta di un ospedale. Egli ha una sola medicina per tutte le malattie e l'ordina a dosi fisse insieme ai giorni di ricovero nell'ospedale.

Voi che avete? Una malattia di cuore – Bene: prenderete 1 litro della medicina unica e starete 17 giorni in ospedale – Ma se fossi guarito al decimo giorno? – Non importa: resterete fino al 17°! – E se al 17° non fossi ancora guarito? – Non importa: uscirete appena scaduto il termine!

E voi che avete? Una polmonite – Bene: prenderete 2 litri e ½ della solita medicina e starete 57 giorni in ospedale e se guarite prima starete dentro lo stesso e se al 57° giorno non sarete guarito, uscirete lo stesso!

***

Così è la nostra giustizia penale, che pretende pesare la 'colpa morale' del delinquente e che pretende avere una dosimetrica per cui la pena sia proporzionata al grado di colpa, non un giorno di più non uno di meno.

E così ne viene la lotta fra giudici e difensori perché la pazzia cioè l'irresponsabilità cioè la mancanza di 'colpa morale' sia o non sia ammessa, da essa dipendendo che l'autore del delitto sia o non sia punito.

***

Tutto questo, come si vede, è assurdo ed è dannoso e pericoloso così per gli individui colpiti dalla giustizia penale come per la società che crede di preservarsi dalla loro malefica attività. Ma tutto questo sarà eliminato quando la giustizia penale si trasformerà, come la scuola positiva sostiene, in una funzione clinica di preservazione sociale dal morbo della criminalità.

Il problema essenziale ed unico, per i giudici, deve essere di provare che l'accusato è veramente l'*autore del delitto.*

Dopo di ciò, o il delitto è lieve e il delinquente non è temibile ed è adatto alla vita sociale (delinquente d'occasione o per passione scusabile) ed allora l'unica forma di sanzione dev'essere l'obbligo rigoroso di *risarcire i danni* alla vittima.

Mandare in carcere per dieci, quindici giorni chi ha ingiuriato o percosso è semplicemente stupido. E il carcere diventa, per questi delinquenti occasionali una scuola di perdizione e di perfezionamento, una specie di stufa Pasteur per la cultura dei microbi... criminali. I delinquenti occasionali diventano delinquenti abituali e la recidiva cronica sta a documentarlo.

O il delitto è grave e il delinquente è pericoloso e non è adatto alla vita sociale e allora il giudice non deve fissare *a priori* il termine della segregazione, ma deve soltanto rinviare delinquenti agli stabilimenti (colonie agricole, manicomi criminali, scuole industriali, riformatori ecc.).

In questi stabilimenti il metodo deve essere 'di cura e non di repressione' perché tutti questi delinquenti, pazzi o no, sono degli anormali, che bisogna guarire (quando non sono inguaribili) e non 'castigare' o 'punire'.

Io non posso, naturalmente, entrare qui nei dettagli tecnici che la scuola positiva propone a garanzia simultanea così dei diritti personali nei delinquenti come delle necessità sociali di preservazione dai loro misfatti.

Ma quello che era importante dedurre come insegnamento dallo scandalo giudiziario delle Assise di Milano, era dunque la prova luminosa, che questo scandalo non dipende da un verdetto bislacco, ma non è invece che l'esponente più vistoso, e perciò più istruttivo delle assurdità sistematiche, su cui si impernia e funziona la giustizia penale. Assurdità sistematiche, che sfuggono l'attenzione del gran pubblico nella miriade dei casi quotidiani e meno interessanti; ma che la scuola criminale positiva da venticinque anni oramai è venuta rilevando e documentando, per sostituire ai vieti ingranaggi della gramola giudiziaria – fatta per maciullare creature umane senza preservare la società dal morbo criminoso – le funzioni tecniche di una clinica di preservazione più umana ma più efficace, appunto perché inspirata alla vera genesi naturale del delitto nell'individuo e nell'ambiente sociale.

***

Per questo il caso dello squartatore di Milano ha confermato, una volta di più, la verità evangelica 'essere utile che avvengano gli scandali' – perché così soltanto si può scuotere la pubblica opinione ed attirare la pubblica attenzione sulle verità altrimenti inascoltate della scienza per le quali soltanto anche la giustizia penale, liberatasi dai residui di vendetta barbara e di espiazione spiritualista, diventerà una vera e propria funzione sociale di sapiente ed umana tutela così degli individui come dell'intera collettività.

Enrico Ferri

[*Avanti!*, 13 June 1904,
The Butcherer of Milan and penal justice

The Dreyfus trial has put under a magnifying glass *judicial errors* to the detriment of the innocent, which are woven into the daily work of criminal justice, even when not contaminated by political influences.

The acquittal verdict of the butcherer at the Assizes of Milan now puts under this same magnifying glass the *systematic absurdities* determined by antiquated concepts of punitive metaphysics.

***

It would be childish and unjust to blame the Milanese jurors for the unexpected verdict and its ridiculous consequence of twelve days in prison for… removal of a corpse.

I have long been against the use of a jury for common crimes – because I believe that criminal justice is or should be a *technical function* for which specialist knowledge is required and is not so much juridical as psychological, psychiatric, anthropological, etc. But I have also argued for a long time that the model of the jury cannot be abolished unless a technical judiciary, possessed of the two essential requirements of *capacity* and *independence*, has first been put in place. Also, because, as I have said, the verdict of a jury often serves to highlight the difference between the judgement of a public conscience and the abstract norms of penal metaphysics. This difference goes unobserved in the three hundred thousand trials that are 'celebrated' every year in Italy (for crimes and contraventions) with no public attention directed towards them, but the contrast leaps out, vital and strident, as soon as a trial, whether because of the ferocity or very strangeness of its facts, stands out from the sleepy monotony of the run of daily judgements.

***

And the Milanese verdict is an eloquent confirmation of these affirmations of the Positivist Criminal School.

It is now evident that Olivo was a 'deviant' – and more specifically, a species of mad and neurotic criminaloid. It is enough to have read about his interrogation at the Court of Assizes, which ended with an epileptic or nervous crisis – clearly not feigned – to perceive in the butcherer Olivo such a species, the like of which I have described dozens of times (on the basis of forensic medical reports) in the psychopathological section of *Murder in Criminal Anthropology*.

Now, faced with a murderer-butcherer whose crime has aroused so much disgust in the public conscience, what is the role of criminal justice inspired by the ancient concepts?

It has just one role: to locate the number of the article of the penal code that best responds to the terms of the *material fact* and that carries the *most severe penalty*... doggedly resisting any attempt to highlight the *personality of the criminal*.

And this is because if we admit that the murderer-butcherer is a madman or a lunatic, according to the old models, he then either cannot be punished at all or must be prescribed a much less strong dose of punishment!

Hence the fierce and unreasonable and scandalous fight between the magistrates (the Public Prosecutor and the President of the Assizes) and the defence to see who will wring the greater or lesser dose of punishment from the jurors!

The President refuses to include the clause 'wounding followed by death' – because the sentence would have been a few years shorter – and treats justice as if it were a game of chance: all or nothing.

And since the jurors – who, in Italy, unlike in England, do not have the power to affirm subordinate hypotheses on their own initiative – feel, at the level of their consciences, that Olivo is not a born criminal but rather a lunatic, they resist the coercion of their conscience and admit instead a material fact of uxoricide but also affirm that Olivo was not completely irresponsible (admitting his partial responsibility in the section relating to the removal of the body), adding, however, that he had not inflicted the blows with the positive intention of killing. If they could, had the President posed the subordinate question, they would have affirmed that the blows inflicted with intent to wound had, however, resulted in death.

And the verdict, in itself, is perfectly logical and, I will also say, in accordance with the personal characteristics of the accused and the circumstances of the fact.

The consequence of the verdict was, however, grotesquely absurd.

***

And note. If the jurors had affirmed the complete insanity of Olivo, the Court could have ordered his delivery to the public security authorities to have him locked up in a mental asylum as a 'dangerous madman'. But because they had instead denied complete insanity but also homicidal intent, Olivo had to be released; also because in the case of partial responsibility (recognised in Olivo), the Court could make him serve the sentence of… twelve days in a 'custody house', but having already served well over twelve days in preventive detention, instead Olivo had to be released.

And what the public consequently sees is a Mephistophelian contrast between the horrific crime and the ridiculous response of the solemn judgement of the court!

***

However, as I have demonstrated, this time the fault is not the jurors'. They have merely brought to light once again the systematic absurdities of the old and metaphysical model of criminal justice, which sees the crime and not the criminal.

In point of fact, what are the moral and legal cornerstones of the old criminal justice system?

They are these: (I) the *moral guilt* of the criminal must be measured, because his legal and criminal responsibility depends on his moral responsibility; (II) the punishment must be *commensurate*, in nuanced terms, with the degree of moral guilt.

Now, both these norms represent two conventional lies, since no judge born of woman can measure 'the moral guilt' of any human creature if he ignores or does not evaluate a myriad organic and psychic conditions, the individual's family history, and social circumstances that have impelled him towards the crime.

The same psychiatric experts are barely *tolerated* in the courts of criminal justice, which see only the crime, not the criminal. And the same experts, disempowered and ill at ease, too often give in, including unconsciously, to the suggestions of judicial opinion behind closed doors, or even to popular opinion in the most sensational cases.

Passanante was declared sane by the psychiatric experts! Olivo has been declared sane by the psychiatric experts!

***

And not only is the judge, who is a human being, not possessed of the omniscience to know and weigh the 'moral guilt' of the criminal – at most, he will appease his conscience with the transaction of mitigating circumstances – but there follows the second concern, that which I have named penal *dosimetry*.

The great preoccupation of the judge is that the criminal may be given twenty rather than fifteen years – ten rather than five!

And our code has led to the grotesqueness of Chineseism – whereby the Chinese laws count the centimetres' length and thickness of the swatches of *bamboo* used to beat the condemned! – the system of calculating the moral and legal responsibility of criminals through arithmetic fractions! And, consistent with various aggravating and extenuating circumstances, the judge turns into an accountant, adding a third and then a quarter, but then taking away a quarter and a sixth, and finally comes up with the astonishing conclusion that all weighed and counted, the 'punishment' proportionate to the 'guilt' of the criminal is this (for example): eight years, five months, thirteen days! No more, no less!

And ninety times out of a hundred, the 'punishment' is prison, more or less *cellular* – a panacea for all crimes, from slander to rape, forgery to murder!

And were that individual sentenced to eight years, five months, thirteen days, be ready once again for civic life after three, four years of segregation, no matter: he must stay until the penal dose has expired! Conditional release is written into the code, but it is almost never applied, precisely because the entire system is based on penal dosimetry.

And if the convict is not fit for civic life by the end of his sentence, no matter: he must be freed, because that is what the dosimetry demands!

Imagine a doctor at the entrance to a hospital. He has only one remedy for all illnesses and dispenses it in fixed doses along with the number of days of hospitalisation.

What's wrong with you? Heart disease. Fine: for you, it will be one litre of the standard medicine and a hospital stay of seventeen days. But what if I'm cured on day ten? No matter: you'll be staying until the seventeenth! And what if by the seventeenth I'm not cured? No difference: you will be released as soon as the term is done!

And what's the matter with you? Pneumonia. Well, for you, it's two and a half litres of the standard medicine, and you will be in the hospital for 57 days, and if you're cured before, you'll stay in anyway, and if on day 57 you're not cured, you will still be released!

***

This is our criminal justice system, which claims to weigh the 'moral guilt' of the criminal and to have a dosimetric system such that the punishment is exactly proportionate to the degree of guilt, not one day more, not one day less.

And so the struggle between judges and defence attorneys arises because madness – that is, irresponsibility – that is, lack of 'moral guilt' – is or is not admitted, and on this, the punishment or otherwise of the perpetrator of the crime depends.

***

All this, as can be seen, is absurd and is harmful and dangerous both for the individuals affected by criminal justice and for the society that believes it is protecting itself from their evil activity. But all this will be eliminated when criminal justice is transformed, as the Positivist School maintains, into a clinical function of social preservation from the disease of criminality.

The essential and only problem for judges must be to prove that the accused is truly the *perpetrator of the crime*.

From that it follows either that the crime is minor and the criminal is not to be feared and indeed is suitable for civic life (the occasional criminal, or excusable based on passion), and then the only form of sanction must be the strict obligation to *compensate* the victim *for damages*.

Sending someone to prison who has slandered or beaten a person, for ten or fifteen days, is simply stupid. And prison becomes, for these occasional criminals, a school for perdition and refinement, a kind of hot air oven for breeding a culture of criminal... microbes. Occasional criminals become habitual criminals, and chronic recidivism is evidence of this.

Either the crime is serious, and the criminal is dangerous and not suited to civic life, and then the judge must not set *a priori* the term of segregation but must only send criminals to certain establishments (agricultural colonies, criminal asylums, industrial schools, rehabilitation, etc.).

In these establishments, the method must be 'cure and not repression', because all such criminals, mad or not, are abnormal individuals who must be cured (when they are not incurable), rather than 'punished' or 'chastised'.

Here I cannot, of course, go into the technical details proposed by the Positivist School to simultaneously guarantee both the personal rights of criminals and societal needs for protection from their misdeeds.

But what is thus important to deduce as a lesson from the judicial scandal of the Milan Assizes is the shining proof that this scandal does not depend on a bizarre verdict but is instead only the most visible, and therefore most instructive, exponent of the systematic absurdities on which criminal justice is based and functions. Systematic absurdities, which escape the attention of the general public in the myriad daily and less interesting cases, but that the positive criminal school has been detecting and documenting for twenty-five years now, to replace the stale mechanisms of the judicial mill – made so as to crush human beings without protecting society from the disease of criminality – with the technical functions of a more humane but more effective preservation clinic, precisely because it is inspired by the true natural genesis of crime within the individual and in the social context.

***

For this reason, the case of the butcherer of Milan has confirmed, once again, the evangelical truth that 'it is useful that scandals occur' – because only in this way can public opinion be shaken and public attention drawn to the otherwise unheard truths of science, for which only criminal justice, freed from the residues of barbaric revenge and spiritualist atonement, will become a true social function of wise and humane protection of individuals as well as of the entire community.

Enrico Ferri]

6

Il secolo, 14/15 giugno 1904, p. 3,
Il caso Olivo [**estratto**]

È orribile il solo pensare che l'Olivo possa tranquillamente vivere in mezzo alla società civile. Egli non prova neppure il rimorso per l'assassinio commesso e per aver tagliata a pezzi la donna che diceva di amare. Il suo cinismo sorpassa ogni limite del credibile.

Per noi è uno dei più pericolosi uomini che passeggino liberamente in mezzo agli altri. Egli dimostrò nell'uxoricidio tanta freddezza di animo che lo si può credere capace di compiere, senza esitare, qualsiasi azione consimile.

Il fantasma della donna che fu sua e che ammazzò a coltellate, non turba le sue notti.

La impressione tattile, rabbrividente, della carne che colle sue mani guastò raspandola dalle ossa della moglie, non gli ha lasciato ricordo maggiore di quello di aver spolpato un pollo per cuocerlo in fricassea: e si divertiva ridendo a fare i salti nella gabbia per dimostrare il tonfo fatto dal corpo della moglie assassinata! Né basta ancora: egli si scaglia contro gli alienisti che non l'hanno giudicato matto, perché, essendo nel pieno possesso delle sue facoltà mentali, desiderava e procurava con ogni arte, di farsi giudicare irresponsabile.

[...]

Quando il suo nome sarà proferito, ciascuno gli farà il vuoto intorno, perché egli, assolto dai giurati per l'ignoranza di un magistrato e per cavilli legulei, è però colpito da una condanna morale che suscita il ribrezzo.

Si allontani da Milano, dall'Italia: si faccia dimenticare.

[*Il secolo*, 14/15 June 1904, p. 3,
The Olivo case [**excerpt**]

It is dreadful to think that Olivo can live peacefully in the midst of civil society. He does not even feel remorse for the murder he has committed and for having chopped into pieces the woman he said he loved. His cynicism surpasses all limits of credibility.

For us, he is one of the most dangerous men who walk freely among others. In his uxoricide, he demonstrated such coldness of spirit that one could believe him capable of carrying out any similar act without hesitation.

The ghost of this woman, his own woman, whom he stabbed to death, does not trouble his nights.

The shuddering, tactile impression of that flesh that he despoiled with his own hands, ripping it from his wife's bones, left him with a memory no more remarkable than had he stripped the flesh of a chicken to cook it in a fricassee; further, he even found it amusing, laughing, to jump about in the dock to demonstrate the thud the body of his murdered wife made! Even this is not enough: he lashes out against those alienists who did not judge him mad, because, being in full possession of his mental faculties, he wanted and sought with every skill he owned to be judged mentally unsound.

[...]

When his name is mentioned, everyone will draw a blank around him because, acquitted by the jurors as a result of a magistrate's ignorance and legalistic loopholes, he nonetheless is tainted by a moral condemnation that arouses disgust.

May he leave Milan, leave Italy: may he let himself be forgotten.]

7

Avanti!, 15 giugno 1904,
Olivo e la difesa sociale

Il caso Olivo ormai è noto a tutti.

Questo strano uomo, che fino a 47 anni aveva condotto una vita illibata, salvo aver da giovinetto ferito *per un pisello* un suo compagno, e che si era mostrato una specie di mattoide geniale, un po' filologo, un po' poeta, un po' matematico, sopratutto contabile; che aveva una grande idea di sé, ma che con tutti gli sforzi più grandi non era riescito che ad un posto secondario di ragioniere, senza una ragione speciale, sposa una mezza prostituta, volgarissima di parole, e di atti, che lo tradisce quasi sotto i suoi occhi e lo insulta coi termini i più atroci di *stupido*, di *mezzano*, ecc., e giunge negli ultimi tempi – fatta ogni giorno più audace dalla speranza di una lucrosa separazione – a provocarlo con schiaffi, con sputi e con minaccia di revolverate e coltellate.

Ed egli che aveva amato ciecamente quella donna, che la riguardava come la sua bambola, che le passava parecchi capricci, mentre stretto da una morbosa avarizia qualche volta le negava il necessario, egli che era di tempra irascibile, reagiva violentemente a schiaffi e ad insulti, aveva tentato la separazione, aveva indietreggiato per la paura delle spese, egli si imbattè in un ultimo litigio che fece traboccare il vaso.

Un giorno essa pretese di voler una maestra; ma egli che si piccava di purismo e per giunta era avaro credeva di supplirvi meglio da sé stesso e non la volle concedere; ma andò da quella maestra, la pregò di congedarsi, ma senza dire che egli ve l'avesse indotta. Costei invece dichiarò nettamente che lasciava l'insegnamento perché costretta da lui. Da qui quella irritazione, che era andata accumulandosi ed aumentandosi da tanti giorni fra loro, toccò il suo colmo; la Beccaro giunse a minacciarlo di coltello, a infamare la sua madre, onde egli la uccide a colpi di coltello; e cade subito dopo, in un accesso di torpore in cui rimane parecchie ore svegliandosi poi senza ricordarsi più di nulla.

Finalmente, ritornato in sé, non vede altro scampo che di far scomparire gli avanzi della consorte, ne scarna e taglia il cadavere con molta abilità. I visceri e le parti più carnose getta in una latrina; dà ad intendere ai vicini che la moglie è andata a Biella; e dopo aver dormito indifferente quattro giorni con le ossa e la testa, scarnificati e disinfettati della sua vittima, porta quei pezzi di cadavere a Genova in una valigia e li getta a mare con così poca accortezza che essi ritornano subito a galla e così vien scoperto, tanto più che lungo la strada la sua invincibile avarizia aveva lasciato numerose traccie della sua presenza. Aveva dato due soldi di mancia al bambino che gli portava la ferale valigia, e questionato sul prezzo col vetturale a Genova.

Arrestato fu giudicato perfettamente normale dai periti, che esclusero però la premeditazione.

Nelle Assise si difese abilmente mostrando una calma notevole, e una grande sincerità, ma si notò però il fenomeno singolare, che egli si preoccupava più della sua fama di letterato e di matematico che dell'accusa di assassino e che egli alternava la poesia più sentimentale colla contabilità veramente comica, non solo delle spese fatte anno per anno, mese per mese, per vitto e alloggio, ma perfino del numero degli sputi – né più né meno – lanciatigli dalla moglie.

Fu poi notevole che, a un tratto, sotto l'esaurimento delle risposte e sotto l'emozione di avere ricostrutta freddamente la scena del delitto fu preso da un accesso epilettoide, in cui nemmeno tre carabinieri bastarono a frenarlo.

L'importanza di questo accesso era grande, perché dalle lettere sequestrate si era già saputo che da giovinetto aveva sofferto di affezioni cerebrali per cui cadeva di notte sotto il letto; che a 20 anni gli si rinnovarono sotto l'insolazione e si complicarono con fenomeni psichici, ronzii alle orecchie, smemoratezza, offuscamento della vista – fenomeni che pare sieno ricomparsi nella notte in cui successe il delitto – e che nel '78 fu per tre volte all'ospedale di Ciriè.

Ora ravvicinando questi fatti alla strana ottusità psichica per cui rimase indifferente davanti al cadavere e ne fece sì triste scempio, ai contrasti così straordinari delle facoltà mentali e psichiche che sono così frequenti negli epilettici e sopratutto alla irascibilità, che lo dominava continuamente contro i vicini, i parenti, perfino contro i clienti del suo padrone, ve n'era abbastanza per conchiudere che si trattava non di un criminale nato, ma di un criminaloide più mattoide che geniale trascinato al delitto dal fondo epilettico insieme e dalla grave provocazione che seguiva ad una serie di cause irritanti, che avrebbero indotto a scoppi violenti un uomo anche più tranquillo di lui.

***

È evidente che egli meritava una pena non gravissima, ma la pena per lo meno per un ferimento seguito da morte o per la uccisione in rissa. Invece la giuria lo ha completamente assolto.

***

Non io che pure ho sostenuto risolutamente trattarsi di un criminaloide e non di un criminale nato, non io approvo questa eccessiva indulgenza; ma la comprendo se non la giustifico dinnanzi alle ingiuste ed eccessive durezze di un Pubblico Ministero che ne voleva fare un volgare assassino, nonché alla miopia di quei periti che non vollero ammettere l'epilessia che pure i giurati ebbero sotto i loro occhi, e nemmeno intravvidero (tranne l'Ellero) i rapporti di questa colle strane condizioni psichiche e affettive di quel criminaloide epilettico. Fecero essi, i giurati, a lor modo e troppo grossolanamente un po' di quella antropologia criminale che gli scienziati e i giuristi non vollero riconoscere e applicare.

***

Io capisco però come debba essersi trovata imbarazzata la giuria, perché mancano nelle nostre leggi le applicazioni più elementari delle scoperte dell'antropologia criminale.

Non parlo del manicomio criminale in cui se si trattava di un vero omicida epilettico avrebbe dovuto l'Olivo essere rinchiuso per tutta la vita o per lo meno fino a completa guarigione. Ma trattandosi di una forma più mite, per lo meno bisognava che i giurati potessero avere la scelta per una pena che equivalesse a quella del ferimento seguito da morte o dalla uccisione non premeditata.

Mancano alla nostra legislazione quei perfezionamenti che si chiamano le pene indeterminate.

Come bene Ferri si espresse, il legislatore considerando il delitto in astratto piuttosto che il delinquente dosava i rimedi penali come il terapeuta una volta le droghe medicinali.

Per ogni malattia esisteva una data cura con una data dose di rimedio; ma anche in medicina la cosa è cambiata: e si studia *la malattia* non solo, ma insieme e più anche il *malato*; e si varia la cura d'una stessa malattia secondo che l'ammalato è anemico o iperemico, pletorico o scrofoloso, sifilitico, ecc.

Così deve essere per la cura dei delinquenti.

E così la differenza di pena per i vari reati non dovrebbe essere soltanto di dose, di anni cioè, di mesi, di giorni; ma dovrebbe variare anche secondo le speciali condizioni personali e sociali del reo, a seconda che la criminalità sia pazzesca o d'occasione o di passione oppure si tratti di criminale nato, che rappresenta la massima pericolosità per la grande probabilità di recidiva.

È evidente che la stessa pena non poteva applicarsi per un assassino indurito come per un uomo che per 47 anni non aveva mai commesso nessun atto colpevole e che al delitto era stato trascinato da una causa gravissima senza né agguato né complici.

D'altra parte l'ottusità morale – mostrata nell'unirsi con una femmina indegna, nel convivere parecchi giorni coi resti della sua vittima, nel parlare e descrivere atti così ripugnanti colla massima indifferenza – doveva esser messa sulla bilancia per un trattamento speciale e dalla risultante di tutti questi giudizi parziali, se non veniva l'invio al manicomio criminale, si sarebbe dovuto infliggere una pena che mettesse il condannato nella impossibilità della recidiva per parecchio tempo.

Ad ogni modo sarà da deplorare la precipitosa ed esagerata indulgenza di questa giuria, ma è anche da deplorare che manchino dei provvedimenti legislativi che potrebbero prevenirla; senza cadere in quegli eccessi opposti a cui si sono abbandonati gli interpreti inflessibili della legge, che non solo ignorano l'antropologia criminale, ma molte volte ignorano la più elementare psicologia.

Cesare Lombroso

[*Avanti!*, 15 June 1904,
Olivo and the social defence

The Olivo case is now known to everyone.

This strange man, who up to the age of 47 had led a blameless life, other than as a young man wounding one of his companions *for the price of a pea*, and who had shown himself to be a sort of brilliant mattoid, part-philologist, part-poet, part-mathematician, above all accountant, with a high opinion of himself but who, despite his greatest efforts, had risen only to an accountant position of minor importance, for no obvious reason marries a quasi-prostitute, vulgar in speech and deed, who betrays him almost before his eyes and insults him with the most atrocious terms, *stupid*, *pimp*, etc., and latterly – emboldened day by day by the hope of a lucrative separation – begins to provoke him through slapping, spitting and the threat of gunshots and stabbing.

And he, who had blindly loved this woman, who had looked at her as his doll, who gave in to her many whims, and while gripped by morbid avarice sometimes denied her what was necessary, he who was of an irascible nature, reacting violently to such slaps and insults, had attempted separation, had backed away through fear of the expense had gotten into one last fight that was the straw that broke the camel's back.

One day she had claimed she wanted a teacher; he, who prided himself on purism and was also tight, believed he could make it up better himself and did not want to grant [her this opportunity]; he went to her teacher and said the lessons were to stop, but without saying that he had induced this decision. By contrast, she clearly stated that the teaching came to an end because she was forced by him to stop it. And so, the irritation, which had been accumulating and growing between them for many days, reached its peak: Beccaro went so far as to threaten him with a knife and to insult his mother, so he killed her with a knife; immediately afterwards, he fell into a torpor in which he remained for several hours, waking up without remembering anything.

Finally, returning to his senses, he sees no other way out than to get rid of his wife's remains, de-boning and dissecting the corpse with great skill. He throws the viscera and fleshiest parts into a latrine; he leads the neighbours to believe his wife has gone to Biella; and having blithely slept for four days with the bones and head nearby, stripped and disinfected of his victim, he takes those pieces of the corpse to Genoa in a suitcase and throws them into the sea with so little foresight that they immediately return to the surface, and so he is discovered, especially since along the way his invincible avarice had left numerous traces of his presence. He had given a two-cent tip to the child who carried the morbid suitcase and had quarrelled over the price with the carrier in Genoa.

Arrested, he was judged perfectly normal by the experts, who nonetheless ruled out premeditation.

At the Assizes, he defended himself skilfully, showing remarkable calm and great sincerity, but of note was the singular phenomenon that he was more concerned about his fame as a man of letters and a mathematician than about the accusation that he was a murderer and that he alternated his more sentimental poetry with truly comical accounting, not only of monthly and annual expenses for food and lodging but also of even the number of times – no more, no less – that his wife spat at him.

It was then notable that, suddenly, under the exhausting strain of his answers and the emotion of coldly reconstructing the scene of the crime, he was gripped by an epileptoid attack that even three carabinieri were not enough to quell.

This attack was of great importance because from letters seized in the investigation, it was already known that as a young man he had suffered from cerebral affections that caused him to fall from the bed at night; that, at the age of twenty, these occurred again because of sunstroke and were complicated by psychic phenomena, ringing in the ears, forgetfulness, blurred vision – phenomena that appear to have resurfaced on the night the crime occurred – and that three times he was taken to Ciriè hospital in '78.

Now, comparing these facts to the strange psychic dullness that rendered him indifferent to the corpse and led him to make such a sad mess of it, to the extraordinary contrasts of his mental and psychic faculties that are so frequent in epileptics, and above all to the irascibility that continually brought him into conflict with his neighbours, relatives, even his master's clients, there was enough to conclude that he was not a born criminal but rather a criminaloid, more mattoid than brilliant, dragged into the crime both by the depths of his epilepsy and the serious repeated provocation that would have led a man calmer yet than him to violent outbursts.

***

It is clear that he did not deserve the most serious punishment, but at least punishment for injury that led to death or for death in a brawl. Instead, the jury completely acquitted him.

***

Even though I resolutely maintain that he was a criminaloid and not a born criminal, I do not approve of this excessive indulgence, but I do understand it, even if I do not seek to justify it in the face of the unjust and excessive harshness of a Public Prosecutor who wanted to make him a vulgar murderer, as well as the shortsightedness of those experts who did not want to admit the epilepsy that even the jurors could see before their own eyes, nor yet – other than Ellero – even glimpse signs of the relationships between this and the strange psychic and emotional conditions of the epileptic criminaloid.

They, the jurors, in their own way and too coarsely, conducted some of the criminal anthropology work that scientists and jurists did not want to recognise and apply.

***

However, I understand that the jury must have been put in a difficult situation because our laws fail to include the most basic application of the discoveries of criminal anthropology.

I'm not talking about the criminal asylum where, if he were a real epileptic murderer, Olivo would have had to be locked up for life, or at least until he was fully cured. But since it was a milder form, at least the jurors needed to be able to have the choice of a punishment equivalent to that of wounding followed by death or unpremeditated killing.

Our legislation lacks those ameliorations known as indeterminate sentences.

As Ferri has well-articulated, the legislator, by abstractly considering the crime rather than the criminal, has measured out penal remedies in the same way that the therapist once dosed medicinal drugs.

For every disease there was a given cure with a given dose of remedy, but even in medicine, things have changed: not only is *the disease* studied, but also the *patient* at the same time, and the treatment of the same disease varies according to whether the patient is anaemic or hyperaemic, plethoric or scrofulous, syphilitic, etc.

The treatment of criminals should be the same.

And so, the difference in punishment for various crimes should not only be in terms of dose, that is, years, months, days; but should also vary according to the particular personal and social context of the offender, depending on whether the crime is one of insanity or opportunity or passion, or whether he is a born criminal who represents maximum danger due to the great probability of recidivism.

It is evident that the same punishment could not be applied to a hardened murderer as to a man who had never committed a culpable act in forty-seven years and was dragged into a crime through a very serious cause and with neither ambush nor accomplices.

On the other hand, the moral obtuseness – shown in his uniting with an unworthy female, in living for several days with his victim's remains, and in speaking of and describing such repugnant acts with the utmost indifference

– must be weighed on the scale for special treatment; and resulting from all these partial judgements, were the sentence not delivery to the criminal asylum, a punishment would have to be measured that would make it impossible for the condemned man to reoffend for a long time.

In any case, the hasty and exaggerated indulgence of this jury is to be deplored, but it is also deplorable that there is a lack of legislative measures to prevent it, albeit without falling into those opposite excesses to which the inflexible interpreters of the law, those who not only ignore criminal anthropology but often also the most elementary psychology, have abandoned themselves.

Cesare Lombroso]

8

I tribunali, 19 giugno 1904, pp. 2–3,
Lettera di Alberto Olivo a Cesare Lombroso [**estratto**]

Ho letto e riletto attentamente il suo articolo, e meditatolo lungamente: e mentre son d'accordo con lei su quello che chiamerò, per così esprimermi, il nocciolo del suo discorso, non posso a meno di rilevare alcune asserzioni inesatte ed arrischiate, che un uomo come lei, posto dalla scienza e dall'ingegno in un posto così eminente, non si sarebbe dovuto lasciar sfuggire dalla penna, ma che trovano forse la loro giustificazione nella fretta di un articolo da giornale. E mi spiego.

***

Anzitutto Ella parla *di scoppi d'ira furibonda per cause lievissime*. Io credo che questa frase le sia stata suggerita dal fatto delle mie frequenti collere con mia moglie a motivo del suo vezzo di annacquarmi il vino. A parte che l'espressione *furibonda collera* è molto iperbolica, non le sembra, *egregio signor Professore*, che un tale fatto, ripetuto tutti i giorni e per molti anni di seguito, coll'intenzione nella colpevole, anzi col deliberato proposito, di far dispetto al marito, di farlo arrabbiare debba, alla perfine far perdere la pazienza anche ad un santo? E basti per ora di ciò.

Ben più grave è la sua accusa contenuta nella frase: *marito disonorato volontariamente*, e nel periodo: *Né si concilia colla sua fierezza l'acquiescenza con cui si adatta ad accettare appunto da questi ex protettori della moglie, somme troppo scarse per un sollievo anche momentaneo, ma pur sempre disonoranti.*

E qui io vorrei anzitutto sapere da quali fatti ella si sia sentito o creduto autorizzato ad ammettere con tanta convinzione e sicurezza che io sapessi dell'infedeltà di mia moglie e mi vi acconciassi acquiescente e quasi quasi compiacente, annuente; mentre all'opposto è emerso dal dibattimento in modo luminosissimo ed inconfutabile che io ne ero affatto all'oscuro; e testimoni serii e di indubbia onestà e sincerità, non solo, ma *bene addentro alle segrete cose*, hanno dichiarato recisamente che si trattava di un'infame calunnia di quella disgraziata, e che io non sono uomo da discendere a simili bassezze, da cadere in tanta abiezione, da dormire tranquillamente e supino sulla prostituzione della moglie.

[...]

Ella si meraviglia come un uomo così fiero potesse dare la stessa importanza agli insulti di mezzano e di stupido ed agli sputi lanciati in viso da mia moglie, ed al fatto che questa mi annacquava il vino. Mi permetta di dirle, esimio signor Professore, che questa cavatina non mi sembra degna di un uomo di tanto acume quale è lei.

Ella sa benissimo come alle volte un semplice atto in apparenza insignificante può offendere più che la plateale delle ingiurie.

Alle ingiurie di mezzano e di stupido io poteva restare anche indifferente per tre buone ragioni: la prima perché sapevo benissimo di non essere né un *souteneur* né uno stupido; la seconda perché le ingiurie, gli oltraggi restavano nel sacro penetrale della casa e non erano pubblici; la terza perché le offese erano figlie della passione.

E poi *verba volant* e non lacerano le carni né lasciano traccia. Invece l'atto di annacquare, di battezzare il vino, così insignificante e ridicolo in apparenza, era all'opposto più grave di quello che a tutta prima non sembri; grave e pel momento e per l'intenzione e la conseguenza. Infatti, il movente: una sete, una passione morbosa per il vino; passione volgare e indegna di una donna che si rispetta; dannosa nei riguardi della salute e del carattere; pericolosa per la pace e la quiete domestica. L'intenzione: il dispetto, sapendo essa mia moglie che non poteva far cosa che più m'indisponesse e m'irritasse, per l'idea dell'inganno di cui ero vittima e della beffa contenuta nell'inganno stesso, e che equivaleva a un'ingiuria, perché equivaleva a trattarmi come un imbecille. Le conseguenze materiali e morali. E *in primis et ante omnia* un doppio sciupo: di vino, cioè che andava a finire, perché guasto e sciupato, nella latrina; di denaro, per un maggior dispendio, che non mi era consentito dalle mie finanze. E dove lascio le questioni e le noje col fornitore del vino, sul quale e sui cui adepti essa rovesciava la responsabilità del vino scadente? E delle conseguenze morali ho già detto poco fa, parlando del movente.

Come Ella vede dunque, da un atto in apparenza così semplice e futile ne derivava a me un'ingiuria, dirò così, complessa e gravissima come quella che mi feriva nell'animo per l'inganno fatto alla mia fiducia, per la continua sfida alla mia pazienza, per il disprezzo opposto alle mie preghiere ed esortazioni; e mi danneggiava nella borsa (offesa gravissima per un avaro) la quale non poteva comportare le continuate offese. Che ne pensa illustrissimo signor professore?

[...]

Né posso sorpassare sulla taccia di *vanitoso, superbo*, che Ella mi azzecca, e sull'appunto che mi fa di *preoccuparmi più della mia fama di contabile, di letterato, di purista, che degli eccessi da me commessi*. In uno stato d'animo e di mente, ed in condizioni di fisico anormali, eccezionali. Mi duole di dover rilevare l'ingiustizia e l'irragionevolezza di tali accuse, che mi sembrano affatto ingiustificate e destituite di serio fondamento.

[...]

Strana poi sulle sue labbra l'osservazione che io mi sia dato ad una *carriera mediocre*, malgrado la mia (ripeto le sue parole) *profonda cultura letteraria*. Troppe cose avrei da dirle su quest'argomento, le quali le spiegherebbero l'enigma. Mi limiterò solo a farle osservare che un impiego quale io occupavo all'epoca della mia disgrazia, e col quale guadagnavo 275 lire il mese, vale a dire *tremilatrecento* lire l'anno (ed oggi ne avrei guadagnate *tremilaseicento*) non si può mediocre. E quando si pensi che io non ho alcun diploma né di ragioniere, né di ingegnere, né di dottore *in utroque* o d'altro, non vien voglia di domandarsi se sia più mediocre ma più desiderabile la carriera di certi avvocati, dottori, medici, professori, ingegneri che guadagnano 1800 o 2000 lire l'anno oppure se non sia più desiderabile perché meno mediocre la carriera di un semplice mortale non laureato, quale io sono, che guadagna il doppio? E notisi che io avevo davanti un avvenire che riserbava a maggiori fastigi?

[...]

Mi è stata poi lanciata l'accusa di non aver mai avuto un pensiero pietoso per la mia povera Ernestina; mai una parola di rammarico e di esecrezione per quello che ho fatto di quelle misere membra.

Errore! Dio solo mi è testimone di quante lacrime ho sparse nella mia cella durante l'anno di reclusione trascorso in quell'ospizio del dolore e di vergogna. Dio solo sa quale lotta terribile e diuturna ho dovuto sostenere contro me stesso e contro la disperazione per non infrangermi la testa contro le pareti della mia cella. Dio solo sa che non è passato giorno che io non abbia dedicato tutto il mio pensiero e tutti gli affetti dell'animo mio a quella disgraziata. Dio solo sa quanto le abbia rimpianto la sua perdita prematura: come io l'abbia pregato di perdonarle come io le ho perdonato e come spero che essa abbia perdonato a me, e di concederle l'eterna celeste beatitudine. Dio solo sa com'io darei volentieri il mio sangue per poterla richiamare in vita, lei che della vita sentiva la *gioia e violenta ed acuta*.

Ma perché io sono un'anima chiusa, punto espansiva, anzi aliena e nemica di ogni manifestazione aperta e clamorosa, di ogni ostentazione; perché ripugna al mio carattere di dare spettacolo delle mie affezioni, dei miei dolori, dello strazio dell'anima mia; perché sento profondamente il pudore della mia debolezza e della mia miseria; perché so piangere più col cuore che con gli occhi; per tutte queste ragioni io sono apparso agli occhi del mondo e sono creduto un uomo insensibile, senza cuore, un cinico sfacciato, uno sfidatore e temerario della pubblica sensibilità, pietà e mortalità.

[...]

Del resto pensi il mondo di me quel che vuole oggi. Tempo verrà che il giudizio degli uomini sul mio conto dovrà completamente mutarsi, e mi sarà resa giustizia. Già da tutte le parti mi piovono attestati di simpatia e di stima; parole di commiserazione e d'incoraggiamento per parte di anime generose e gentili, che non ho nemmeno il bene di conoscere e che pensano, giudicano e parlano come il cuore e la sana ragione lor detta.

[...]

Alberto Olivo

[*I tribunali*, 19 June 1904, pp. 2–3,
Letter from Alberto Olivo to Cesare Lombroso [**excerpt**]

I have read and reread your article carefully and thought about it at length, and while I agree with you on what I will call, as it were, the core of your speech, I cannot help but point out some inaccurate and risky assertions, which a man like you, placed by science and intelligence in such an eminent position, should not have let slip from his pen, but which perhaps find their justification in the haste of a newspaper article. And let me explain.

***

First of all, You speak *of outbursts of furious anger for very slight causes*. I believe that this phrase was suggested to you because of my frequent anger with my wife for her habit of watering down my wine. Apart from the fact that the expression *furious anger* is very hyperbolic, does it not seem to you, *esteemed Mr Professor*, that such a fact, repeated daily and for years on end, with the intention in the guilty party, indeed the deliberate purpose, of spiting the husband, of making him angry, should, in the end, make even a saint lose his patience? But enough on that for now.

Much more serious is your accusation contained in the phrase: *husband dishonoured voluntarily*, and in the passage: *Nor is the acquiescence with which he is willing to accept, from these very former protectors of his wife, sums too small for even momentary relief, but still dishonourable, compatible with his pride.*

[...]

And here I would first of all like to know by what facts you felt or believed yourself authorised to proclaim with such conviction and certainty that I knew of my wife's infidelity and that I was acquiescent and almost complacent, nodding along, when, on the contrary, it emerged from the debate, in the clearest and most irrefutable way, that I was completely unaware of it; and serious witnesses not only of undoubted honesty and sincerity but also *well-versed in matters of secrecy*, have declared decisively that it was an infamous slander by that unfortunate woman, and that I am not the man to descend to such depths, to fall into such abjection, as to sleep peacefully and supine upon the prostitution of his wife.

[...]

You are astonished that a man of such pride could accord the same importance to the insults of pimp and idiot, and the spitting in my face by my wife as to the fact that she watered down my wine. Allow me to tell you, esteemed Mr Professor, that this little refrain of yours seems unworthy of a man of such acumen as you.

You know very well how sometimes a simple act of apparent insignificance can offend much more than blatant insults.

I could have remained indifferent to the insults of pimp and fool for three good reasons: first, because I knew very well that I was neither a *souteneur* nor a fool; second, because the insults, the outrages, remained in the sacred depths of the home and were not in public; third, because the offences were offshoots of passion.

And, moreover, *verba volant*, not renting the flesh nor leaving any trace. By contrast, the act of watering down, of baptising, the wine, however insignificant and ridiculous it may appear, was much more grave than at first it seems – grave in motive, in intention, and in consequence. Indeed, the motive is a thirst, a morbid passion for wine; a vulgar passion, unworthy in a respectable woman; harmful both to health and character; dangerous for the peace and quiet of the household. The intention: spite, my wife knew she could do nothing to upset and irritate me more than through the very conception of the deception of which I was the victim and the mockery contained in the deception itself, which was equivalent to an insult because it was equivalent to treating me like an imbecile. The material and moral consequences. And *in primis et ante omnia*, a double wastage: of wine, that is, because, spoilt and wasted, it ended up in the latrine; of money, because of the higher expenditure, which my finances did not permit. And where do I even begin with the questions for, and irritations with, the wine supplier, onto whom and his employees she shifted the responsibility for the poor quality of the wine? And I have already spoken of the moral consequences a little while ago, in speaking of the motive.

As you can see, then, on the basis of an act that seemed so minor and trivial, I suffered an injury, in my view, of a complexity and gravity equivalent to that which wounded my soul through the betrayal of my trust, the continuous challenge to my patience, the contempt shown to my prayers and exhortations; and it damaged me in my purse (a very serious offence for a parsimonious man), which was unable to bear the continued offences. What do you think, oh most illustrious Mr Professor?

Nor can I overlook the accusations *vain*, *haughty*, that You adjoin to me and your criticism of me that *I am more concerned with my reputation as an accountant, a man of letters, a purist, than with the excesses I have committed*. In an abnormal, exceptional state of mind and spirit, and in abnormal physical conditions. I regret having to point out the injustice and unreasonableness of such accusations, which seem to me to be completely unjustified and devoid of serious foundation.

[...]

Furthermore, it is strange to hear from your lips the observation that I have given myself to a *mediocre career*, despite my (to repeat your words) *profound literary culture*. I have too many things to say to you on this subject to explain to you this enigma. I will limit myself to pointing out to you that the type of job I had at the time of my misfortune, which earned me 275 lire a month, that is to say *three thousand three hundred* lire a year (and in today's terms that would be earning me *three thousand six hundred*), cannot be mediocre. And when you consider that I have no qualification, not as an accountant, nor an engineer, nor a doctor *in utroque* nor anything else, does it not make you want to ask yourself whether the career of certain lawyers, doctors, physicians, professors, engineers, earning 1800 or 2000 lire a year is more mediocre, but more desirable, or whether in fact the career of a simple mortal without a degree, such as I, who earns twice that, is not more desirable because it is less mediocre? And you note that I had before me a future that promised greater glories?

[...]

Then I was accused of never having had a single pitying thought for my poor Ernestina; no word of regret nor execration for what I did to those miserable limbs.

Mistake! God alone is my witness to the number of tears I shed in my cell during the year of confinement spent in that hospice of pain and shame. God alone knows what a terrible and long-lasting struggle I had to sustain against myself and against despair in order not to smash my head against the walls of my cell. God alone knows that not a day went by that I did not dedicate all my thoughts and all the affections of my soul to that unfortunate woman. God alone knows how much I regretted her premature loss, how I prayed to Him to forgive her as I have forgiven her, and how I hope that she has forgiven me, and to grant her eternal celestial bliss. God alone knows how I would willingly give my blood to be able to bring her back to life, she who felt the *joy* of life, *both violent and acute*.

But because I am a closed soul, not at all expansive, indeed alien and hostile to any open and clamorous manifestation, to any ostentation; because it is repugnant to my character to make a spectacle of my affections, my pains, the torment of my soul; because I feel deeply the shame of my weakness and my misery; because I know how to cry more with my heart than with my eyes – for all these reasons I have appeared in the eyes of the world and am believed to be an insensitive man, heartless, a brazen cynic, challenging of and reckless with regard to public sensitivity, piety, and mortality.

[...]

Besides, let the world think of me what it will today. The time will come when the judgement of men upon me will have to completely change and justice will be done to me. Already from all sides I am showered with attestations of sympathy and esteem: words of commiseration and encouragement from generous and kind souls, who I do not even have the good fortune to know and who think, judge, and speak as their heart and sound reason dictate.

[...]

Alberto Olivo]

9

L'illustrazione italiana, 25 luglio 1904,
L'assoluzione di Alberto Olivo

Veramente è stato peggio che una assoluzione! i signori giurati non si sono accontentati di un verdetto iniquo: hanno voluto aggiungere alla mostruosità morale dell'assoluzione per l'omicidio, l'ironia della parziale condanna per lo scempio fatto del cadavere: e così il Presidente delle Assise – giustamente sorpreso e indignato – è stato costretto a leggere l'inverosimile sentenza con cui si assolve un uomo che ha ucciso la moglie e... lo si condanna per averne sotratto il cadavere!

Alessandro Dumas è *enfoncé*. Il suo famoso *Uccidila!* – che aveva fin troppo suggestionato i giurì francesi e italiani – rientra nei ferrivecchi della psicologia giudiziaria. Adesso, i mariti si crederanno in diritto non solo di ammazzare le mogli, ma anche di squartarle. Tanto, questa allegra funzione non conta che 12 giorni di carcere e 125 lire di multa!

Non sembra possibile che un simile scandalo sia avvenuto nella città di Milano, dove è diffusa la coltura e dove è grande il buon senso. E coloro che si dilettano a trovar le ragioni giuridiche di quanti fenomeni immorali e patologici, danno la colpa al Presidente o ai rappresentanti dell'accusa pubblica e privata i quali – ritenendo certissima l'intenzione omicida dell'imputato – non elevarono nei quesiti l'ipotesi dell'omicidio preterintenzionale. Se quest'ipotesi – si dice – fosse stata offerta ai giurati, essi l'avrebbero accolta, e lo scandaloso verdetto sarebbe stato evitato.

Io mi permetto di trovare ingenua questa spiegazione. Intanto, il modo con cui l'Olivo uccise sua moglie, mi pare dimostri limpidamente egli non voleva *soltanto* colpirla o ferirla. Ma poi, il contegno susseguente dell'imputato rivela una tale *analgesìa morale*, che è ridicola, oltre che ingenuo, il supporre che quest'uomo *fosse pentito* d'aver ucciso. Infatti chi vuol soltanto ferire e per disgrazia uccide, non avrà certo il pensiero né la *possibilità fisica* di squartare e spolpare la persona... ch'egli non aveva intenzione di uccidere! Lo scempio che Alberto Olivo fece del corpo di sua moglie morta è la prova suprema della intenzione omicida che guidava i suoi colpi sul corpo della moglie viva.

Era quindi naturale che né il Pubblico ministero né la Parte Civile pensassero ad offrire ai giurati l'ipotesi della preterintenzionalità. Sarebbe stato non solo un rimpicciolire. ma un falsare la causa!

*

Eppure, quest'ipotesi sembra abbia guidato il verdetto dei giurati, i quali, non trovandola prospettata nei quesiti loro sottoposti, dimenticarono l'orrore del delitto, e arrivarono all'assurdo dell'assoluzione.

Vi arrivarono... forse senza saperlo. Giacché la spiegazione più semplice e più vera dei non rari verdetti assurdi dei giurati consiste appunto nella dolorosa constatazione che quelle dodici egregie persone non sanno sempre quello che si fanno quando – chiuse nella camera delle loro deliberazioni – devono amministrare giustizia.

Io penso che a loro abbia giocato un brutto tiro tutta la discussione – non solo dei periti e degli avvocati, ma dei giornali – sulla responsabilità morale di Alberto Olivo. Essi si sono convinti d'avere dinanzi a sé un uomo *non certo normale*. Un epilettico? un criminaloide, come vuole Lombroso? un caratteristico, come avrebbe voluto Silvio Venturi? Non importa la precisione della diagnosi. Essi hanno sentito l'*eccezionalità* di quel tipo di delinquente; ne hanno visto, anche per gli attacchi del male in Corte d'Assise, lo squilibrio fisico, – e hanno logicamente e giustamente concluso *ch'egli non era un uomo come tutti gli altri*.

Orbene, data questa conclusione, essi si sono trovati di fronte a un Codice il quale, per la responsabilità completa dell'individuo, esige ch'egli sia padrone della sua volontà, senza alcuna malattia che ne renda anche parzialmente inferma la mente: – e confondendo le constatazioni della scienza psichiatrica colle esigenze della difesa sociale – i giurati non si sono sentiti in grado di affermare sul loro onore e sulla loro coscienza che Alberto Olivo avesse liberamente voluto uccidere sua moglie.

Questa è, secondo me, la spiegazione psicologica dello strano verdetto.

Una spiegazione che divide equamente la colpa dello sproposito giudiziario fra i cervelli non troppo colti dei signori giurati e il nostro Codice che par fatto apposta per offrire delle facili scappatoje ai grandi delinquenti, mentre si restringe in una maglia fittissima ed infrangibile per i delinquenti poco pericolosi.

So bene che il pubblico accusa indirettamente di queste vergognose assoluzioni la scuola positiva di diritto penale. So bene che si grida a Lombroso e ai suoi seguaci: 'Siete voi che, facendo passare per matti tutti i maggiori birbanti, ne favorite l'assoluzione!'

Ma a questo pubblico che ci addossa con tanta disinvoltura una colpa tanto grave noi rispondiamo: 'Sì, è vero: secondo noi l'uomo che commette un atroce delitto come quello dell'Olivo non è, non può essere, un uomo normale: ma quando noi constatiamo l'anormalità di un individuo, non ne constatiamo affatto l'irresponsabilità. Noi vorremmo che questi individui anormali ma pericolosi fossero segregati dal consorzio umano: noi diciamo: sono dei pazzi, sono degli ammalati: ma soggiungiamo: *bisogna rinchiuderli*. Siete voi che prendendo soltanto la nostra diagnosi, senza avere la lealtà di aggiungervi le conseguenze sociali che noi proponiamo, arrivate all'assurdo dell'assoluzione. È – cioè – il vostro cervello di spiritualisti, di credenti nel libero arbitrio, che si rifiuta a condannare un uomo perverso e pericoloso quando la scienza vi dimostra ch'egli non è un uomo normale. Accusate dunque la vostra logica spiritualista, non la nostra scienza di queste assoluzioni che rimettono in circolazione individui pericolosissimi i quali potranno domani ripetere quello che oggi hanno commesso col vostro perdono, anzi col vostro applauso'.

Pur troppo, queste semplici parole che varrebbero a togliere molti pregiudizi e… ad evitare molti verdetti scandalosi, non le ho mai sentite pronunciare dai rappresentanti del Pubblico Ministero, i quali preferiscono tuonare contro la scuola positiva, e sostenere che l'imputato è sempre un uomo normalissimo. 1 difensori – si sa, essi fanno ciò che torna conto al loro cliente! – prendono delle nostre idee quello che serve alla loro tesi; e fra i due fuochi il povero giurato perde spesso la bussola e si lascia guidare dalle suggestioni dell'ambiente.

E intanto Alberto Olivo passeggia come un libero cittadino, meravigliato certo – egli più d'ogni altro! – che costi così poco uccidere squartare e spolpare una moglie!

Scipio Sighele

[*L'illustrazione italiana*, 25 July 1904,
The acquittal of Alberto Olivo

It was actually worse than an acquittal! The gentlemen jurors were not satisfied with an unfair verdict: they wanted to add to the moral monstrosity of the acquittal for murder the irony of the partial conviction for the mutilation of the corpse, and so the President of the Assizes – rightly surprised and indignant – was forced to read out the unlikely sentence by which a man who killed his wife is acquitted and… is condemned for the theft of her corpse!

Alexandre Dumas is *enfoncé*. His famous *Kill her!* – which had overly influenced the French and Italian juries – is part of the old junk of judicial psychology. Now, husbands will believe they have the right not only to kill their wives but also to butcher them. After all, this cheerful function merits only twelve days in prison and a 125-lira fine!

It does not seem possible that such a scandal could have occurred in the city of Milan, a cultured city where good sense abounds. And those who delight in finding the legal reasons for so many immoral and pathological phenomena blame the President or the representatives of the public and private prosecution who – considering the murderous intention of the accused to be very sure – did not include among their questions the hypothesis of unintentional homicide. Had this hypothesis – it is said – been offered to the jurors, they would have accepted it, and the scandalous verdict would have been avoided.

I allow myself to find this explanation naive. Meanwhile, the way in which Olivo killed his wife seems to me to clearly demonstrate that he did not *just* want to hit or wound her. But then, the subsequent behaviour of the accused reveals such a *moral analgesia* that it is ridiculous, as well as naive, to suppose that this man *repented* for having killed. Indeed, any person who seeks only to hurt, and unfortunately kills, certainly would not think – or engage in the *physical possibility* – of butchering and stripping the flesh from that person... who he had no intention of killing! The havoc that Alberto Olivo wreaked on the body of his dead wife is supreme proof of the homicidal intent that guided the blows that rained on the body of his still-living wife.

It was therefore natural that neither the Public Prosecutor nor the Civil Party thought to offer the jurors the hypothesis of preterintentionality. It would have been not only belittling but also a falsification of the motive!

*

And yet, this hypothesis seems to have guided the verdict of the jurors, who, finding it not presented to them in the counts submitted, forgot the horror of the crime and arrived at the absurdity of acquittal.

They arrived there... perhaps without realising. Because the simplest and truest explanation of the not infrequently absurd verdicts of juries rests precisely in the painful observation that these twelve distinguished individuals do not always know what they are doing when – enshrined in their deliberating chamber – they must administer justice.

I believe that the entire discourse – not only that of the experts and lawyers, but that of the newspapers too – around the moral responsibility of Alberto Olivo played a bad trick on them. They convinced themselves that they had before them a man who was *certainly not normal*. An epileptic? A criminaloid, as Lombroso would have it? A characteristic type, as Silvio Venturi would have wanted it? The precision of the diagnosis does not matter. They felt the *exceptionality* of that type of criminal; they saw, including in the attacks of his malady in the Court itself, his physical instability, – and they logically and rightly concluded *that he was not like everyone else*.

Well, given this conclusion, they found themselves faced with a Code that requires that, for an individual to bear total responsibility, he must be master of his own will, without any illness that renders his mind even partially infirm: and, confusing the findings of psychiatric science with the needs of social defence, the jurors did not feel able to swear on their honour and their conscience that Alberto Olivo had freely elected to kill his wife.

This, in my opinion, is the psychological explanation for this strange verdict.

An explanation that divides the blame for the judicial blunder equally between the not-so-cultured minds of the gentlemen jurors and our Code, which seems to have been deliberately designed to offer an easy escape to the serious criminal but contracting into a tight, unbreakable mesh around the less dangerous.

I know full well that the public indirectly holds the Positivist School of Criminal Law responsible for these shameful acquittals. I know full well that people cry out to Lombroso and his followers, 'It is you who, by painting all the biggest scoundrels as madmen, favour their acquittal!'

But to this public that so casually places such serious blame on us, we respond, 'Yes, it is true: in our opinion, the man who commits a crime as heinous as Olivo's is not, and cannot be, a normal man: but when we observe the abnormality of an individual, we do not in any way observe his irresponsibility. We would like these abnormal but dangerous individuals to be segregated from the human community: we say: they are mad, they are ill: but we add: *and they must be locked up*. It is you who, hearing only our diagnosis without holding on to hear the social consequences we propose, arrive at the absurdity of absolution. It is – that is – your spiritualist brain, believers in free will, that refuses to condemn a perverse and dangerous man when science shows you that he is not a normal man. Therefore, accuse your spiritualist logic, not our science, of these absolutions that return to society very dangerous individuals who tomorrow can repeat what they committed today, with your forgiveness, indeed, with your applause'.

Unfortunately, I have never heard these simple words, which would remove many prejudices and… avoid many scandalous verdicts, uttered by the representatives of the Public Prosecutor, who prefer to thunder against the Positivist School and always maintain that the accused is a thoroughly normal man. The defence lawyers – we all know they do what is in their client's interest! – take from our ideas that which is useful for their argument; and, standing between these twin fires, the poor juror often loses his compass and allows himself to be guided by environmental suggestion.

And in the meantime, Alberto Olivo strolls the world as a free citizen, surely amazed – he more than anyone else! – that the killing, butchery, and stripping of the flesh of a wife costs so little!

Scipio Sighele]

Bibliography

Primary Sources

Periodicals

Avanti!, 12 June 1904.

Avanti!, 3 December 1904.

Avanti!, 8 December 1904.

Caffaro, 14 June 1904.

Corriere della Sera, 25 November 1903.

Corriere della Sera, 27 May 1903.

Corriere della Sera, 18 July 1903.

Corriere della Sera, 25 November 1903.

Corriere della Sera, 2 June 1904.

Corriere della Sera, 7 June 1904.

Corriere della Sera, 9 June 1904.

Corriere della Sera, 10 June 1904.

Corriere della Sera, 2 December 1904.

Corriere della Sera, 7 December 1904.

Corriere della Sera, 8 December 1904.

Il buon cuore, 1 (1904).

I grandi processi illustrati, 1904, I-XIII.

Il Foro Italiano, 18/2 (1893).

Il Giornale d'Italia, 1 June 1904.

Il Giornale d'Italia, 2 June 1904.

Il Giornale d'Italia, 3 June 1904.

Il Giornale d'Italia, 4 June 1904.

Il Giornale d'Italia, 5 June 1904.

Il Giornale d'Italia, 7 June 1904.

Il Giornale d'Italia, 8 June 1904.

Il Giornale d'Italia, 27 November 1904.

Il Giornale d'Italia, 29 November 1904.

Il Giornale d'Italia, 4 December 1904.

Il Giornale d'Italia, 8 December 1904.

Il Messaggero, 14 June 1904.

Il Secolo, 1–2 June 1904.

Il Secolo, 3–4 June 1904.

Il Secolo, 7–8 June 1904.

Il Secolo, 8–9 June 1904.

Il Secolo, 9–10 June 1904.

Il Secolo, 10–11 June 1904.

Il Secolo, 11–12 June 1904.

Il Secolo, 12–13 June 1904.

Il Secolo, 14–15 June 1904.

Il Secolo, 22–23 November 1904.

Il Secolo XX, July 1904.

I Tribunali, 5 June 1904.

I Tribunali, 12 June 1904.

L'Illustrazione Italiana, 19 June 1904, n. 25.

L'Illustrazione italiana, 11 December 1904.

La Civiltà cattolica, 55 (1904).

La Giustizia penale, 10 (1904).

La Stampa, 27 May 1903.

La Stampa, 1 June 1904.

La Stampa, 2 June 1904.

La Stampa, 3 June 1904.

La Stampa, 4 June 1904.

La Stampa, 5 June 1904.

La Stampa, 7 June 1904.

La Stampa, 8 June 1904.

La Stampa, 10 June 1904.

La Stampa, 11 June 1904.

La Stampa, 12 June 1904.

La Stampa, 13 June 1904.

La Stampa, 14 June 1904.

La Stampa, 24 June 1904.

La Stampa, 20 July 1904.

La Stampa, 20 November 1904.

La Stampa, 23 November 1904.

La Stampa, 27 November 1904.

La Stampa, 2 December 1904.

La Stampa, 3 December 1904.

La Stampa, 4 December 1904.

La Stampa, 6 December 1904.

La Stampa, 7 December 1904.

La Tribuna, 12 June 1904.

La Tribuna, 27 November 1904.

La Tribuna, 30 November 1904.

La Tribuna, 6 December 1904.

La Tribuna, 8 December 1904.

Pasquino, 19 June 1904, n. 25.

Manuscripts

Milan State Archive, Assise, 1904–1906, 1904, Sentenze, 2134.

#LOMBROSOProject, Online resource, <https://lombrosoproject.unito.it/en/correspondence-results/>, source held in Turin, Museo di antropologia criminale 'Cesare Lombroso', University of Turin, 15 September 1904, 27 September 1904, 12 December 1904 [accessed 30 April 2024]

Law Sources

Codice civile del Regno d'Italia: corredato della relazione del Ministro Guardasigilli fatta a S. M. in udienza del 25 giugno 1865 (Turin: Botta, 1865).

Il codice penale per il Regno d'Italia, ed. by Giulio Crivellari (Turin: Unione Tipografico-Editrice, 1889).

Codice penale per il Regno d'Italia (Rome: Stamperia Reale, 1889).

Collezione Completa dei Moderni Codici Civili (Turin: Minerva Subalpina, 1845).

Digest 24.1.51, *Pomponius 5 ad Quintus Mucius.*

Law 19 May 1975, n. 151.

Books and Journal Articles

Alimena, Bernardino, *I limiti e i modificatori dell'imputabilità*, 4 vols (Turin: Bocca, 1894–1899), II (1896).

Antonini, Giuseppe, *I precursori di Cesare Lombroso* (Turin: Bocca, 1900).

Balestrini, Raffaello, *Aborto, infanticidio ed esposizione d'infante: studio giuridico-sociologico* (Turin: Bocca, 1888).

Bianchi, Augusto Guido, Guglielmo Ferrero and Scipio Sighele, eds, *Il mondo criminale italiano*, 2 vols (Milan, Omodei Zorini, 1893), I.

Bossi, Luigi Maria, *A proposito di malattie utero-ovariche e psicopatie: urgenza di riforme nel sistema manicomiale* (Varese: Premiata Tipografia Cooperativa Varesina, 1912).

Browne, Thomas, *Christian Morals* (Cambridge: Cambridge University Press, 1716).

Browne, Thomas, *Religio Medici: Or, the Christian Religion, as Professed by a Physician; Freed from Priest-Craft and the Jargon of Schools*, 2 vols (London: Curll, 1736), II.

Bruno, Tommaso, *La condizione giuridica della donna nella legislazione italiana: studio teorico-pratico* (Florence: Barbera, 1894).

Cabanis, Pierre Jean George, *Rapports du physique et du moral de l'homme* (Paris: Fortin, Masson, 1843 [1802]).

Carcano, Giovanni, *Il codice civile austriaco ed i suoi caratteri* (Milan: Manini, 1860).

Carmignani, Giovanni, *Juris criminalis elementa*, 5th ed. (Pisa: Nistri, 1833 [1808]).

Carmignani, Giovanni, *Teoria delle leggi della sicurezza sociale*, 3 vols (Pisa: Nistri, 1831–1832), II.

Carrara, Francesco, *Programma del corso di diritto criminale*, 2 vols (Florence: Cammelli, [1857] 1907), I.

Casorati, Luigi, *La nuova legge sul giurì* (Prato: Giacchetti, 1874).

Crivellari, Giulio, *La giuria in Italia* (Mantua: Segna, 1872).

Dante, *The Divine Comedy*: Inferno III, 136.

Dante, *The Divine Comedy*: Paradiso VI, 140–42.

Darwin, Charles, *The Descent of Man, and Selection in Relation to Sex* (London: Murray, 1871).

De Rolandis, Giuseppe Maria, 'Lettre de M. le docteur De Rolandis, de Turin, a M. le docteur Fossati, sur un criminel convaincu de plusieurs viols, suivis de meurtre', *Journal de la Société Phrénologique de Paris*, 3 (1835), 244–48.

Della Porta, Giambattista, *De humana physiognomonia libri sex*, ed. by Alfonso Paolella (Naples: Edizioni scientifiche italiane, 2013).

Ellero, Pietro, *Opuscoli criminali* (Bologna: Fava and Garagnani, 1874).

Esquirol, Jean-Étienne Dominique, *Note sur la monomanie-homicide* (Paris: Baillière, 1827).

Esquirol, Jean-Étienne Dominique, *Della alienazione mentale o Della pazzia in genere e in ispecie*, 2 vols, trans. by Luigi Calvetti (Milan: Rusconi, 1827).

Ferri, Enrico, *Cenni critici sulla giuria in Italia* (Venice: Fontana, 1880).

Ferri, Enrico, *La scuola positiva di diritto criminale: prelezione al corso di diritto e procedura penale nella R. Università di Siena pronunciata il 18 novembre 1882* (Siena: Torrini, 1883).

Ferri, Enrico, *Sociologia criminale*, 3rd ed. (Turin: Bocca, 1892).

Ferriani, Lino, *La infanticida nel codice penale e nella vita sociale: considerazioni* (Milan: Dumolard, 1886).

Filangieri, Gaetano, *La scienza della legislazione*, 8 vols (Milan: Borroni and Scotti, 1856 [1780–1791]), II.

Foramiti, Francesco, *Enciclopedia legale ovvero lessico ragionato di gius naturale, civile, canonico*, 4 vols (Venice: Co' Tipi del Gondoliere, 1842), II.

Forlani, Francesco, *L'isterismo nei suoi rapporti colla follia e colla responsabilità. Memorie medico-legali* (Vienna-Turin-Florence: Loescher, 1869).

Forti, Francesco, *Trattati inediti di giurisprudenza* (Florence: Viessieux, 1854).

Fowler, Lorenzo, *Marriage, its History and Ceremonies, with a Phrenological and Physiological Exposition of the Functions and Qualifications for Happy Marriages* (New York: Fowlers and Wells, 1848).

Franceschini, Lorenzo, *I giurati secondo la nuova legge 8 giugno 1874: osservazioni e commenti* (Rome: Barbera, 1874).

Frassati, Alfredo, *La Nuova Scuola di Diritto penale in Italia e all'estero* (Turin: Paravia, 1891).

Gabba, Carlo Francesco, *Della condizione giuridica delle donne nelle legislazioni francese, austriaca e sarda. Studio di legislazione comparata* (Milan: Redaelli, 1861).

Galeotti, Leopoldo, *Discorso intorno agli scritti editi e inediti di Francesco Forti*, in Forti, *Trattati inediti di giurisprudenza*, pp. IX–XXVI.

Gall, Franz Joseph, and Johann Gaspar Spurzheim, *Anatomie et physiologie du système nerveux en général, et du cerveau en particulier*, 4 vols (Paris: Schoell, 1810–19 [1812]), II.

Galton, Francis, *Inquiries into Human Faculty and its Development* (London: Macmillan, 1883).

Gambarotta, Guglielmo, *Inchiesta sulla donna* (Turin: Bocca, 1899).

Gambarotta, Guglielmo, *L'adulterio e la teorica dei diritti necessari* (Turin: Bocca, 1898).

Georget, Etienne-Jean, *De la physiologie du système nerveux, et spécialement du cerveau*, 2 vols (Paris: Baillière, 1821).

Giuriati, Domenico, *Le leggi dell'amore* (Turin: Roux and Favale, 1881).

Impallomeni, Giovanni Battista, *Della giuria* (Palermo: Lo Statuto, 1895).

Lavater, Johann Kaspar, *Physiognomy, Or, the Corresponding Analogy between the Conformation of the Features and the Ruling Passions of the Mind* (London: Tegg, 1866).

Lombroso, Cesare, *Criminal Man, according to the classification of Cesare Lombroso, briefly summarised by his daughter Gina Lombroso-Ferrero, with an introduction by Cesare Lombroso* (New York: Putnam, 1911).

Lombroso, Cesare, *L'uomo bianco e l'uomo di colore* (Padua: Sacchetto, 1871).

Lombroso, Cesare, and Guglielmo Ferrero, *La donna delinquente, la prostituta e la donna normale* (Turin: Roux, 1893).

Lombroso, Cesare, and Guglielmo Ferrero, *La donna delinquente, la prostituta e la donna normale*, 4th ed., with notes by Gina Lombroso (Turin: Bocca, 1923).

Lombroso, Cesare, *Tatto sensibilità generale e dolorifica, e tipo degenerativo in donne normali, criminali e alienate: seduta del 2 gennaio 1891* ([n. p..]: [n. pub.], 1891).

Lombroso, Gina, *L'anima della donna*, 3 vols (Bologna Zanichelli, 1917–1926), I.

Lombroso, Paola, 'Superiorità organica della donna', *L'Italia femminile: corriere delle donne italiane: mode, letteratura, arte, varietà*, I/1, 15 January 1899.

Lombroso, Paola, *Caratteri della femminilità* (Turin: Bocca, 1909).

Manfredini, Giuseppe, *Il giurato italiano dopo il primo gennaio 1875* (Padua: Salmin, 1875).

Mantegazza, Paolo, *Fisiologia del piacere* (Milan: Bernardoni, 1874 [1854]).

Mantegazza, Paolo, *Fisiologia della donna*, 2 vols (Milan: Bietti, 1945 [1893]), II.

Mazzini, Giuseppe, *Dei doveri dell'uomo* (Milan: RCS, 2010 [1860]).

McGrigor Allan, James, 'On the Real Differences in the Minds of Men and Women', *Journal of the Anthropological Society of London*, 7 (1869), cxcv–ccxix.

McGrigor Allan, James, *Woman Suffrage, Wrong in Principle, and Practice: An Essay* (London: Remington & Company, 1890).

Melegari, Dora, *Il sonno delle anime* (Milan: Treves, 1903).

Melegari, Dora, *Il destarsi delle anime* (Milan: Treves, 1915).

Mellusi, Vincenzo, *La madre delinquente: studio di psicologia morbosa* (Rome: Loescher, 1897).

Negri, Giovanni Maria, *Dei difetti del Codice Civile Italico, che porta il titolo di Codice Napoleone e dei pregj del Codice Civile Austriaco* (Vicenza: Parise, 1815).

Olivo, Alberto, *Dal culmine all'abisso: dramma in tre atti e un epilogo* (Milan: Grassi, 1906).

Olivo, Alberto, *Ira fatale. Autobiografia di un uxoricida*, ed. by Ermanno Cavazzoni (Milan: Bollati Boringhieri, 1988).

Olivo, Alberto, *La mia difesa contro il professor Cesare Lombroso* (Milan: Società Editoriale Milanese, 1905).

Orano, Giuseppe, *La recidiva nei reati* (Rome: Carlo Voghera, 1883).

Ottolenghi, Salvatore, *La sensibilità della donna* (Turin: Bocca, 1896).

Pagani, Carlo, and Filippo De Ferrari, *Il cittadino giurato innanzi alla corte d'assisie (sic!)* (Florence: Stamperia Reale, 1866).

Pagani, Cesare, 'Osservazioni sull'articolo dell'avv. Luigi Stella', *La Legge, monitore giudiziario e amministrativo del Regno d'Italia*, 3/12 (1872), 160–6.

Patrizi, Mariano Luigi, *Sensazione postuma e oscillazione vascolare conseguenti allo stimolo termico freddo. Nuove ricerche col guanto volumetrico* (Modena: Società Tipografica, 1905).

Pazzi, Muzio, *Per la profilassi dell'aborto criminoso e dell'infanticidio* (Bologna: Poligrafico Emiliano, 1913).

Porto, Vito, *Progetto del codice penale presentato dal Ministro Zanardelli alla Camera dei Deputati nella Seduta del 22 novembre 1887* (Rome: Stamperia dell'opinione, 1888).

Renazzi, Filippo Maria, *Elementa juris criminalis*, 4 vols (Bologna: Francisci Cardinali and Caroli Frulli, 1826 [1773–75]), I-II.

Rossi, Pellegrino, *Trattato di diritto penale*, 2 vols (Milan: Borroni and Scotti, 1832), I.

Roussel, Pierre, *Sistema fisico e morale della donna*, 2 vols (Naples: Manzi, 1829 [1775]), II.

Scotti, Antonio, 'Dell'autorizzazione maritale e giudiziale secondo il codice civile italiano', *Archivio giuridico*, IV (1869), 387–435.

Sergi, Giuseppe, *Per l'educazione del carattere*, 2nd ed. (Milan: Dumolard, 1893 [1884]).

Sergi, Giuseppe, 'Sensibilità femminile. Lettera all'illustre Prof. C. Lombroso', *Archivio di psichiatria, scienze penali ed antropologia criminale per servire allo studio dell'uomo alienato e delinquente*, 13/1 (1892), 1–8.

Setti, Augusto, *Manuale per il giurato* (Milan: Hoepli, 1903).

Sighele, Scipio, *Letteratura tragica* (Milan: Treves, 1906).

Stella, Luigi, 'Alcune considerazioni sulla minore responsabilità penale della donna', *Archivio Giuridico*, 4 (1869), 76–83.

Veratti, Bartolomeo, 'Della mitigazione delle pene per le femmine delinquenti', in *Opuscoli religiosi, letterarj e morali*, serie II, I (Modena: Soliani 1863), pp. 78–103.

Viazzi, Pio, *Sui reati sessuali* (Turin: Bocca, 1896).

Zecchini, Petronio Ignazio, *Dì geniali della dialettica delle donne ridotta al suo vero principio* (Bologna: S. Tommaso D'Aquino, 1771).

Secondary Sources

Abu-Odeh, Lama, 'Comparatively Speaking: The "Honor" of the "East" and the "Passion" of the "West"', *Utah Law Review* (1997), 287–307.

Altheide, David L., and Robert P. Snow, *Media Logic* (Beverly Hills: SAGE, 1979).

Altheide, David L., 'Media Logic, Social Control, and Fear', *Communication Theory*, 23/3 (2013), 223–38.

Alù, Giorgia, and Sarah Patricia Hill, 'Mini special Issue: Violence Against Women in Italian Literature', *Italian Studies*, 76/3 (2021), 302–06.

Ambroise-Rendu, Anne-Claude, 'Le Chroniqueur, la justice et l'opinion publique: les faits divers à la fin du XIXe siècle', *Histoire de la justice*, 20/1 (2010), 69–80.

Ambroise-Rendu, Anne-Claude, *Crimes et délits. Une histoire de la violence de la Belle Époque à nos jours* (Paris: Nouveau Monde Éditions, 2006).

Anzalone, Lina, *Storia di Rastignac. Un calabrese protagonista e testimone del suo tempo* (Soveria Mannelli: Rubbettino, 2005).

Asp, Kent, 'News Media Logic in a New Institutional Perspective', *Journalism Studies*, 15/3 (2014), 256–70.

Augello, Massimo M., Marco E. L. Guidi, Giovanni Pavanelli, eds, *Economia e opinione pubblica nell'Italia liberale: gli economisti e la stampa quotidiana* (Milan: FrancoAngeli, 2016).

Azara, Liliosa, and Luca Tedesco, eds, *Donna delinquente e la prostituta: l'eredità di Lombroso nella cultura e nella società italiane* (Rome: Viella, 2019).

Bandelli, Daniela, *Femicide, Gender and Violence: Discourses and Counterdiscourses in Italy* (Cham: Palgrave, 2017).

Banti, Alberto Mario, *La nazione del Risorgimento. Parentela, santità e onore alle origini dell'Italia unita* (Turin: Einaudi, 2000).

Banti, Alberto Mario, 'Discorso nazional-patriottico e ruoli di genere (Europa, secoli XVIII-XIX)', in *Innesti. Donne e genere nella storia sociale*, ed. by Giulia Calvi (Rome: Viella, 2004), pp. 121–46.

Banti, Alberto Mario, 'Media e immagini nel mondo contemporaneo (XIX-XXI sec.)', *Società e storia* (2016), 529–32.

Banti, Alberto Mario, 'Nations, Sexuality, and Violence in Nineteenth-Century National Narratives', in *European Modernity and the Passionate South. Gender and Nation in Spain and Italy in the Long Nineteenth Century*, ed. by Xavier Andreu-Miralles and Mónica Bolufer-Peruga (Leiden: Brill, 2022), pp. 73–91.

Baral, Simone, 'Il frenologo in tribunale. Nota per una ricerca sul caso italiano', *Criminocorpus, Folie et justice de l'Antiquité à l'époque contemporaine* (2016) [accessed 30 April 2024].

Barbagli, Marzio, ed., *Famiglia e mutamento sociale* (Bologna: Il Mulino, 1977).

Barbagli, Marzio, *Sotto lo stesso tetto. Mutamenti della famiglia in Italia dal XV al XX secolo* (Bologna: Il Mulino, 1984).

Baroutsis, Aspa, 'Understanding Media Mentalities and Logics: Institutional and Journalistic Practices, and the Reporting of Teachers' Work', *Discourse: Studies in the Cultural Politics of Education*, 40:4 (2019), 545–59.

Becker, Peter, and Richard F. Wetzell, eds, *Criminals and Their Scientists: The History of Criminology in International Perspective* (Cambridge: Cambridge University Press, 2013).

Beam, Sara, 'Gender and the Prosecution of Adultery in Geneva, 1550–1700', in *Women's Criminality in Europe, 1600–1914*, ed. by Manon van der Heijden, Marion Pluskota, Sanne Muurling (Cambridge: Cambridge University Press, 2020), pp. 91–113.

Bellassai, Sandro, *L'invenzione della virilità. Politica e immaginario maschile nell'Italia contemporanea* (Rome: Carocci, 2011).

Bellomo, Manlio, *La condizione giuridica della donna in Italia. Vicende antiche e moderne* (Rome: Il Cigno, 1996 [1970]).

Beirne, Piers, 'Between Classicism and Positivism: Crime and Penalty in the Writings of Gabriel Tarde', *Criminology*, 25/4 (November 1987), 785–820.

Berrios, German E., *The History of Mental Symptoms: Descriptive Psychopathology Since the Nineteenth Century* (Cambridge: Cambridge University Press, 1996).

Bettaglio, Marina, Nicoletta Mandolini and Silvia M. Ross, eds, *Rappresentare la violenza di genere: sguardi femministi tra critica, attivismo e scrittura* (Milan: Mimesis, 2018).

Bettoni, Antonella, '"Fama", Shame Punishments and the History of Justice in the Sixteenth and Seventeenth Centuries', in *Shame, Blame, and Culpability*, pp. 32–43.

Borzacchiello, Assunta, 'La grande riforma. Breve storia dell'irrisolta questione carceraria', *Rassegna penitenziaria e criminologica* (2005), 83–147.

Bourdieu, Pierre, *Distinction: A Social Critique of the Judgment of Taste* (Cambridge: Harvard University Press, [1979] 1984),

Bourdieu, Pierre, *The Logic of Practice* (Stanford: Stanford University Press, 1990).

Bourdieu, Pierre, *Masculine Domination* (Bloomington: Stanford University Press, [1998] 2002).

Braunmühl, Caroline, 'Theorizing Emotions with Judith Butler: Within and beyond the Courtroom', *Rethinking History*, 16/2 (2012), 221–40.

Burke, Peter, *The Historical Anthropology of Early Modern Italy* (Cambridge: Cambridge University Press, 1987).

Butler, Judith, *Gender Trouble. Feminism and the Subversion of Identity* (London: Routledge, 1990).

Buttitta, Antonino, *Semiotica e antropologia* (Palermo: Sellerio, 1979).

Caccia, Patrizia, '"Giustizia sia fatta: e giustizia sia". Giustizia e avvocati nella letteratura popolare milanese', in *Avvocati a Milano*, pp. 179–89.

Caesar, Ann, Gabriella Romani, and Jennifer Burns, eds, *The Printed Media in Fin-de-Siècle Italy: Publishers, Writers, and Readers* (Abingdon: Routledge, 2017).

Calanca, Daniela, *Storia della famiglia italiana: ruoli e passioni nel XX secolo* (Pesaro: Metauro, 2005).

Cantarella, Eva, 'Homicides of Honor: The Development of Italian Adultery Law over Two Millennia', in *The Family in Italy: From Antiquity to the Present*, ed. by David I. Kertzer and Richard P. Saller (New Haven/London, Yale University Press, 1991), pp. 229–44.

Cantarella, Eva, *L'ambiguo malanno: condizione e immagine della donna nell'antichità greca e romana* (Rome: Editori riuniti, 1981).

Carbone, Angela, 'Il dibattito sul divorzio nel lungo Ottocento: Stato, Chiesa e opinione pubblica nel Mezzogiorno d'Italia', *Chronica Mundi*, 15 (2021), 103–29.

Carbone, Angela, ed., *Scritti in onore di Giovanna Da Molin. Popolazione, famiglia e società in età moderna* (Bari: Cacucci, 2017).

Cartuyvels, Yves, and Aniceto Masferrer, 'The Making of Insane Offenders in the Western Tradition: A Comparative Approach to the Birth and Enforcement of Criminological Positivism (1870–1940)', *GLOSSAE. European Journal of Legal History*, 20 (2023), pp. 1–27.

Casanova, Cesarina, *Per forza o per amore: storia della violenza familiare nell'età moderna* (Rome: Salerno, 2016).

Casella, Laura, 'Foramiti, Francesco', in *Dizionario biografico dei giuristi italiani (XII-XX secolo)*, 2 vols (Bologna: Il Mulino, 2013), I, pp. 886–7.

Casetta, Abele, ed., *Pietro Ellero un grande pordenonese nella cultura giuridica, sociale e politica dell'Ottocento*, Atti del convegno di Pordenone 26 novembre 2005 (Pordenone: Comune di Pordenone, 2007).

Castronovo, Valerio, ed., *La nascita dell'opinione pubblica in Italia. La stampa nella Torino del Risorgimento e capitale d'Italia (1848–1864)* (Rome-Bari: Laterza, 2004).

Castronovo, Valerio, and Nicola Tranfaglia, eds, *Storia della stampa italiana*, 5 vols (Rome-Bari, Laterza, 1979), III, *La stampa italiana nell'età liberale*.

Cavina, Marco, 'Il dolo latente nell'animo. Filippo Maria Renazzi nel dibattito giuridico intorno alla graduazione del dolo fra XVIII e

XIX secolo', in *Filippo Maria Renazzi: università e cultura a Roma tra Settecento e Ottocento*, ed. by Paolo Alvazzi Del Frate, Maria Rosa Di Simone, and Carla Frova (Bologna: Il mulino, 2019), pp. 227–39.

Cavina, Marco, *Nozze di sangue: storia della violenza coniugale* (Rome-Bari: Laterza, 2011).

Cazzetta, Giovanni, *Praesumitur seducta. Onestà e consenso femminile nella cultura giuridica moderna* (Milan: Giuffrè, 1999).

Chemotti, Saveria, and Maria Cristina La Rocca, eds, *Il genere nella ricerca storica*, 2 vols (Padua: Il Poligrafo, 2015).

Cohen, Thomas V., 'The Lay Liturgy of Affront in Sixteenth-Century Italy', *Journal of Social History*, 25 (1991), 857–77.

Colao, Floriana, 'Le scuole penalistiche', in *Enciclopedia italiana. Il Contributo italiano alla storia del pensiero. Diritto* (Rome: Enciclopedia Italiana Treccani, 2012), pp. 349–56.

Comanducci, Paolo, 'La scuola criminalistica pisana tra Sette e Ottocento', in *Illuminismo e dottrine penali*, ed. by Luigi Berlinguer and Floriana Colao (Milan: Giuffrè, 1990), pp. 241–304.

Connell, Raewyn W., *Masculinities* (Cambridge: Polity Press, 1995),

Connell, Raewyn W., *Gender and Power. Society, the Person, and Sexual Politics* (Cambridge: Polity Press, [1987] 2002).

Corradi, Consuelo, and Heidi Stöckl, 'Intimate Partner Homicide in 10 European Countries: Statistical Data and Policy Developments in Cross-national Perspective', *European Journal of Criminology*, 11/5 (2014), 601–18.

Corradi, Morena, and Silvia Valisa, eds, *La carta veloce. Figure, temi e politiche del giornalismo italiano dell'Ottocento* (Milan: Franco Angeli, 2021).

Crescenzi, Victor, 'L'autorizzazione maritale e il problema storico della capacità della donna coniugata di disporre dei propri beni', in *Mujeres y derecho. Una perspectiva histórico-jurídica. Encuentro de historiadores del derecho. Actas*, ed. by Francisco L. Pacheco Caballero (Barcelona: Associació Catalana d'História del Dret, 2015), pp. 127–85.

Cross, Susan E., and Ayşe K. Üskül, 'The Pursuit of Honor: Novel Contexts, Varied Approaches, and New Developments', in *Handbook of Advances in Culture & Psychology*, ed. by Michele J. Gelfand, Chi-Yue Chiu and Ying-Yi Hong (Oxford: Oxford University Press, 2022), pp. 189–243.

D'Cruze, Shani, Efi Avdela and Judith Rowbotham, eds, *Problems of Crime and Violence in Europe 1750–2000: Essays in Criminal Justice* (Lewiston: Mellen, 2010).

D'Onofrio, Salvatore, 'Onore e disonore in Sicilia', in *La antropologia como pasión y como práctica: ensayos in honorem Julian Pitt-Rivers*, ed. by Honorio M. Velasco, Dominique Fournier, Luiz Díaz Viana (Madrid: CSIC, 2004), pp. 201–28.

Daumas, Maurice, *Adulteri e cornuti. Storia della sessualità maschile tra Medioevo e modernità* (Bari: Dedalo, 2008).

Davies, Pamela, Peter Francis and Chris Greer, eds, *Victims, Crime and Society* (London: Sage, 2007).

Dawson, Myrna, and Michelle Carrigan, 'Identifying Femicide Locally and Globally: Understanding the Utility and Accessibility of Sex/Gender Related Motives and Indicators', *Current Sociology* (2020), 1–23.

De Fort, Ester, *Scuola e analfabetismo nell'Italia del '900* (Bologna: Il Mulino, 1995).

De Giorgio, Michela, 'Madri del "secol novo". Sfide, lotte, scelte', in *Di Generazione in generazione: le italiane dall'Unità a oggi*, ed. by Maria Teresa Mori, Alessandra Pescarolo, Anna Scattigno, Simonetta Soldani (Rome: Viella, 2014), pp. 139–66.

De Romanis, Roberto, and Rosamaria Loretelli, eds, *Il delitto narrato al popolo. Immagini di giustizia e stereotipi di criminalità in età moderna* (Palermo: Sellerio, 1999).

Della Peruta, Franco, *Il giornalismo italiano del Risorgimento* (Milan: FrancoAngeli, 2011).

Delmedico, Sara, '"He Saw what He Wanted to See': Reputation, Jealousy and the Law. The Uxoricide of Giselda Zanolo', *Papers of the British School at Rome* (2021), 319–33.

Delmedico, Sara, and Manuela Di Franco, 'Fascism and "Italians Abroad": National Identity and the Building of the Fascist State', *Chronica Mundi*, 14 (2019–2020), 81–119.

Delmedico, Sara, '"I Forgive my Sons for any Disgust They Might Have Caused Me'. Alvise I Mocenigo and the Decline of Paternal Authority in Nineteenth-Century Venice', *Journal of Family History*, 44/4 (2019), 347–65.

Delmedico, Sara, '"Molto meno se la donna non può provare d'essere stata sorpresa". Donne, onore e seduzione nel Regno delle Due Sicilie di metà Ottocento', in *La donna, il matrimonio e la famiglia Aspetti sociali dal XVI al XX secolo*, ed. by Giovanna Da Molin and Angela Carbone (Bari: Cacucci, 2022), pp. 185–97.

Delmedico, Sara, *Opposing Patriarchy: Women and the Law in Action in Pre-Unification Italy (1815–1865)* (London: Institute of Modern Languages Research, 2021).

Demartini, Anne-Emmanuelle, and Dominique Kalifa, eds, *Imaginaire et sensibilités au XIX siècle: Études pour Alain Corbin* (Paris: Créaphis, 2005).

Dezza, Ettore, and Pio Caroni, *L'ABGB e la codificazione asburgica in Italia e in Europa* (Milan: Cedam, 2006).

Di Simone, Maria Rosa, 'L'influenza di Beccaria nello Stato pontificio: il trattato di Filippo Maria Renazzi', *Rivista di storia del diritto italiano*, 87 (2014), 365–98.

Di Simone, Maria Rosa, 'Le italiane tra Code Napoléon e Allgemeines Bürgerliches Gesetzbuch', *Cittadinanze incompiute: la parabola dell'autorizzazione maritale*, ed. by Stefania Bartoloni (Rome: Viella, 2021), pp. 35–53.

DiCristina, Bruce, 'Criminology and the "Essence" of Crime: The Views of Garofalo, Durkheim, and Bonger', *International Criminal Justice Review*, 26/4 (2016), 297–315.

Dolza, Delfina, *Essere figlie di Lombroso. Due donne intellettuali tra '800 e '900* (Milan: Franco Angeli, 1990).

Donato, Maria Clara, and Lucia Ferrante, eds, *Violenza. Genesis*, IX/2 (2010).

Eagle Russett, Cynthia, *Sexual Science: The Victorian Construction of Womanhood* (Cambridge, MA: Harvard UP, 1989).

Eamon, William, 'The Scientific Renaissance', in *A Companion to the Worlds of the Renaissance*, ed. By Guido Ruggiero (Oxford: Blackwell, 2002), pp. 403–24.

Fayer, Carla, *La familia romana: aspetti giuridici ed antiquari*, 3 vols (Rome: "L'Erma" di Bretschneider, 1994), II.

Fazio, Ida, 'Valori economici e valori simbolici. Il declino della dote nell'Italia dell'Ottocento', *Quaderni storici*, 78 (1992), 291–317.

Feci, Simona, and Laura Schettini, 'Storia e uso pubblico della violenza contro le donne', in *La violenza contro le donne nella storia: contesti, linguaggi, politiche del diritto (secoli XV-XXI)*, ed. by Simona Feci and Laura Schettini (Rome: Viella, 2017), pp. 7–39.

Ferguson, Eliza Earle, *Gender and Justice: Violence, Intimacy, and Community in Fin-de-Siècle Paris* (Baltimora: John Hopkins University Press, 2010).

Ferguson, Eliza Earle, 'Judicial Authority and Popular Justice: Crimes of Passion in Fin-de-Siecle Paris', *Journal of Social History*, 40 (2) (2006), 293–315.

Ferrari Occhionero, Marisa, ed., *Dal diritto di voto alla cittadinanza piena* (Rome: Casa editrice Università La Sapienza, 2008).

Ferrero, Ida, '"Eva delinquente": la scuola positiva e l'imputabilità al femminile', in *Donne ristrette*, ed. by Giulia Mantovani (Milan: Ledizioni, 2018), pp. 489–501.

Fioravanzo, Monica, 'L'autorizzazione maritale e la sua abrogazione nel quadro europeo tra guerre e rivoluzioni (1919–1945)', *Cittadinanze incompiute: la parabola dell'autorizzazione maritale*, ed. by Stefania Bartoloni (Rome: Viella, 2021), pp. 223–42.

Fioravanzo, Monica, 'Sull'autorizzazione maritale. Ricerche attorno alla condizione giuridica della donna nell'Italia unita', *Clio*, 30 (1994), 641–725.

Forno, Mauro, *Informazione e potere: storia del giornalismo italiano* (Rome: Laterza, 2012).

Foucault, Michel, *Discipline and Punish: The Birth of the Prison* (New York: Pantheon, 1977).

Frevert, Ute, 'Defining Emotions: Concepts and Debates over Three Centuries', *Emotional Lexicons. Continuity and Change in the Vocabulary of Feeling 1700–2000*, ed. by Ute Frevert, Christian Bailey, Pascal Eitler, Benno Gammerl, Bettina Hitzer, Margrit Pernau, Monique Scheer, Anne Schmidt, and Nina Verheyen (Oxford: Oxford University Press, 2014), pp. 1–31.

Galeotti, Giulia, 'L'autorizzazione maritale nel primo codice civile unitario: un istituto "estraneo" alla tradizione italiana?', *Dimensioni e problemi della ricerca storica*, 2 (2005), 155–82.

Galeotti, Giulia, *Storia del voto alle donne in Italia* (Rome: Biblink, 2006).

Galfré, Monica, *Tutti a scuola! L'istruzione nell'Italia del Novecento* (Rome: Carocci, 2017).

Gamberi, Cristina, 'Retoriche della violenza. Il femminicidio raccontato dai media italiani', in *La violenza contro le donne nella storia*, ed. by Simona Feci and Laura Schettini (Rome: Viella, 2017), pp. 261–78.

Gammerl, Benno, 'Emotional Styles – Concepts and Challenges', *Rethinking History*, 16/2 (2012), 161–75.

Garland, David, *The Culture of Control: Crime and Social Order in Contemporary Society* (Chicago: University of Chicago Press, 2001).

Garlati, Loredana, 'Honour and Guilt. A Comparative Study on Regulations on Infanticide between the Nineteenth and Twentieth Century', in *Family Law and Society in Europe from the Middle Ages to the Contemporary Era*, ed. by Maria Gigliola Di Renzo Villata (Cham, NY: Springer International Publishing, 2016), pp. 257–81.

Geri, Marco P., 'Il magistero di un criminalista di foro. Giovanni Carmignani "avvocato professore di Leggi"' (Pisa: ETS, 2015).

Gibson, Mary, *Born to Crime: Cesare Lombroso and the Origins of Biological Criminology* (Westport, CT; London: Praeger, 2002);

Gibson, Mary, 'On the Insensitivity of Women: Science and the Woman Question in Liberal Italy, 1890–1910', *Journal of Women's History*, 2/2 (1990), 11–41.

Gilmore, David, *Manhood in the Making: Cultural Concepts of Masculinity* (New Haven: Yale University Press, 1990).

Giomi, Elisa, 'Introduzione', in *Relazioni brutali. Genere e violenza nella cultura mediale*, ed. by Elisa Giomi and Sveva Magaraggia (Bologna: il Mulino, 2017), pp. 14–15.

Giomi, Elisa, and Sveva Magaraggia, eds, *Relazioni brutali. Genere e violenza nella cultura mediale* (Bologna: Il Mulino, 2017).

Gius, Chiara, and Pina Lalli, '"I loved her so much, but I killed her". Romantic love as a representational frame for intimate partner femicide in three Italian newspapers', *ESSACHESS. Journal for Communication Studies*, 7, 2/14(2014), 53–75.

Goldstein, Jan E., *Console and Classify: The French Psychiatric Profession in the Nineteenth Century* (Chicago: University of Chicago Press, 1987), pp. 152–96.

Graziosi, Marina, 'Infirmitas sexus. La donna nell'immaginario penalistico', *Jura gentium*, I/I (2005), electronic resource [accessed 15 October 2024].

Grossi, Paolo, *A History of European Law* (Chichester: Wiley-Blackwell, 2010).

Guarnieri, Patrizia, *Individualità difformi. La psichiatria antropologica di Enrico Morselli* (Milan: Franco Angeli, 1986).

Guarnieri, Patrizia, '"La volpe e l'uva": cultura scientifica e filosofia del positivismo italiano', *Physis*, XXV (1983), 301–36.

Guerci, Luciano, *La discussione sulla donna nell'Italia del Settecento: aspetti e problemi* (Turin: Tirrenia Stampatori, 1987).

Guerci, Luciano, *La sposa obbediente: donna e matrimonio nella discussione dell'Italia del Settecento* (Turin: Tirrenia Stampatori, 1988).

Gulotta, Guglielmo, *Famiglia e violenza: aspetti psicosociali* (Milan: Giuffrè, 1984).

Habermas, Jürgen, *Storia e critica dell'opinione pubblica* (Rome: Laterza, 2000 [1962]).

Hepp, Andreas, 'Mediatization and the 'Molding Force' of the Media', *Communications: The European Journal of Communication Research*, 37/1 (2012), 1–28.

Herzfeld, Michael, *Cultural Intimacy: Social Poetics in the Nation-State* (London: Routledge, 1997).

Horn, David G., *The Criminal Body. Lombroso and the Anatomy of Deviance* (London: Routledge, 2003).

Jayewardene, Cleobis H. S., 'The English Precursors of Lombroso', *The British Journal of Criminology*, 4/2 (1963), 164–70.

Johnson, Sharon P., 'Cultural Blindness and Ambiguity: Reading (for) and Writing about Rape', *French Cultural Studies*, 27/2 (2016), 113–34.

Kalifa, Dominique, *Crime et culture au XIXe siècle* (Paris: Perrin, 2005).

Kalifa, Dominique, *L'Encre et le sang. Récits de crimes et société à la Belle Époque* (Paris: Fayard, 1995).

Kalifa, Dominique, *Les bas-fonds. Histoire d'un imaginaire* (Paris: Éditions du Seuil, 2013).

Kalifa, Dominique, and Philippe Artières, *Vidal le tueur de femmes. Une biographie sociale* (Paris: Perrin, 2001).

Kilby, Jane, and Larry J. Ray, eds, *Violence and Society: Toward a New Sociology* (Malden: Wiley-Blackwell, The Sociological Review, 2014).

Kimmel, Michael S., *The Gendered Society* (Oxford: Oxford University Press, 2011).

Kimmel, Michael S., 'Invisible Masculinity', *Society*, 30 (1993), 28–35.

Knepper, Paul, 'Laughing at Lombroso: Positivism and Criminal Anthropology in Historical Perspective', in *The Wiley Handbook of the History and Philosophy of Criminology*, ed. by Ruth Triplett (Hoboken, NJ: Wiley-Blackwell, 2018), pp. 49–66.

Knepper, Paul, and Per Jørgen Ystehede, eds, *The Cesare Lombroso Handbook* (London: Routledge, 2013).

Lagarde, Marcela, '*Identidades de género y derechos humanos. La construcción de las humanas*', VII curso de verano, *Educación, democracia y nueva ciudadanía*, Universidad Autónoma de Aguascalientes, 1997, Cátedra UNESCO de Derechos Humanos de la UNAM, online resource <http://www.derechoshumanos.unlp.edu.ar/assets/files/documentos/identidad-de-genero-y-derechos-humanos-la-construccion-de-las-humanas.pdf> [accessed on 30 April 2024].

Landucci, Giovanni, *Darwinismo a Firenze. Tra scienze e ideologia (1860–1900)* (Florence: Olschki, 1977).

Landucci, Giovanni, *L'occhio e la mente. Scienza e filosofia nell'Italia dell'Ottocento* (Florence: Olschki, 1987).

Lantéri-Laura, Georges, *Histoire de la phrénologie* (Paris: PUF, 1970).

Lévy, René, and Amy Gilman Srebnick, eds, *Crime and Culture: An Historical Perspective* (Farnham: Ashgate, 2005).

Lippmann, Walter, *L'opinione pubblica* (Rome: Donzelli, 2004 [1922]).

Loconsole, Matteo, 'Laws and Sexual Prejudices in the Italian Positivist Culture: Murderous Mothers and the Education to Infanticide', *Studi sulla Formazione*, 22/2 (2019) 355–74.

Lombardo, Giovanni Pietro, Marco Duichin, and François Azouvi, eds, *Frenologia, fisiognomica e psicologia delle differenze individuali in Franz Joseph Gall: antecedenti storici e sviluppi disciplinari* (Turin: Bollati Boringhieri, 1997).

Luengo López, Jordi, 'El siniestro gusto literario del Neronismo. Un estudio comparativo en la producción franco-española sobre la violencia contra las mujeres', *AnMal Electrónica*, 31 (2011), <https://dialnet.unirioja.es/servlet/articulo?codigo=4043411> [electronic resource, accessed on 28 October 2024].

MacDonald, Katherine, 'Humanistic Self-Representation in Giovan Battista Della Porta's "Della Fisonomia Dell'Uomo": Antecedents and Innovation', *The Sixteenth Century Journal*, 36/2 (2005), 397–414.

Maclean, Ian, *The Renaissance Notion of Woman: A Study in the Fortunes of Scholasticism and Medical Science in European Intellectual Life* (Cambridge: Cambridge University Press, 1980).

Mc Mahon, Richard, ed., *Crime, Law and Popular Culture (1500–1900)* (Portland: Willan Publishing, 2009).

McDougall, Sara, 'The Transformation of Adultery in France at the End of the Middle Ages', *Law and History Review*, 32/3 (2014), 491–524.

McLaren, Angus, *The Trials of Masculinity: Policing Sexual Boundaries, 1870–1930* (Chicago: University of Chicago Press, 1997).

Mancia, Giuseppe, 'Scipione Riva-Rocci', *Clinical Cardiology*, 20/5 (1997), 503–04.

Mandolini, Nicoletta, *Representations of Lethal Gender-based Violence in Italy between Journalism and Literature* (London: Routledge, 2021).

Mandolini, Nicoletta, Caroline Williamson Sinalo, eds, *Representing Gender-Based Violence: Global Perspectives* (Cham: Palgrave, 2023).

Manzin, Gregoria, and Barbara Pezzotti, 'Women and Violence in Italian Literature', *Spunti e Ricerche*, 33 (2018), 1–168.

Maschietto, Beatrice, 'II problema penale nella dottrina italiana del secondo Settecento: Filippo Maria Renazzi', in *Criminalità e giustizia in Germania e in Italia. Pratiche giudiziarie e linguaggi giuridici tra tardo medioevo ed età moderna*, ed. by Marco Bellabarba, Gerd Schwerhoff, and Andrea Zorzi (Bologna: Il Mulino, 2001), pp. 235–52.

Melograni, Piero, and Lucetta Scaraffia, eds, *La famiglia italiana dall'Ottocento a oggi* (Rome and Bari: Laterza, 1988).

Mills, Martin, and Amanda Keddie, 'Cultural Reductionism and the Media: Polarising Discourses around Schools, Violence and Masculinity in an Age of Terror', *Oxford Review of Education*, 36/4 (2010), 427–44.

Missiroli, Mario, 'Rastignac e il suo tempo', in *Uomini e giornali. I grandi giornalisti di ieri negli scritti dei giornalisti di oggi*, ed. by Silvio Negro and Andrea Lazzarini (Florence: Salani, 1947), pp. 165–73.

Montaldo, Silvano, ed., *Cesare Lombroso. Gli scienziati e la nuova Italia* (Bologna: il Mulino, 2010).

Montaldo, Silvano, *Donne delinquenti. Il genere e la nascita della criminologia* (Rome: Carocci, 2019).

Montaldo, Silvano, 'Lombroso: The Myth, The History', *Crime, Histoire & Sociétés / Crime, History & Societies*, 22/2 (2018), 31–61.

Montaldo, Silvano, 'The Medicalisation of the Corpse in Liberal Italy. National Legislation and the Case of Turin', in *Public Uses of Human Remains and Relics in History*, ed. by Silvia Cavicchioli and Luigi Provero (New York-Abingdon: Routledge, 2019), pp. 230–45.

Monti Rossi, Martino, 'Fisiognomica e grazia: da Bernardo di Chiaravalle a Giovan Battista Della Porta', *Bruniana & Campanelliana* 21, 2 (2015), 330–45.

Mosse, George, *The Image of Man. The Creation of Modern Masculinity* (Oxford: Oxford University Press, 1996).

Muravyeva, Marianna, '"Verguenza, Vergogne, Schande, Skam and Sram": Litigating for Shame and Dishonour in Early Modern Europe', in *Shame, Blame, and Culpability: Crime and Violence in the Modern State*, ed. by Marianna Muravyeva, David Nash, and Judith Rowbotham (Abingdon: Routledge, 2013), pp. 17–32.

Muravyeva, Marianna, David Nash and Judith Rowbotham, *Shame, Blame, and Culpability: Crime and Violence in the Modern State* (Abingdon: Routledge, 2013).

Murialdi, Paolo, *Storia del giornalismo italiano. Dalle gazzette a Internet* (Bologna: Il Mulino, 2006).

Musumeci, Emilia, *Emozioni, crimine, giustizia: un'indagine storico-giuridica tra Otto e Novecento* (Milan: Franco Angeli, 2015).

Musumeci, Emilia, 'L'amore in tribunale: la rilevanza delle emozioni nel diritto penale in Italia tra Otto e Novecento', in *History and Law Encounters. Lezioni per pensare da giurista II*, ed. by Elisabetta Fusar Poli, Aldo Andrea Cassi, Federica Paletti (Turin: Giappichelli, 2022), pp. 167–88.

Musumeci, Emilia, 'New Natural Born Killers? The Legacy of Lombroso in Neuroscience and Law', in *The Cesare Lombroso Handbook*, ed. by Paul Knepper and Per Jørgen Ystehede (London: Routledge, 2013), pp. 359–73.

Natale, Alberto, *Gli specchi della paura: il sensazionale e il prodigioso nella letteratura di consumo (secoli XVII-XVIII)* (Rome: Carocci, 2008).

Natale, Alberto, 'Paura mediatica e propaganda', *Griselda. Il portale di letteratura* (2016). <https://site.unibo.it/griseldaonline/it/approfondimenti/alberto-natale-paura-mediatica-propaganda> [accessed on 30 April 2024].

Nye, Robert A., 'Heredity or Milieu: The Foundations of Modern European Criminological Theory', *Isis*, 67/3 (1976), 335–55.

Oddone, Cristina, *Uomini normali: Maschilità e violenza nell'intimità* (Turin: Rosenberg & Sellier, 2020).

Pallottino, Paola, *Storia dell'illustrazione italiana: cinque secoli di immagini riprodotte* (Florence: Usher Arte, 2011).

Panico, Guido, 'La violenza giustificata. Il racconto dell'uccisione di una femme fatale: un case study', in *Il genere nella ricerca storica*, ed. by Chemotti and La Rocca, II, pp. 889–900.

Parmigiani, Giovanna, *Feminism, Violence, and Representation in Modern Italy: "We are Witnesses, not Victims"* (Bloomington: Indiana University Press, 2019).

Passarella, Claudia, 'Between Leniency and Severity. Family Life and Criminal Behaviours at the Court of Assize of Venice, 1871–1898', *Crime, Histoire & Sociétés/Crime, History & Societies*, 24/2 (2020), 97–120.

Penedo, Cristine, 'O Crime nos Media. Impacto e valor simbólico das historias transgressivas', *Media & Jornalismo*, 3 (2003), 89–102.

Pescarolo, Alessandra, *Il lavoro delle donne nell'Italia contemporanea* (Rome: Viella, 2019).

Piccone, Simonetta Stella, and Chiara Saraceno, eds, *Genere. La costruzione del femminile e del maschile* (Bologna: Il Mulino, 1996).

Pireddu, Nicoletta, 'Paolo Mantegazza: ritratto dell'antropologo come esteta', in *Paolo Mantegazza: medico, antropologo, viaggiatore: selezione di contributi dai Convegni di Monza, Firenze, Lerici*, ed. by Cosimo Chiarelli and Walter Pasini (Florence: Florence University Press, 2002), pp. 1–11.

Pitt-Rivers, Julian, 'Honour and Social Status', in *Honour and Shame: The Values of Mediterranean Society*, edited by J. Peristiany (London: Weidenfeld and Nicholson, 1965), pp. 19–77.

Plesset, Sonja, *Sheltering Women: Negotiating Gender and Violence in Northern Italy* (Stanford: Stanford University Press, 2006).

Poskett, James, *Materials of the Mind: Phrenology, Race, and the Global History of Science, 1815–1920* (Chicago: University of Chicago Press, 2019).

Prosperi, Adriano, *Dare l'anima. Storia di un infanticidio* (Turin: Einaudi, 2005).

Prosperi, Adriano, *Infanticide, Secular Justice, and Religious Debate in Early Modern Europe* (Turnhout: Brepols, 2016).

Örnebring, Henrik, and Anna Maria Jönsson, 'Tabloid Journalism and the Public Sphere: A Historical Perspective on Tabloid Journalism', *Journalism Studies*, 5/3 (2004), 283–95.

Radford, Jill, and Diana E. H. Russell, eds, *Femicide. The Politics of Woman Killing* (New York: Twayne, 1992).

Radica, Christel, 'Onore, follia e amore: storie di assassini e Firenze (1866–1914)', *Genesis*, XVIII, 2 (2019), *Maschilità e violenza di genere*, 63–82.

Rafter, Nicole Hahn, 'Introduction', *Theoretical Criminology*, 18/2 (2014), 128–33.

Rafter, Nicole Hahn, *The Criminal Brain: Understanding Biological Theories of Crime* (New York: New York University Press, 2008).

Refini, Eugenio, 'Bodily Passions: Physiognomy and Drama in Giovan Battista Della Porta', *Renaissance and Reformation*, 40, 1 (2017), 121–39.

Reiner, Robert, 'Media Made Criminality: The Representation of Crime in the Mass Media', in *The Oxford Handbook of Criminology*, ed. by Rod Morgan, Mike Maguire, and Robert Reiner (Oxford: Oxford University Press, 2007), pp. 376–416.

Renneville, Marc, *Le langage des crânes: histoire de la phrénologie* (Paris: Institut d'edition Sanofi-Synthelabo, 2000).

Rinaldi, Cirus, *Maschilità, devianze, crimine* (Milan: Meltemi, 2018).

Rizzelli, Giunio, *Lex Julia de adulteriis, Studi sulla disciplina di adulterium, lenocinium, stuprum* (Lecce: Edizioni del Grifo, 1997).

Rizzo, Domenico, and Laura Schettini, eds, *Maschilità e violenza di genere, Genesis*, XVIII/2 (2019).

Rodler, Lucia, *Il corpo specchio dell'anima: teoria e storia della fisiognomica* (Milan: Mondadori, 2000).

Roselli, Maria Gloria, 'Paolo Mantegazza: la prima cattedra di Antropologia in Italia e la fondazione del Museo', in *L'Istituto di Studi Superiori e la cultura umanistica a Firenze*, 2 vols, ed. by Adele Dei (Ospedaletto-Pisa: Pacini, 2016), II, pp. 601–55.

Rosenwein, Barbara, 'Problems and Methods in the History of Emotions', *Passions in Context*, I/1 (2010), 1–32.

Rossi-Doria, Anna, *Diventare cittadine. Il voto alle donne in Italia* (Florence: Giunti, 1996).

Ruff, Julius R., *Violence in Early Modern Europe* (Cambridge: Cambridge University Press, 2001).

Ruggiero, Guido, *The Boundaries of Eros: Sex Crime and Sexuality in Renaissance Venice* (Oxford: Oxford University Press, 1989).

Russell, Diana E.H., and Roberta Harmes, eds, *Femicide in Global Perspective* (New York: Teacher's College Press, 2001).

Russell, Diana E.H., 'Femicide: Politicizing the Killing of Females', in *Strengthening Understanding of Femicide: Using Research to Galvanize Action and Accountability*, Report of the Conference held in Washington on 14–16 April 2008, pp. 26–31.

Samoggia, Alessandra, and Francesco Scalone, eds, *La famiglia tra mutamenti demografici e sociali* (Udine: Forum, 2019).

Savoia, Paolo, *Early Modern Surgery: Faces, Men, and Pain* (London: Routledge, 2020).

Schettini, Laura, 'La violenza maschile contro le donne', *Storia delle donne nell'Italia contemporanea*, ed. by Silvia Salvatici (Rome: Carocci, 2022), pp. 135–61.

Scoliere, Margherita, 'Il giureconsulto Filippo Maria Renazzi: presentazione di un inedito', *Studi Romani*, 46/3 (1998), 375–98.

Serafini, Stefano, *Gothic Italy. Crime, Science, and Literature after Unification, 1861–1914* (Toronto: University of Toronto Press, 2024).

Serafini, Stefano, 'Immagini e criminalità nell'Italia di fine secolo tra stampa, letteratura e scienza', *The Italianist*, 42/1 (2022), 1–23.

Seymour, Mark, *Debating Divorce in Italy. Marriage and the Making of Modern Italians, 1860–1974* (New York: Palgrave Macmillan, 2006).

Seymour, Mark, 'Emotional Arenas: From Provincial Circus to National Courtroom in Late Nineteenth-Century Italy', *Rethinking History*, 16/2 (2012), 177–97.

Seymour, Mark, *Emotional Arenas: Life, Love, and Death in 1870s Italy* (Oxford: Oxford University Press, 2020).

Shepherd, Laura J., ed., *Handbook on Gender and Violence* (Cheltenham: Edward Elgar, 2019).

Siegel, Reva B., "The Rule of Love': Wife Beating as Prerogative and Privacy', *The Yale Law Journal*, 105/8 (1996), 2117–207

Simpson, Thomas, *Murder and Media in the New Rome: The Fadda Affair* (New York: Palgrave Macmillan, 2010).

Siraisi, Nancy G., *History, Medicine, and the Traditions of Renaissance Learning* (University of Michigan Press, 2007).

Siraisi, Nancy G., *Medicine and the Italian Universities: 1250–1600* (Leiden: Brill, 2001).

Smith, Laurajane, Margaret Wetherell and Gary Campbell, eds, *Emotion, Affective Practices, and the Past in the Present* (Oxon and New York: Routledge, 2018), pp. 1–22.

Soldani, Simonetta, eds, *L'educazione delle donne. Scuole e modelli di vita femminile nell'Italia dell'Ottocento* (Milan: Franco Angeli, 1989).

Soldani, Simonetta, *Nascita della maestra elementare*, in *Fare gli italiani. Scuola e cultura nell'Italia contemporanea*, ed. by Simonetta Soldani e Gabriele Turi, 2 vols (Bologna: Il Mulino, 1993), I, pp. 67–130.

Spierenburg, Pieter, ed., *Men and Violence: Gender, Honor, and Rituals in Modern Europe and America* (Columbia: Ohio State University Press, 1998).

Storti, Claudia, and Cristina Danusso, eds, *Figure del Foro lombardo tra XVI e XIX secolo* (Milan: Giuffrè, 2006).

Suresh, Nikitha, and Lucy Sara George, 'Trial by Media: An Overview', *International Journal of Law Management and Humanities*, 4/2 (2021), 267–72.

Tagliavini, Annamaria, 'Il fondo oscuro dell'anima femminile', in *La donna nelle scienze dell'uomo: immagini del femminile nella cultura scientifica italiana di fine secolo*, ed. by Valeria P. Babini, Fernanda Minuz, and Annamaria Tagliavini (Milan: Franco Angeli, 1986), pp. 78–113.

Taylor, Paul M., and Cesare Marino, 'Paolo Mantegazza's Vision: The Science of Man behind the World's First Museum of Anthropology (Florence, Italy, 1869)', *Museum Anthropology*, 42 (2019), 109–24.

Taylor, Trip Finity, Kortni MacDonald, 'The criminalization of madness', in *The Origins of Criminological Theory*, ed. by Omi Hodwitz (London: Routledge, 2022), pp. 92–110.

Tatasciore, Giulio, 'Per una storia culturale del crimine. Alcuni recenti studi francesi', *Storica*, 60 (2014), 92–110.

Tosh, John, 'What Should Historians Do with Masculinity? Reflections on Nineteenth-Century Britain', *History Workshop Journal*, 38 (1994), 179–202.

Triplett, Ruth, ed., *The Wiley Handbook of the History and Philosophy of Criminology* (Hoboken, NJ: Wiley-Blackwell, 2018).

Twine, Richard, 'Physiognomy, Phrenology and the Temporality of the Body', *Body & Society*, 8/1 (2002), 67–88.

Ungari, Paolo, *Il diritto di famiglia in Italia dalle costituzioni giacobine al Codice civile del* 1942 (Bologna: Il Mulino, 1970).

Ungari, Paolo, *Storia del diritto di famiglia in Italia (1796–1942)* (Bologna: Il Mulino, 1974).

Unia, Marco, 'I periodici giuridici milanesi dal 1848 al 1946', in *Avvocati a Milano: sei secoli di storia*, ed. by Ada Gigli Marchetti, Alceo Riosa and Francesca Tacchi (Milan: Skira, 2004), pp. 191–97.

Vagnoli, Carlotta, *Maledetta sfortuna: vedere, riconoscere e rifiutare la violenza di genere* (Milan: Fabbri, 2021).

Valsecchi, Chiara, *L'avvocatura veneta tra diritto comune e codici: il caso del vicentino Giovanni Maria Negri*, in *Avvocati e avvocatura nell'Italia dell'Ottocento*, ed. by Antonio Padoa Schioppa (Bologna: Il Mulino, 2009), pp. 521–624.

Van Whye, John, 'The Authority of Human Nature: The "Schädellehre" of Franz Joseph Gall', *The British Journal for the History of Science*, 35/1 (2002), 17–42.

Verplaetse, Jan, *Localising the Moral Sense: Neuroscience and the Search for the Cerebral Seat of Morality, 1800–1930* (Dordrecht: Springer, 2009).

Villa, Renzo, 'Lombroso and his School. From Anthropology to Medicine and Law', *The Cesare Lombroso Handbook*, ed. by Knepper and Ystehede, pp. 8–29.

Vinci, Stefano, 'Insanity and Criminal Justice in Italy at the End of the 19th Century', *GLOSSAE. European Journal of Legal History*, 20 (2023), 28–44.

Warner, Michael, 'Introduction: Fear of a Queer Planet', in *Fear of a Queer Planet. Queer Politics and Social Theory*, ed. By Michael Werner (Minneapolis: University of Minnesota Press, 1993), pp. vii–xxxiii.

Weil, Shalva, Consuelo Corradi and Marceline Naudi, eds, *Femicide across Europe: Theory, Research and Prevention* (Bristol: Bristol University Press, 2018).

West, Kate, 'Visual Criminology and Lombroso: In Memory of Nicole Rafter (1939–2016)', *Theoretical Criminology*, 21/3 (2017), 271–87.

Wetherell, Margaret, Laurajane Smith and Gary Campbell, 'Introduction: Affective Heritage Practices', in *Emotion, Affective Practices, and the Past in the Present*, pp. 1–22.

Index of Names

EUROPA PERIODICA

STUDIES ON PERIODICALS AND NEWSPAPERS

Edited by
Patrizia Delpiano, Fabio Forner, Giovanni Iamartino,
Sabine Schwarze and Corrado Viola

Volume 1 Fabio Forner / Franz Meier / Sabine Schwarze (ed.): I periodici settecenteschi come luogo di comunicazione dei saperi. Prospettive storiche, letter-arie e linguistiche. 2022.

Volume 2 Lucia Berti: Scientific Crosscurrents between Italy and England. Italian Contributions to the Philosophical Transactions of the Royal Society, Seventeenth to Nineteenth Centuries. 2023.

Volume 3 Domenico Cecere / Alessandro Tuccillo (eds): Communication and Politics in the Hispanic Monarchy: Managing Times of Emergency. 2023.

Volume 4 Domenico Cecere / Fabio Ruggiano / Sabine Schwarze (eds): Tradizioni del discorso sulla lingua nella stampa periodica italiana dal Settecento a oggi. 2024.

Volume 5 Sara Delmedico: Representing Violence against Women. A Case Study from Early Twentieth-Century Italy. 2025.

www.ingramcontent.com/pod-product-compliance
Ingram Content Group UK Ltd.
Pitfield, Milton Keynes, MK11 3LW, UK
UKHW041824031026
15587UKWH00002B/551

9 783631 906293